PRAISE FOR

THE LIGHTHOUSE OF STALINGRAD

**Winner of the Gold Award,
the 2023 Military History Matters
Book of the Year**

"Splendid . . . MacGregor writes with great fluency and narrative drive, and his account of the context to the battle and the complexity of its fraught swings of fortune and misfortune is compellingly terse."

—*The New Statesman* (UK)

"Brisk and dramatic . . . Meticulous yet action-packed, this will thrill World War II buffs."

—*Publishers Weekly*

"MacGregor's wonderful book shines important new light on the most horrific, and arguably the most important, battle of the twentieth century. It is a story of 'backs to the wall' defense of the Motherland that modern Russians, with the boot now on the other foot, would do well to study."

—*The Telegraph* (UK)

"MacGregor takes us right into the war on and below the ground. . . . A gripping and knowledgeable account."

—*The Spectator* (UK)

"Peeling back the layers of myth surrounding the Battle of Stalingrad is a tall order. In *The Lighthouse of Stalingrad*, Iain MacGregor brilliantly dissects the story of Pavlov's House, the building supposedly defended by a small group of Soviet men against overwhelming odds."

—*History Today*, Books of the Year 2022

"An utterly gripping read."
— Tom Holland, author and host of *The Rest Is History* podcast

"The finest of military history, utterly riveting, based on revelatory and superb research, and a heartrending account of arguably the most impactful battle to defeat Nazism in World War II. A wonderful and important and timely book."
— Alex Kershaw, *New York Times* bestselling author of *The Bedford Boys*

"The best and richest book yet written about the battle for Stalingrad and what it means today."
— *The Critic* (UK)

"Compelling . . . MacGregor effectively uses primary sources, including the archived personal stories of Soviet veterans and the unpublished memoir of German officer Friedrich Roske, who come fully alive in these pages."
— *Kirkus Reviews*

"As well as being . . . a fine narrative history of the titanic battle, it is about the complicated relationship between reality, legend, and myth in war."
— *Country Life* (UK)

"A superb evocation: MacGregor strips away the layers of myth—using a powerful array of sources—and takes us to the brutal heart of this pivotal battle."
— Michael K. Jones, author of *Stalingrad: How the Red Army Triumphed*

"In the midst of Moscow's bloody war on Ukraine, with Putin invoking the 'glorious victories' of World War II to inspire his country, Iain MacGregor's vivid, dramatic, day by day account reminds us that the awful reality of Stalingrad for soldiers on both sides was: 'The lucky ones bled, froze, or starved to death in temporary field hospitals set up in bunkers or cellars.'"
— William Taubman, Pulitzer Prize–winning author of *Khrushchev: The Man and His Era*

"If you thought you knew all about the Battle of Stalingrad, Iain Mac-Gregor's gripping account will put you right. Drawing on a remarkable range of diaries, letters, and memoirs, many of which have never been published before, he provides an illuminating, authoritative, and unforgettable insight into the decisive days of that most terrible struggle on the banks of the Volga."

—Jonathan Dimbleby, BBC broadcaster and *Sunday Times* bestselling author of *Barbarossa: How Hitler Lost the War*

"Stunning. History at its very best: a blend of impeccably researched scholarship, genuinely revelatory primary sources, and a beautifully written narrative. The grim brutality of the conditions in which the men of both sides fought—and died—is brought back to life with immense clarity; one can almost smell the smoke and stench of death. Iain MacGregor's superb book is the most compellingly readable account yet written of this iconic, notorious battle."

—James Holland, author of *Normandy '44: D-Day and the Battle for France*

"If you believe there is nothing fresh to be written about the most decisive battle of the Second World War, Iain MacGregor's *The Lighthouse of Stalingrad* will be something of a revelation. . . . The sheer brutal intimacy of his descriptions of this fighting are extraordinary. . . . This is a chilling, vivid account that helps to explain not just the Third Reich's defeat at Stalingrad but also the myths that persist in Russia to this day—for better and, most recently, for worse."

—Frederick Taylor, author of *Dresden: Tuesday, February 13, 1945*

ALSO BY IAIN MacGREGOR

Checkpoint Charlie: The Cold War, the Berlin Wall, and the Most Dangerous Place on Earth

THE LIGHTHOUSE
OF STALINGRAD

THE HIDDEN TRUTH AT THE HEART OF
THE GREATEST BATTLE OF WORLD WAR II

Iain MacGregor

SCRIBNER

New York   London   Toronto   Sydney   New Delhi

Scribner
An Imprint of Simon & Schuster, Inc.
1230 Avenue of the Americas
New York, NY 10020

First Scribner trade paperback edition December 2023

For information about special discounts for bulk purchases,
please contact Simon & Schuster Special Sales at 1-866-506-1949
or business@simonandschuster.com.

The Simon & Schuster Speakers Bureau can bring authors to
your live event. For more information or to book an event,
contact the Simon & Schuster Speakers Bureau at 1-866-248-3049
or visit our website at www.simonspeakers.com.

Interior design by Kyle Kabel

Manufactured in the United States of America

1   3   5   7   9   10   8   6   4   2

Library of Congress Cataloging-in-Publication Data

Names: MacGregor, Iain, author.
Title: The Lighthouse of Stalingrad : the hidden truth at the heart
of the greatest battle of World War II / Iain MacGregor.
Other titles: Hidden truth at the heart of the greatest battle of World War II
Description: First Scribner hardcover edition. | New York : Scribner,
2022. | Includes bibliographical references and index.
Identifiers: LCCN 2022017235 (print) | LCCN 2022017236 (ebook) |
ISBN 9781982163587 (hardcover) | ISBN 9781982163600 (ebook)
Subjects: LCSH: Stalingrad, Battle of, Volgograd, Russia, 1942–1943. | Dom
Pavlova (Volgograd, Russia)—History. | Soviet Union.
Raboche-Krestʹianskaia Krasnaia Armiia. Gvardeĭskaia strelkovaia
diviziia, 13-ia. | Germany. Heer. Infanterie-Division, 71. | World War,
1939–1945—Campaigns—Eastern Front.
Classification: LCC D764.3.S7 M334 2022 (print) | LCC D764.3.S7 (ebook) |
DDC 940.54/21747—dc23/eng/20220427
LC record available at https://lccn.loc.gov/2022017235
LC ebook record available at https://lccn.loc.gov/2022017236

ISBN 978-1-9821-6358-7
ISBN 978-1-9821-6359-4 (pbk)
ISBN 978-1-9821-6360-0 (ebook)

I have left the obvious, essential fact to this point, namely, that it is the Russian Armies who have done the main work in tearing the guts out of the German army.

—Prime Minister Winston Churchill
House of Commons, August 2, 1944, "War Situation"

As Commander-in-Chief of the Armed Forces of the United States of America I congratulate you on the brilliant victory at Stalingrad of the armies under your Supreme Command. The one hundred and sixty-two days of epic battle for the city which has forever honored your name and the decisive result which all Americans are celebrating today will remain one of the proudest chapters in this war of the peoples united against Nazism and its emulators.

—Memo from Franklin D. Roosevelt to
Premier Joseph Stalin, February 6, 1943

For Cameron and Isla

Contents

Pavlov's House is a symbol of the heroic struggle of all defenders of Stalingrad. It will go down in the history of the defense of the glorious city as a monument to the military skill and valor of the guards.

—Lieutenant Juliy Petrovich Chepurin, correspondent
for 62nd Army, Stalingrad, October 31, 1942[1]

Chronology

April 5, 1942
Hitler Directive No. 41 on the German offensive in Southern Russia

April 24, 1942
Alexander M. Vasilevsky takes over as chief of the Soviet General Staff (formally appointed to the post June 26, 1942)

May 12, 1942
Beginning of the Soviet offensive at Kharkov

May 17, 1942
The Germans counterattack at Kharkov

May 23–24, 1942
Encirclement and destruction of Soviet armies involved in their failed Kharkov offensive

June 28, 1942
Beginning of German offensive (*Case Blue*) in Southern Russia

July 1–4, 1942
Fall of Sevastopol to German Eleventh Army (von Manstein)

July 6, 1942
Voronezh on the Don captured by the Germans

July 9, 1942
German Army Group South command split between Army Group A and Army Group B

July 12, 1942
Formation of "Stalingrad Front" Soviet army group

July 23–24, 1942
German forces take Rostov-on-Don

July 23, 1942
Hitler Directive No. 45 orders simultaneous main offensives on Stalingrad and toward the Caucasus

July 28, 1942
Stalin issues Order No. 277 ("Not One Step Back!")

August 9, 1942
The Maikop oil fields are captured by the Germans

August 19, 1942
Paulus leads Sixth Army toward Stalingrad from their positions on the Don Bend

August 23–24, 1942
The Luftwaffe begins carpet-bombing of Stalingrad

August 26, 1942
General Georgy Zhukov appointed deputy supreme commander of the Soviet Armed Forces

September 3, 1942
German troops reach outskirts of Stalingrad

September 10, 1942
The Sixth Army reaches the Volga River and splits the 62nd and 64th Soviet Armies apart

September 12, 1942
Lieutenant General Vasily Chuikov takes command of the 62nd Army

September 13, 1942
Beginning of the battle for Stalingrad city center

September 13–14, 1942
Major General Rodimtsev's 13th Guards Rifle Division begins its crossing of the Volga into the center of Stalingrad

September 24, 1942
Colonel General Halder replaced by Zeitzler as chief of the Army General Staff

September 24, 1942
Junior Sergeant Pavlov's "storm unit" of the 42nd Regiment recaptures the "House of Specialists," beginning the siege of "Pavlov's House"

September 26, 1942
Most of central Stalingrad in German hands

October 9, 1942
System of dual political-military command in the Red Army (the Institute of Commissars) abolished

October 14, 1942
Climax of the German effort to take Stalingrad

November 8, 1942
Hitler announces in Munich that Stalingrad is in his hands

November 11, 1942
The last major German offensive in Stalingrad (Operation Hubertus)

November 19, 1942
Beginning of the Soviet counteroffensive (Operation Uranus)

November 23, 1942
German Sixth Army plus Axis allies encircled in Stalingrad

November 24, 1942
Hitler orders the Sixth Army to fight on in Stalingrad

November 25, 1942
Beginning of Soviet offensive against Army Group Center (Operation Mars)

November 25, 1942
Beginning of airlift by the Luftwaffe to Stalingrad

November 30, 1942
Paulus promoted to colonel general

December 12, 1942
Beginning of Field Marshal von Manstein's Operation Winterstorm to rescue the Sixth Army

December 16, 1942
The Soviets launch Operation Little Saturn

December 20, 1942
Operation Mars aborted

December 23, 1942
German relief operation to Stalingrad called off

December 28, 1942
German Army Group A ordered to retreat from the Caucasus

January 8, 1943
Soviets issue ultimatum to Sixth Army to surrender—but refused

January 10, 1943
Beginning of Soviet operations against the encircled Sixth Army

January 17, 1943
Repeat of Soviet surrender ultimatum—again refused

January 25, 1943
Further Soviet offer of surrender terms—refused

January 30, 1943
Adolf Hitler promotes Paulus to field marshal

January 31, 1943
Surrender of Paulus and the Sixth Army in the southern-central pocket

February 2, 1943
Surrender of remaining German forces in Stalingrad in the northern pocket

Cast of Characters

Author's note: The following officers and other ranks, on both sides, appear in chronological form as the campaign in 1942 progressed. Many would be promoted, as I shall note in the narrative.

GERMAN

Adolf Hitler—German Commander in Chief

Colonel General Franz Halder—Chief of the General Staff, Army High Command

Colonel General Kurt Zeitzler—Chief of the General Staff, Army High Command

Field Marshal Fedor von Bock—Commander, Army Group South

Field Marshal Paul Ludwig Ewald von Kleist—Commander, Army Group A

General Field Marshal Wolfram Freiherr von Richthofen—Commander, Luftflotten IV

General Friedrich Wilhelm Ernst Paulus—Commander, Sixth Army

Colonel Wilhelm Adam—Aide-de-camp to General Paulus, Sixth Army

Major General Alexander von Hartmann—Commander, 71st Infantry Division

Lieutenant Colonel Friedrich Roske—Commander, Infantry Regiment 194

Captain Gerhard Münch—Third Battalion of Infantry Regiment 194

First Lieutenant Gerhard Hindenlang—Adjutant, Infantry
  Regiment 194
Sergeant Albert Wittenberg—Pioneer, 50th Infantry Division

SOVIET
Joseph Vissarionivich Stalin—Chairman of the Council of People's
  Commissars
General Georgy Zhukov—Deputy Commander in Chief, Red Army
Nikita Sergeyevich Khrushchev—Military Commissar, Stalingrad
  Front
Colonel General Andrey Ivanovich Yeremenko—Commander,
  Southeastern and Stalingrad Fronts
Lieutenant General Vasily Ivanovich Chuikov—Commander, 62nd
  Army
Lieutenant General Mikhail Stepanovich Shumilov—Commander,
  64th Army
Major General Alexander Ilyich Rodimtsev—Commander, 13th
  Guards Rifle Division
Colonel Ivan Pavlovich Elin—Commander, 42nd Guards Rifle
  Regiment
Senior Lieutenant Alexei Efimovich Zhukov—3rd Battalion, 42nd
  Guards Rifle Regiment
Lieutenant Anton Kuzmich Dragan—1st Battalion, 42nd Guards Rifle
  Regiment
Lieutenant Anatoly Grigoryevich Merezhko—Staff Officer, 62nd
  Army
Lieutenant Ivan Filippovich Afanasiev—3rd Battalion, 42nd Guards
  Rifle Regiment
Junior Sergeant Yakov Fedotovich Pavlov—3rd Battalion, 42nd
  Guards Rifle Regiment

THE LIGHTHOUSE
OF STALINGRAD

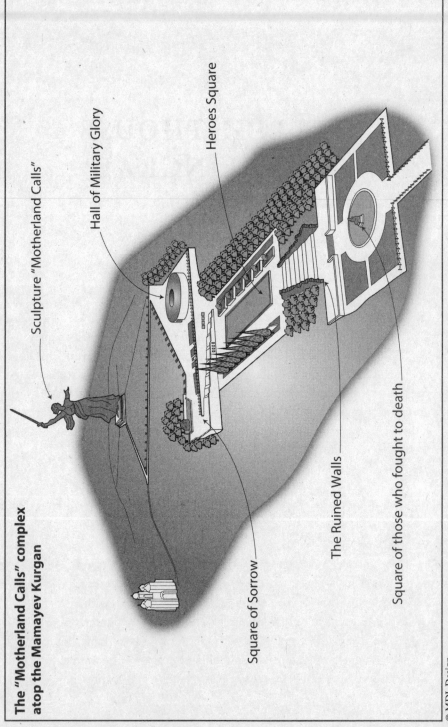

The "Motherland Calls" complex atop the Mamayev Kurgan

Sculpture "Motherland Calls"

Hall of Military Glory

Heroes Square

Square of Sorrow

The Ruined Walls

Square of those who fought to death

© MDL Design

We Bury Our Own

The most memorable event in my grandfather's life was, of course, the Battle of Stalingrad. [When he died] he wanted to lie in the ground next to his soldiers."[1] As we talk on the phone, Nikolai Chuikov's voice suddenly breaks, lost in his memories of the day the citizens came out onto the streets of the city that had decided the fate of the Second World War in Europe, to say farewell to their adopted son.

Nikolai is a direct descendent of one of the greatest military names in Russian modern history, Vasily Ivanovich Chuikov. Every child in the country, and indeed the majority of military history students across the globe, know his name—the commander of the army that saved the "Hero City." A peasant boy from outside Moscow,[2] Chuikov commanded a regiment of revolutionaries at the raw age of nineteen and would eventually rise to become a highly decorated marshal of the Soviet Union. He had led his men of the 8th Guards Army from Stalingrad, through the Ukraine and Poland, defeating the best armies Hitler could muster before accepting the Third Reich's unconditional surrender in Berlin in May 1945.[3] A hard, stocky, belligerent man, he was known for an explosive temper. The stick he carries in images from the celebrations at Stalingrad in February 1943 was well known to the backs of many of his subordinates. His own bravery was without question, but one could argue that his carelessness with his men's lives was perhaps a different matter. His relentless counterattacks in the defense of Stalingrad bled Nazi Germany's Sixth Army, but also almost wiped out his own. Despite this, after the war, he was beloved. With tousled black hair, deep-set eyes, and a sullen expression only brightened by his gleaming gold teeth, Chuikov's was a face one certainly remembered.

Joseph Stalin himself wanted this man to command the Soviet Union's premier formation of the Kiev District in 1949—a barrier to any western attack in the future.[4] Elevated to high office in March 1969, Chuikov was sent by First Secretary Leonid Brezhnev to head a four-man delegation to represent the Kremlin at the funeral of fellow warrior and ex-President of the United States Dwight D. Eisenhower in Washington, DC. On a windswept winter's day by the Volga it was now his turn to be given a soldier's farewell from the people of the city that had made all this possible.

Chuikov had been ill for some time, his eighty-two-year-old body still ravaged by the shrapnel wounds he'd received in active service fighting the Finns in the Winter War of 1940, as well as the multiple mini-strokes he had suffered later in life. However, it was a heart attack on March 18, 1982, that finally claimed his life. His dying wish was to be buried in the city.[5] It was a unique honor, granted by a Kremlin used to burying its generals' ashes in its own walls within Red Square. The Mamayev Kurgan[6] ("Hill of Mamai") or "Height 102," one of Chuikov's most famous command posts during the battle for Stalingrad,[7] right on the front line, had been dug into the earth at the city's highest point. For weeks it had been fought over with artillery, duels, aerial bombing, and brutal hand-to-hand combat. The ancient Tartar burial mound was now a giant memorial complex dedicated to the tens of thousands who had perished there as well as the hundreds of thousands of others who had died in the battle overall. The grassy hill had been scorched black during the fighting, was devoid of vegetation for years after the battle, and remains littered with the detritus of warfare and human bones to this day. When Field Marshal Friedrich Paulus, commander of the German Sixth Army, surrendered at the end of January 1943, his first question of his Red Army captors of the 64th Army had been where was "CP 62"?[8] By that he meant the command post on the Mamayev Kurgan.

Bestowed with honors, and twice a hero of the Soviet Union, Chuikov had been heavily involved in the postwar reconstruction of the site in the late 1950s, working alongside the renowned sculptor Evgenii Viktorovich Vuchetich[9] to produce a now world-famous memorial complex, the Motherland Calls.[10] He was a man who knew his place in the history of the Great Patriotic War, and like many of his contemporaries he ensured that he would be chief among equals when it came to celebrating the heroes of his country's greatest victory. The giant statue that dominated one of the squares in the Mamayev complex was unmistakably the face of Chuikov, much to the chagrin of his Stalingrad contemporaries.[11] He had stolen the show at the complex's official opening back in October 1967, when the people of the city cried out for him instead of the local politicians to address them. Reluctantly, he was permitted to speak, last: "My brothers, the Stalingradians!" he began, to be met by a tidal wave of shouts and cheers. Now his last wish had been granted: to be buried with his men on Height 102, the commander of the old 62nd Army to lie forever with his troops.

The Kremlin had signed his public obituary celebrating his military and political deeds, with First Secretary Leonid Brezhnev, though himself too ill to attend the funeral, sending his key men from the Central Committee to pay homage alongside local Volgograd Party dignitaries. As the easterly breeze cut through the gathering crowd waiting along the banks of the river, some sitting in trees and atop parked buses to get the best view, the most senior men in the Soviet Union had flown in from Moscow, and now they stood solemnly next to Chuikov's coffin, lying in state in the Central House of the Soviet Army on Suvorovskaya Square. The head of the KGB, Yuri Andropov, gazed past Chuikov's family and the honor guard around his coffin, toward the double-fronted glass doors. The crowd was pressing toward the entrance to get a better look. Next to him stood Foreign Minister Andrei Gromyko, lost in his thoughts. Representing the Soviet Armed Forces was the defense minister Dimitry Ustinov, who amiably talked to the younger man on his right, a rising star of the Party, recently elevated to secretary of the Central Committee—Mikhail Sergeyevich Gorbachev.

Brezhnev had long admired Chuikov, the "Legendary One." While he himself had made his way up the ladder during the Great Patriotic

War as a political commissar, it had not stopped him from inflating his own contribution to the war effort, awarding himself the military honors that commanders such as Chuikov had spilled blood for. Both men had endured an uneasy relationship with Brezhnev's predecessor as first secretary—Nikita Khrushchev. Brezhnev respected Chuikov's bluntness, and laughed at the way he had publicly questioned where Khrushchev had been during the fighting in Stalingrad.[12] And more important, Brezhnev had counted on his support when the time came to oust the erratic leader and take control of the Central Committee himself in 1962. He owed Chuikov.

After a morning of lying in state, it was time. The procession, in step with the Red Army brass band, followed the coffin, now atop a polished metal gun carriage and drawn by an armored car. The cold snap had struck the steppe countryside surrounding the city the week before, blanketing it in snow, with the numbing cold still holding Volgograd in its grip. Moisture rising from the flowing river created an eerie mist along the riverbank, adding to the funereal scene. Chuikov's family led the way, followed by the Central Committee men, other local dignitaries, a column of young Soviet guardsmen who would carry Chuikov's coffin, and finally a growing mass of civilians, including hundreds of Stalingrad veterans. The entire route was lined with thousands of residents of the city, standing five deep in some places, all wishing to see the commander's last journey.

Nikolai Chuikov continued: "My grandfather, of course, remembered and talked about veterans all his life, until the very last days, when, after multiple strokes, he was already very unwell. At his eightieth birthday, a full courtyard of veterans gathered under the windows of his apartment on Granovsky Street in Moscow. He saw them, went down, and they literally clung to him. Then he invited them home in groups to clink glasses with each one. 'We remembered our dead comrades!' my grandfather declared, as if addressing ghosts: 'I will come to you soon.' It was a moving sight."[13]

The procession had arrived at the pathway to the enormous memorial complex, which covered 1.3 square miles of the eastern slope of the Mamayev. Before they would reach their destination, the mourners were now faced with a series of terraces to ascend, each with sculptures eulogizing a stage of the battle.[14] They began by walking up the 100-meter (328-foot) path, before climbing up the two hundred steps, representing the two hundred days of the battle, which took the cortege and the multitude of followers up to the Avenue of Lombardy Poplars. They were now walking through a circular piazza enclosed by birch trees, giving the mourners a dominating view across the Volga that emphasized how crucial in commanding the high ground this position had been to both sides.

Without stopping, the procession climbed a second set of granite steps past Heroes Square and then through the cavern-like Hall of Military Glory (the Pantheon), built into the hillside, with grass covering its roof. The vaulted ceiling, marbled floor, and brick walls of the hall created a deliberate reverential atmosphere. In the light of the large, eternal flame, they could see the paneled walls where more than seven thousand of the fallen names were inscribed, a fraction of the battle's death toll. How many faceless comrades had disappeared into the fires of the battle? Following a pathway winding its way up the side of the Pantheon took the mourners into the Square of Sorrow. Now, as the mourners blinked into the natural light, there she was! Seemingly towering two hundred feet above them stood the giant statue of the Motherland Calls, sword in her hand, pointing toward the west, dominating the skyline. The wind blew in from the east over the Volga, against the backs of the mourners. Flakes of snow began to fall. They were almost there.

The young guardsmen came to a halt. A murmur now rose from the throng behind them, as dozens of elderly men emerged from the crowd. Some were in their old olive-drab dress uniforms from their service days, others in their smartest civilian dark suits. All were festooned with medals, buffed and dazzling in the wintry light, and hanging from their ribbons in three, sometimes four, rows, stretching in some cases from their collar lapels down as far as their last jacket button, showcasing a lifetime of service to the Motherland. The unsung heroes of the 62nd Army, silent and dignified.

Quietly they made their way alongside the young coffin bearers, now standing stock-still, and stepped in to replace them. They were the survivors of the 62nd Army, who had fought for Chuikov, beaten the finest modern army of its day, and driven it back to Berlin. They would carry their commander to his final resting place on the eastern slopes of the mound. A dozen formed up, flanking the coffin, with a man at the front to lead the way and another bringing up the rear. Another group would walk behind them to step in should one, or all, become unable to carry the load. Their faces betrayed nothing other than grim determination to carry out their task, though they walked slowly, much slower than the younger guardsmen whom they had replaced minutes earlier. The atmosphere was now charged as they brought their old general to his final resting place and the ceremonial music filled the air. The leader of the pallbearers turned his head back toward his men and let out a command. The procession came to a sudden halt. Two men stepped out of line and were replaced in order that the coffin be held securely—perhaps, more than the physical exertion itself, the ceremony had been too much for them. They stepped back into the crowd, one wiping his brow with his jacket sleeve. His old comrades surrounded him, squeezing his arm and patting his head in thanks.

The band had stopped playing. As family and dignitaries formed up, Marshal Kulikov, commander in chief of Warsaw Pact Forces, now stepped forward to give the farewell speech from a grateful nation and Party. Chuikov's wife, Valentina Petrovna, and extended family stood alongside local Party bosses and the veteran sniper and hero of the Soviet Union Vasily Zaitsev.[15] A friend of the family, Zaitsev reached to comfort Petrovna, pointing back down the hill toward the giant statue in the circular piazza, of a bare-chested giant clutching his PPSh-41 machine gun in one hand and a hand grenade in the other, guarding the entrance to the square they had just walked through.[16] The statue's face uncannily resembled the granite features of her husband in his prime, during the battle of 1942, his slogan declaring, "Stand to the Death!"

* * *

After four hours, it was time to lay Chuikov to rest. The final eulogies were spoken over his grave. Shots rang out as volley fire broke the silence in tribute. The local police had tried to keep the public back a respectful distance, but as the family and officials returned to their cars, the onlookers broke ranks to quietly make their way to the graveside to pay their own tribute in silence.

"To the heroes of the Battle of Stalingrad," a lone voice proclaimed.

The snow turned heavier as mist now shrouded from the mourners' view the dense forests on the eastern bank of the Volga. As the ordinary citizens walked back into the city center shielding themselves from the biting wind, the derelict monument of a red-bricked four-storey warehouse loomed in the distance. It had been the scene of what they had all been taught over the years was one of the final defensive redoubts of Chuikov's army as it clung to the western shore during the battle. Standing nearby was a series of modern apartment blocks overlooking the large open park—9th January Square. One apartment block in particular was pointed out by parents to their children as they walked by, the place where a small band of Chuikov's men had performed superhuman heroics to thwart the German Army's push to the river and capture the city—"Pavlov's House."

Introduction

The square of combat and the house
at 61 Penzenskaya Street

It is another crisp, winter's morning in Volgograd. I am walking along the Volga near to the Panorama Museum, which overlooks the great river and whose exhibits tell the story of the Battle of Stalingrad. A restored T-34 tank stands sentinel at its gates. To the right of the main entrance, hidden from view behind large double-ironed gates, is a two-storey modern building housing the museum's archives. I am spending the week there as a guest to research the oral testimonies of Red Army survivors of the battle. Just as at Chuikov's funeral, the wind whips into my face. Great clouds of steam rise off the icy flow of the river. I have been walking for an hour or so, taking in the places by the embankment in the central sector, reminded everywhere I turn that I am standing in what was once a major battlefield. The Central Landing, overlooking the Volga, is a stone's throw away from the museum, and to a Russian means just as much as Omaha Beach in Normandy might to an American. Now standing on the shoreline, I am enveloped by the icy mist. I look back toward the embankment wall towering approximately thirty feet over me. All residents of the city today know this wall, a former salt pier, on which a Red Army guardsman belonging to the 13th Guards Rifle Division daubed Russian words in tar in 1943 that translated read: "Here they stood to death, Rodimtsev's Guardsmen, having defended, they conquered death!" Just one of dozens of tributes, statues, gardens of remembrance, and squares that are dotted throughout the city to remember the fallen.

I want to inspect a large public square and a particular building nearby, one which has held my imagination since as a boy I read of the ferocious battle fought here in the Second World War. Like the city itself, since the death of Stalin and the later fall of Communism, the street I am walking down has been renamed. It is now Sovetskaya Street. The building I am looking for, Number 39, lies in the heart of the city of Volgograd, a modern, four-storey apartment block nestled close to a busy road that runs along the central section of the Volga. One end of the block overlooks Lenin's Square to the west, while the other, to the east, is a stone's throw from the museum. Next to the museum sits the impressively ruined shell of the famous Gerhardt's Mill, preserved today as it was left after the bitter fighting for the city in 1942–43. Unlike its historic neighbor, the well-maintained yellow-fronted apartment complex was the first to be rebuilt from the ruins in 1943 and put to good use for the inhabitants. To passersby it is an ordinary, though quite smart, residential building designed in the style of the city's prewar architecture. As I walk along the street, keeping the river to my right, I quickly spot what I have been hoping to see, revealed red brick, in stark contrast to the building's autumnal yellow, almost clinging to its corner and side. Carved into the brick, a message in Russian reads (in translation): "In this building fused together heroic feats of warfare and of labor. We will defend / rebuild you, dear Stalingrad!"

I walk the length of the building taking in its dimensions, recreating in my mind's eye how it would have been garrisoned as a mini fortress during the bitter house-to-house fighting, its many windows bricked up and used as firing points, the entrances to the cellars below which sheltered the Soviet defenders from German bombardments and armored attacks.

Dominating the entrance to the rear of Lenin's Square is a huge stone mausoleum, built in the Soviet modernist style. A semi-circular series of columns at its center overlooks a series of flower beds and a memorial wall. A two-dimensional figure of a Red Army soldier, again in the classic Soviet modernist style, is chiseled into the wall, a guardian to the house behind it. Below the figure, taking up almost the entire width of the memorial wall, is a list of the defenders of this house. Pavlov's House. Perhaps the most famous house in the Battle of Stalingrad.

There is a passion for the Battle of Stalingrad. It is seen by many as the key European battle of the Second World War. As the historian John Erickson concludes:

> By the end of the Stalingrad campaign Germany and its Axis allies on the Eastern Front had suffered casualties of a million and a half dead, wounded and captured. Nearly 50 divisions—almost the whole of five armies—had been lost. . . . The Soviet victory at Stalingrad was the turning point in the war on the Eastern Front and the Eastern Front was the main front of the Second World War.[1]

Across the old Soviet Union, and specifically Putin's Russia today, the victory in the city named after the old dictator represents the turning point in the Great Patriotic War of 1941–45. The sacrifices made, the casualties suffered in the war, and the victory gained in its most famous battle define modern Russia.[2] The United States of America suffered 419,000 killed in action after it entered the war at the end of 1941. The United Kingdom sustained a higher figure of 451,000 dead. The Soviets suffered more than 27,000,000 dead. From the fall of Crete in May 1941 to the invasion of Italy in September 1943, the Red Army was the only force engaged in battle with the bulk of German forces on European soil.[3] Putin's own elder brother perished in the siege of Leningrad and his father was severely wounded in 1942 defending the city. Like millions of his fellow countrymen, Putin has a deep, personal connection with and a passion for the conflict, which extends to the war's greatest battle and the Red Army's finest victory. There it resisted Hitler's plans for the conquest and occupation of the Soviet Union's vital oil fields in the Caucasus, the capture of its vital supply route on the Volga River, and the splitting of the country in two.

President Putin has visited what is now Volgograd[4] many times, often for official events, such as to commemorate the seventy-fifth anniversary of the victory on February 2, 2018. He always makes time to speak and be photographed with veterans, often at the Panorama Museum. It is part publicity to link Putin's nationalist platform to Russia's greatest battle, but also to reinforce the Soviet cult of the Great Patriotic War itself, where every action, sacrifice, death, and of course victory is justified and venerated. Perhaps, like Khrushchev, Brezhnev, Gorbachev, and Yeltsin before him, Putin recognizes the acclaim Stalin himself achieved in his postwar years, both at home and abroad, as a direct result of the victory at Stalingrad.[5]

The Russian president evokes these memories to cement his position as a strong leader, in much the same way as Joseph Stalin, seeing the country through difficult times, both economic and political. Wrapping himself in the Russian flag and celebrating the wartime deeds of his forebears guarantees him a strong base of support with patriotic Russians of all generations. At the time of editing this book in the spring of 2022, when relations between Russia and the West are as low as at any time since the end of the Cold War, over Putin's invasion of Ukraine, this domestic support (or suppression of any internal criticism) is even more critical. "Victory in Europe Day" is Russia's second biggest national holiday, and in a recent poll[6] Russians voted the victory at Stalingrad ahead of the defense of Moscow in 1941 and the subsequent victory at Kursk in 1943 as the most important event in the Second World War.

There are certain cities, fortresses, buildings, and people that are sacrosanct to the official Russia storyline that predates Putin's rise to power; their reputations evolved during the Second World War and have been burnished ever since: the defense of the Brest Fortress (in what is now Belorussia) in the early days of Operation Barbarossa in 1941; the heroism of the citizens of Leningrad, besieged, bombed, and starved for 872 days; and the men of the Red Army who would ultimately capture the biggest prize of Berlin in May 1945. The desire to venerate this collective and individual effort and link it to current events has always been paramount. This was achieved through powerful use of Soviet propaganda at the time and has been maintained in the postwar years. Stalingrad was and is the ultimate touchstone for any Russian leader—it is to the country what Dunkirk is for the British, the Alamo[7] is to Americans, or Verdun[8] is to the French. But the mythologizing of the struggle for Stalin's city can sometimes distort the true history, which in itself is unambiguously heroic.

Of the catastrophic losses in Russian lives during the course of the Second World War, sixteen million of them were civilians, and more than seven million between the ages of nineteen and twenty-five. Practically every Soviet family was left mourning a loved one. In European Russia, seventy-eight thousand cities, towns, and villages were destroyed, and the nation's transport and communication infrastructure was devastated. But Stalingrad, at an enormous cost in human life, broke the cycle of continual German victories, thus ensuring that it was now a case of *when* and not *if* the Allies would eventually defeat the Nazis. But the cost to the Russian forces was enormous, as Brandon M. Schecter concluded in *The Stuff of Soldiers*:

> By war's end, 11,273,026 were permanently lost and 34,476,700 had been drafted (on average there were about 11 million persons in uniform every year). . . . The army at the front had gone through 488 percent of its average monthly strength from 1941 to 1943. In other words, it had been rebuilt five times.[9]

Though the German summer offensive commenced in July 1942, the battle for the city itself raged from early September to February 2, 1943. It would end with the annihilation of arguably the Wehrmacht's most experienced formation, the Sixth Army.[10] This powerful force had been at the vanguard of the conquest of the Low Countries and France in 1940 and the initial invasion of Russia in June 1941. From their destruction at Stalingrad, the German forces and their Axis allies in the east would be on the defensive, and the Red Army, previously thought a spent force, would grind inexorably westward toward Berlin. As John Erikson surmises in *The Road to Stalingrad*: "If the battle of Poltava in 1709 turned Russia into a European power, then Stalingrad set the Soviet Union on the road to being a world power."[11] The five-month-long battle was a culmination of Hitler's summer offensive to strike south toward Russia's oil fields in the Caucasus with more than a million troops, catching Stalin and his military council Stavka[12] by surprise, given that they expected the Germans to repeat their direct assault on Moscow. Weeks of bloodletting through the high summer of 1942 (as the Red Army frantically threw in its reserves to stem the advance of the German Army Group South) would ultimately lead to the banks of the Volga River, the arterial transport route of the country—and the city—with a Communist showpiece on its shoreline that was now a giant wartime factory.

German forces reached the Volga north of Stalingrad on August 23 and established defensive lines around the city before launching coordinated attacks. The Luftwaffe would reduce vast areas of the city to rubble and kill thousands of civilians. From September 13 onward, a weakened Red Army did its utmost to defend within the city vital strongholds that would become legendary–the Grain Elevator, the Barrikady Gun Factory, the Tractor Factory, and Railway Station No. 1—but against relentless German armored and infantry assaults the Red Army was pushed back until it clung to a few narrow bridgeheads.

Casualties on both sides were staggering as hundreds of thousands of troops fought tooth and claw, with incessant artillery and aerial bombardments adding to the inferno. The German's field-gray tunics were so coated with dust and debris that they were often mistaken for Russian khaki. *Rattenkrieg*—"Rat's War"—became the Sixth Army's cynical nickname for their bloody struggle to advance street by street, house by house, room by room, and beneath the city streets itself, in the sewers. By late September, three weeks into the battle, the Red Army had switched tactics to tie down greater numbers of Germans, bleed their strength, and neutralize their superior aerial and armored firepower, with their troops "hugging their enemy" to maximize German casualties and deter artillery and aerial strikes.

Such fighting would herald the use of Russian storm groups comprising teams of between four and eight men, armed with grenades, machine guns, bayonets, and even sharpened spades, to clear out a building before being heavily reinforced to repel enemy counterattacks and set the building up as a mini fortress. Several of these could turn a weakened defensive line into a deadly killing ground. And so it was that a five-man team from the 42nd Guards Regiment, a Soviet "Band of Brothers," that belonged to the 13th Guards Rifle Division, was ordered to retake an apartment block that overlooked a vital section of the Russian lines within the center of the city, which had been viciously fought over since the start of the battle. The storm group was led by a twenty-four-year-old junior sergeant, Yakov Fedotovich Pavlov. Of peasant stock, from Novgorod Oblast in northwest Russia, he was renowned both for his rather dandyish fur cap and his tenacity in defense against overwhelming odds.

The fight for the city center would see two key opposing units come to the fore in Stalingrad. The German 71st Infantry Division, commanded by Major General Alexander von Hartmann, like many others, would be destroyed in the fight for the city, but not before it was involved in ferocious combat with an equally legendary formation—the 13th Guards Rifle Division of Major General Alexander Rodimtsev. Both men would lead their respective formations against each other in five months of bitter fighting for the heart of the city itself. The stories we read today of the savage, almost medieval combat both sides meted out in this house-to-house struggle are what makes the Battle of Stalingrad so appealing to historians like myself. One such story focuses on Pavlov, who has since been elevated to quite a unique position; I will discuss his story with fresh insight and testimonies from other men who fought alongside him.

Junior Sergeant Pavlov's storm group that took control of the building knew their position now protruded from their lines into German territory—affording their artillery spotters excellent positions to bring down accurate salvos on the enemy as they formed up to launch dawn attacks each day. The building also provided cover for one of the crossing points over the Volga where a landing platform had been constructed for troops and supplies to be funneled to the front line. Whoever held it controlled the bridgehead. The building would be continually attacked by German infantry and armor, and bombed from the air, even as the garrison was continually reinforced, with men and materiel, and casualties mounted.

Although strewn with the dead and dying, compared to the main event, this was a relatively insignificant battle. Once it was reported in a local newspaper during the continuing battle, however, Pavlov would become a legend and the actual events would have a new storyline inspired by the writers working for the political section of the Red Army,[13] a storyline that has little to do with reality but is accepted as fact to this day. The building on the Volga was christened "Pavlov's House" by the Soviet press, who lionized the peasant fighter's spirit as typical of the *Frontoviki*[14] on the front line of the Motherland's greatest test yet against the fascist invader. In reality, the position was code-named the "Lighthouse."

Eager to dull the reality that the Germans occupied 90 percent of the city by mid-November, the Soviets desperately required stories that would suggest the exact opposite.[15] Their reporters on the ground now wrote articles praising the heroics of Stalingrad civilians and the defending Red Army. The first mention of "Pavlov's House" appeared in the 62nd Army's newspaper *Stalin's Banner* on October 31, 1942, before being heralded after the battle in a social movement of reconstruction. The combatants were named in the *Banner* story, their ethnic origins praised, a multicultural melting pot of the Soviet Union, and artistic license was taken with the timeline of events. The piece was popular among local troops needing a feel-good story, but soon it was elevated to national status, with a similar article appearing in *Pravda*[16] on November 19, 1942, the day Operation Uranus, orchestrated by General Georgy Zhukov, set in train the encirclement and ultimate destruction of the German Sixth Army. Later the story was recounted on national radio.

Once victory had been achieved at Stalingrad, there was international celebration, with widespread praise for the Soviets. The *Daily Mail*[17] proclaimed on its front page: "Stalingrad Army Wiped Out," while across the Atlantic the *New York Times* heralded the destruction of "the flower of Adolf Hitler's army . . . [with] Axis casualties on the Volga since last Fall to [be] more than 500,000 in dead and captured alone."[18] At the Tehran Conference in November 1943, Prime Minister Winston Churchill presented on behalf of King George VI the "Sword of Stalingrad," inscribed "From a grateful British people" to Joseph Stalin.[19]

Socialist realism was the official government-approved style of art—in all its forms—that dominated Soviet Russia from the days of Lenin in the 1920s all the way through until nearly the fall of the Berlin Wall and the end of the Cold War in the 1990s. Writers, artists, sculptors, poets, and filmmakers all came under its sphere of influence in order to perfect the socialist ideal of life in the country. A key element of this doctrine was the embellishment of truth in order to support whatever Party line was taken. What would happen after the Battle of Stalingrad, to report the story of the defense of one house as a metaphor for the suffering of the city and of Russia itself, fit perfectly into the socialist realism policy.

This apocalyptical fight came to life on screen as soon as 1943 with the release of the "official" government propaganda epic *The City That Stopped Hitler: Historic Stalingrad*, directed by Leonid Varlamov and narrated by the voice of the country's iconic radio broadcaster Yuriy Levitan.[20] Stalin was the star, naturally, armed with an almost Napoleonic grasp of tactics and beloved by his troops and generals, making the key decisions to guarantee victory for a grateful nation.[21] That final part probably was indeed art imitating life in the totalitarian society that was postwar Russia and behind the "Iron Curtain" that had descended across Eastern Europe. But the sacrifices of Russia's people and its Red Army had been lauded across the globe up until that point. In France alone more than 150 streets or avenues were renamed after Stalingrad as the Communists won control in local elections from Lille to Cannes, and Bordeaux to Grenoble. A station on the Paris Metro was named after Stalin's city, and a square in the 19th arrondissement of the French capital was titled Place de la Bataille-de-Stalingrad.

There had been a wealth of reporting on the front line of the Eastern Front during the fighting, as Russia's finest writers donned olive drab to serve in the Red Army and produce for their official daily newspaper,

Red Star, what in any other country would have been award-winning prose.[22] But, as with Western writers and correspondents, sharing a trench with like-minded colleagues fostered a desire to tell the truth as they witnessed it—good or bad.

Vasily Grossman was one such writer. A chemical engineer originally from the Ukraine, he had joined up in late 1941 after hostilities began and would report on the major battles right up until the capture of Berlin in 1945. His twelve articles—some of which will be referenced later in this narrative—earned him the respect of the ordinary Red Army soldier. He captured their lives on the front line and in battle, and Stalingrad was to be the pinnacle of his war. The lives he brought to life on the page would go on to inhabit his fictional prose also, especially his finest novel, *Life and Fate,* which he completed in 1959. The honesty of his narrative describing the weaknesses of Stalin's performance in the war meant predictably that the novel would be dubbed "anti-Soviet" by the authorities and never see the light of day. Grossman died in 1964 of cancer. In 1980, his seminal work would be smuggled out of Russia and finally published to great acclaim,[23] thus pushing Stalingrad into Western audiences' consciousness as a popular subject.

As the Cold War developed, in Communist-led countries, parks, factories, housing estates were all renamed or newly constructed to celebrate the pivotal victory. Around the world, plays about the Great Patriotic War were performed to packed houses. By the 1970s, as relations between the Soviet Union and the West were thawing, two major documentary series gave due credit to the terrible cost Russia had paid to defeat Hitler. They both combined the strategic overview with the personal experience of a variety of eyewitnesses to the critical events. The multi-award-winning twenty-six-part chronicle of the conflict *The World at War* was released in 1973, narrated by Sir Laurence Olivier and with a whole episode given over to Stalingrad. It was at the time the most expensive documentary series ever produced. In 1978, Hollywood legend Burt Lancaster fronted an American answer to its British-made predecessor; a twenty-part series focusing only on the Great Patriotic War itself, with Lancaster filmed by the Volga recounting the brutal, epic nature of the fighting.[24]

In the more than thirty years since the end of the Cold War, the battle has been dramatized to audiences of millions. In 2011 the BBC produced a flagship adaptation of *Life and Fate*,[25] and three films, including the Hollywood blockbuster *Enemy at the Gates*, have given audiences a taste of the scale of destruction that was wrought on the city. And historians have also analyzed and appraised the battle, with Antony Beevor's international bestseller *Stalingrad*, David M. Glantz's *Stalingrad* trilogy, and perhaps one of the best recent titles to capture the last original voices, *Stalingrad: The City That Defeated the Third Reich* by Christopher Tauchen and Jochen Helbeck.

Pavlov's House has radically evolved in the reporting from the defense of one single building as chronicled in a Red Army newspaper, to becoming embedded in modern Russian folklore and elevated as a cornerstone of not only the battle but the entire Great Patriotic War itself. It would be then used as a symbol for a local movement of women and young pioneers to rebuild Stalingrad, which itself became a national story that would inspire similar groups in every town and city across Russia that had been damaged or destroyed by the war.[26] Sergeant Pavlov would become the poster boy of the movement, and his image is recognized by new generations in the twenty-first century.

There is a "Pavlov's House" level in the multimillion-dollar PlayStation franchise *Call of Duty* (complete with Junior Sergeant Pavlov himself), thus teaching the next generation (my teenage son among them), an erroneous version of the battle's story. In 2018, on the seventy-fifth anniversary of the victory, while on his state visit to Volgograd, President Putin stood alongside a specially selected group of students ("Victory Volunteers") to launch a nationwide, interactive, educational video game, funded by a presidential grant, which took the viewer on a virtual reality tour of the key places in the Battle of Stalingrad, including Pavlov's House.[27]

The Lighthouse of Stalingrad looks at the legend of this building, seen through the eyes of those men and women who inhabited 61 Penzenskaya Street. With the death of Stalin in 1953 came a relinquishing of government censorship, ushered in by his successor Nikita Khrushchev, and veterans were invited by the Panorama Museum's director to submit their personal stories, wherever they had fought in the city and whatever their rank. The vast majority of these testimonies have remained untouched for decades in the archives, but they vividly capture the many iconic moments of the battle, and also offer up a unique insight into what these men and women were experiencing. Yes, there was a degree of Soviet censorship in terms of the language used and what memories people felt safe to put down on paper, but nevertheless, these testimonies make for fascinating reading.

Against the backdrop of the overall campaign itself in 1942–43, and the many voices I will introduce, I will analyze the legend of Junior Sergeant Pavlov and the key figures for the fighting in the city center. The truth is in some cases quite different from what *Pravda* and other Soviet media handlers wanted the Russian public to know. To be clear, this was still a prolonged fight for a key position on the battlefield, and Pavlov himself was a brave, highly decorated soldier who would be seriously wounded three times by war's end. But the story developed a life of its own both during and after the Great Patriotic War.

The facts that have been accepted since 1943 are these: the garrison was a small "band of brothers" who were a perfect cultural mix of eleven ethnic groups drawn from across the Soviet Union and fought off overwhelming odds for fifty-eight straight days, killed hundreds of the enemy, and were commanded by Pavlov. Such was the significance of the building to the overall fighting in the battle that Field Marshal Paulus even had it marked up on Sixth Army maps. This is the official story that all Russians are aware of and indeed has been repeated in countless histories of the battle. Yet this narrative is not accurate, and the real story is far more revealing about the individuals involved, the timeline of events, and the fate of those who survived. And then there is the question of the role of Pavlov himself.

Pavlov's fame was guaranteed by press recognition and then a high-level endorsement from his old commander of the 62nd Army, Marshal Chuikov, in 1945 and from his own divisional commander, the hero of the 13th Guards Rifle Division, Major General Alexander Rodimtsev.

Both men repeated the *Pravda* storyline in their own memoirs published in the 1960s. Needing living heroes to elevate, a grateful Soviet leadership generously rewarded Pavlov with their highest military honors: the Hero of the Soviet Union, the Order of Lenin, two Orders of the Red Star, and numerous other medals. After the war, he joined the Communist Party, was elected to political office, and maintained a high profile within the Party and across the country.[28] This would be in sharp contrast to the men from his company (many of whom were killed in the siege and in subsequent later operations within the city), whose story has never been told, nor their actions rewarded. Indeed, there is currently a campaign by local historians in Volgograd to have Pavlov's House renamed for the real commander who held the garrison together but who was severely injured and later invalided out of the army. His story will be told in these pages.

With the upcoming eightieth anniversary of the battle, what will no doubt be the final gathering of veterans will take place. As few as they are, they will travel from all parts of Russia and rightly be given pride of place at various events. Amid international media attention and military ceremony, Volgograd, as it has for the past eight years, will revert to its wartime name of "Hero City Stalingrad"[29] to celebrate a great victory and commemorate the unimaginable losses. As Putin declared in his speech on the previous anniversary, five years before, atop the Mamayev Kurgan complex: "Stalingrad was turned into an invincible, impregnable fortress to halt the progress of Nazism. . . . Our soldiers turned every street, trench, house, and firing point into a fortress."

The historian in Putin has seen him publicly express the need for "patriotic education" of the country's youth and his government issue edicts that historical texts for Russian schools be rewritten and standardized to provide the "true" version of events—branding dissenting interpretations as "anti-Russian." Since the international success of Anthony Beevor's *Stalingrad* in the 1990s, he has sought to methodically limit access to the country's official archives in Podolsk[30] (which Putin's predecessor Boris Yeltsin had opened) and wholeheartedly engaged in the kind of agitprop[31] that used to be the specialty of the country's *zapolity.*[32] It is the historian's role to push against any form of censorship when writing about Russian history amid such restrictions.

This book was derived from research trips I took to Volgograd, Moscow, and Berlin, studying dozens of testimonies of the men who battled in the city and interviewing, among others, the son of Junior Sergeant Pavlov and the grandson of Marshal Chuikov. Incredibly, from the German side, I have discovered an unpublished memoir left by the last German commander of the southern pocket, who housed, protected, and acted as confidant to Field Marshal Paulus during the last fateful days. Combat veteran Major General Friedrich Roske of the 71st Infantry Division was an eyewitness to some of the key moments across five months of battle in the center of the city. Despite countless operations leading his men, he survived the battle. He was awarded a battlefield promotion from Lieutenant Colonel by Paulus during the last days of the fighting. His handwritten memoir has lain dormant for decades, until now, and sheds new light on the German assault into the city that September, the brutal fighting over the following months, and the pivotal last days of Paulus's command of the Sixth Army. From both sides, this will be a story of heroism, dogged determination against overwhelming odds, and despair as comrades are killed.

The Lighthouse of Stalingrad will, I hope, give an understanding as to why this city at the gateway to Asia was in the path of the German offensive, bring new voices to the established storyline, and specifically reveal the true legacy of the house at 61 Penzenskaya Street.

PART I

BLACK SUMMER
FOR THE RED ARMY

We had no strength to hold the defence. If we had been given an order to hold out, we would have stayed, but the command preferred to save us. We felt desperation and anger because of our helplessness, and we also wondered: *Why do they let us not fight the enemy properly? Why do we keep on withdrawing?*

—Anatoliy Grigoryevich Mereshko,
Lieutenant, 62nd Army[1]

CHAPTER ONE

Rolling the Dice—
The Battle of Moscow 1941

When Barbarossa commences the world will hold its breath
and make no comment.

—Adolf Hitler, February 1941

Today at 4 a.m. . . . without a declaration of war, Germany attacked
our country . . . Ours is a righteous cause. The enemy shall be
defeated. Victory will be ours!"[1] The monotone drone of Vyacheslav
Molotov, Stalin's minister of foreign affairs, boomed from Moscow radio
across the nation on June 22, 1941. The attack from the west that Stalin
had warned the Russian people of in the 1930s was now upon them.
His courting of Adolf Hitler over the previous two years, their mutual
carving up of Poland in 1939, and his eagerness to remain neutral and
supply the German war machine with valuable supplies had led him
to ignore the signs of imminent invasion. Millions of Axis troops were
now pouring over the border to strike deep into the country as Red
Army frontier units were overwhelmed, supply dumps captured, and
the air force destroyed.[2] Soviet fighters and bombers had been neatly
lined up in rows on the runways, giving German pilots easy targets.
Command and control centers, communication hubs, and arterial roads
running up to the border were targeted and destroyed by the Luftwaffe
to maximize the confusion. The slaughter of the first-day attacks would
continue as the armored formations of the Wehrmacht surged into the

country's heartland. The Nazi regime's "Crusade against Bolshevism," the term coined by the German propaganda minister Joseph Goebbels, was underway.

Blitzkrieg ("lightning war") had swept all before it across Poland in 1939, France and the Low Countries the following summer, and the Balkans in the spring of 1941.[3] Hitler now turned to what had always been his ultimate goal—the destruction of Bolshevik Russia. On July 31, 1940, toward the end of a conference held at his Bavarian retreat in Berchtesgaden to decide the fate of Operation Sea Lion, the invasion of Great Britain, Hitler declared that a showdown with Russia would have to take place the following spring. The intention was to repeat the timetable that had proved so successful in France that summer; speed was of the essence to defeat Stalin's European armies.

The military planning was delegated by Hitler's head of the German army Field Marshal Walther von Brauchitsch to his chief of the general staff General Franz Halder at the high command of the armed forces—*Oberkommando der Wehrmacht* (OKW). Several draft versions were analyzed, discussed, and redrawn until September, when a blueprint was ready, overseen by personnel of the Operations Division under the direction of the new assistant chief of staff, Major General Friedrich Paulus. Over the weeks leading up to Christmas the plan was war-gamed by Paulus's department, requests by the designated army group commanders were taken in, logistical advisers consulted, plans again revised and then, finally, signed off on.

On December 18, 1940, Hitler was presented with the final draft by Lieutenant General Alfred Jodl, chief of the Armed Forces Operation Staff—code-named Operation Barbarossa.[4] Critically, in the draft plans Hitler had ignored the economic concerns raised, which highlighted the issues that would come back to haunt German progress over the next twelve months. Russia's poor transportation infrastructure would need to be rapidly overhauled. Raw materials and oil reserves in the south would have to be acquired intact. Though advances had been made in domestic production quotas, by 1941 Germany was reliant on Romanian and Russian supplies through trade agreements. The former country would now be Germany's main ally to invade the latter.

Food production also had to be maintained to avoid the specter of famine. In November Hitler was confronted with the mathematics of supply. His tanks would run out of fuel, food, and ammunition after twenty days of operation once the invasion began. Significantly, this limit of fuel would reduce their scope of advance into Russia to eight hundred kilometers (five hundred miles).[5] Once they halted, it would take several weeks for the army groups to be replenished and continue their operations along the whole front, while at the same time teams of pioneers would need to adapt the bigger gauges of Russian railway lines as well as ensure that roads were passable for heavy armor and other traffic. In fact, once the invasion was well underway and the army groups were forging into enemy territory, the plunder and enemy supplies they captured would enable the Wehrmacht to continue their advances for longer than their supplies allowed.

With Russian road and rail networks poor to non-existent in southern Russia, the hard facts of resupply would hinder the Wehrmacht as it sought to defeat the Red Army in a single summer campaign. German military intelligence, often weak in terms of supplying a true picture, did at least reveal two major Russian concentrations in the western theater—seventy divisions based in the Ukraine and sixty divisions in White Russia near the border and west of Minsk, with only thirty divisions in the Baltic States—but German intelligence reports over-emphasized the effect of the reorganization that had followed the Red Army's performance in the Winter War with Finland in 1940. True, in the higher echelons of the military the cull had been dramatic and brutal, but the actual fighting ability of the rank and file was still intact in 1941.[6]

Though its industrial capacity to mass produce tanks would be successfully established by the summer of 1942, Soviet armor in 1941 amounted to fewer than than two thousand operated vehicles in the western theater. Though they would maul both German armored and motorized divisions,[7] their crews' lack of radio communications and the Red Army's inability to coordinate serious attacks doomed them to offer only sporadic and isolated resistance to the armored German juggernaut in the first weeks. The saving grace for the Red Army was their dominance in artillery, outnumbering the Germans by a ratio of 4-to-1, and what the Soviet artillerymen lacked in experience they made up for in power, making the invader pay a serious price.[8]

Unlike his educated and well-trained German counterpart, the average Soviet soldier in 1941 had only basic skills in weaponry to fall back on, with few receiving more complex instruction in communication systems and how to work alongside artillery and air support.[9] What German intelligence crucially failed to assess, and senior army commanders failed to consider, was the number of reserves available to Russia—approximately fourteen million could be called up to serve when hostilities began. The reservists were not well trained, but they were still capable of fighting, and millions of Russians now flocked to report for duty. Irrespective of what materials and tools were required, for Hitler and his closest advisers this was to be a very different kind of conflict. Outlining his primary goals, Adolf Hitler instructed a conference of the German General Staff that the Soviet Union was to be abolished, with the coming conflict to be a war of "annihilation." Joseph Goebbels wrote in his diary: "The Fuhrer says that be it right or wrong, we must win . . . for when we win, who is to question us about our method? We already have so much on our conscience as it is that we just have to win."[10]

There was still intense high-level debate, questioning, and even to a lesser degree dissent from some of the men who would lead the spearheads of Barbarossa. Field Marshal Gerd von Rundstedt, who had played a key role in Poland and France's defeats, was selected to command Army Group South. A veteran from the Great War in Eastern Europe, von Rundstedt enjoyed enough familiarity with the Fuhrer that he felt able to question Hitler whether he knew what it meant to invade Russia. He noted in his diary:

> This war with Russia is a non sensical idea to which I can see no happy ending. But if for political reasons the war is unavoidable then we must face the fact that it cannot be won in a single summer campaign. Just

look at the distances involved. We cannot possibly defeat the enemy and occupy the whole of western Russia from the Baltic to the Black Sea within a few short months. We should prepare for a long war. And go for our objectives step by step.[11]

With other leading officers, von Runstedt suggested a more balanced approach to the coming invasion, but his proposal, like all others, was rejected by Hitler, who held firm in his belief that the Bolshevik grip on the Russian state and its armed forces would crumble once hostilities began.[12] Compounding his hubristic opinion of the Red Army was his sense of destiny, driven by his instincts as a politician. He was well aware that after Germany's stunning victories in 1940, his national prestige was riding high and had given him this one moment when such a gamble would be permitted. It might not come again. The planning continued unabated. The capture of Soviet communication and industrial hubs such as Leningrad, Minsk, and Moscow were vital, but the destruction of the Russian armed forces and their ability to regenerate new ones was the priority. This ambition was supported by Hitler and commander in chief of the Luftwaffe Hermann Göring's belief that it would be a rapid campaign. The need for strategic bombing by the Luftwaffe was sidestepped in favor of a ground attack strategy to seek out and destroy the Red Army in the field. Once Russia was knocked out of the war, or at least severely crippled, Germany would only then turn west to finish off Great Britain.

To achieve this goal, Operation Barbarossa would deploy three Army Groups (North, Center, and South) comprising more than 3.8 million troops, organized into 170 German and Axis divisions, 150,000 of the elite Waffen-SS (the combat wing of the SS), and abetted by a pool of 1.2 million replacements. The forces would be supported with nearly four thousand German tanks (primarily Panzer IIs, IIIs, and IVs) and complemented by more than eight hundred captured French and Czech ones. Six hundred thousand motor vehicles and several hundred thousand horses[13] would also be in support. Though on paper the Red Army outnumbered the three German army groups by a significant margin, the single factor that would tip the balance was airpower. Each of the army groups would enjoy the protection and aerial ground support of their own powerful air fleets (*Luftflotten* 1, 2, and 4) numbering more than 3,500 aircraft and fielding 1.7 million personnel. In addition, the German Luftwaffe was undoubtably the world's most powerful and experienced air force, and it would now focus on clearing Soviet airspace on June 22, 1941.

Even though both sides were evenly matched in numbers, Stalin ignored his own diplomatic and military intelligence as to the locations of the German concentrations and ordered the Red Army to man the whole frontier, the bulk of the forces being first-year recruits with limited combat experience. By bringing such overwhelming force to targeted areas, the three German army groups would achieve rapid breakthroughs, advancing behind the Red Army's rear to then encircle and destroy them. Once that was achieved, the German Army as a whole would move forward to set up a second line so far from the territory of the Reich that it would be impossible to launch any speculative bombing raids. Ultimately, there would be an advance to a third line taking the Wehrmacht past Moscow, with their frontier stretching from Archangel in the north down to the Volga River itself, cutting the country in two and making it possible to then send the Luftwaffe to seek out and destroy Russia's industrial base beyond the Ural Mountains. Only when this final operation had succeeded would the bulk of German troops be withdrawn and preparations to deal with Great Britain begin.

Army Group North would move from their forward bases in East Prussia and advance along the length of the Baltic coast to capture and destroy Leningrad, and German expectations were the local populations would then rise up against their Russian occupiers who had previously invaded in June 1940. Army Group Center meanwhile would launch their attack from their positions in Poland close to the Soviet zone to capture the key transport hubs of Minsk and Smolensk and then drive on to Moscow. Army Group South would speed down into the Ukraine to seize its capital, Kiev, occupy its agricultural and industrial bases, and surge southward to the Caucasus region to capture the oil fields and naval ports on the Black Sea coast. The city of Stalingrad, lying by the Volga, was for now just a name on the operational map.

Even on paper the plan presented an incredibly tough nut for Army Group South to crack. The Caucasus was a massive landmass, broken up by a significant mountain range, not easy terrain to navigate and occupy, particularly if pressed by the Red Army coming from the south and the east. The Germans would be tackling a force whose strength in troops was still unknown and whose armor outgunned the attackers by a ratio of at least 2 to 1. Hitler instead focused on seizing 10 percent of Russia's overall oil production. By taking the Caucasus, Army Group South could then look to traverse the mountains to move on Transcaucasia, an even greater prize: heavy with industry, densely populated, and the Soviet's main base for oil production—twenty-four million tons in 1942 alone.[14] Added to this were the large gas deposits providing 65 percent of Russia's natural gas supplies. As well, German economists and steel magnates coveted the world's largest deposits of manganese, enabling cities such as Stalingrad to become vast industrial centers of steel manufacturing and subsequently weapons citadels. Economically, industrially, and agriculturally it all made sense to now focus on acquiring southern Russia and denying its resources to an already weakened Red Army. On paper at least . . .

Beneath the surface of Barbarossa's military strategy lay a darker policy: the Nazi leadership's ideological campaign to destroy Communism and conduct a race war against the Jews and Slavic peoples living in the territories its armies would occupy. On May 13, Hitler issued a decree, drawn up by Chief of the General Staff Franz Halder, effectively exempting German troops from punishment for any atrocities they might commit on their campaign.[15]

Two weeks before Barbarossa commenced, with troops massed on the Russian border, a second communiqué was issued, this time only to senior commanders of the Wehrmacht: *Guidelines on the Treatment of Commissars.* What became known as the "Commissar Order" would give carte blanche to German troops to deal with captured Red Army political officers as they saw fit. The leaflet stipulated that commissars "are as a matter of principal to be finished off with their weapons at once," a clear violation of international law. The German military leadership ensured as few copies as possible were distributed, with senior commanders to verbally instruct their units personally.

Not only was the deadly fate of commissars officially sanctioned by the Nazi leadership, with the connivance of the armed forces, but so too was the destruction of East European Jewry and the enslavement of the Slavic races. By the time of the fighting in Stalingrad in the autumn of 1942, more than two million Jews in the occupied territories would already be dead. The Sixth Army and the Fourth Panzer Army, heading to their own destruction in the city, became the willing enablers of many of the sanctioned massacres. The Sixth's original commander, Field Marshal Walther von Reichenau, told his men they must undertake "the complete annihilation of the Bolshevik heresy," and by following orders they would be "liberating the German people from the Asiatic-Jewish danger once and for all." Whereas the Fourth's commander, General Hermann Hoth, exhorted his men: "Russia is not a European state, but an Asiatic state. . . . Europe, and especially Germany must be freed from the pressure, and from the destructive forces of Bolshevism, for all time."[16] A few German commanders voiced their concerns at such harsh, un-Prussian methods, and would cancel von Reichenau's directive, including General Paulus once he took command of the Sixth Army in early 1942.

Stalin had been playing a high-stakes game to appease Hitler's obvious intentions to attack the Soviet Union at some point in the future. He had sidestepped getting involved with the German advances into the Balkans and Greece and had signaled to the German leader his willingness to maintain their cordial relationship by signing a neutrality agreement with Hitler's new ally Japan.[17] His denying diplomatic status in Moscow to the governments-in-exile of Belgium, Norway, and Yugoslavia further displayed his allegiance to the Germans, which he then magnified by doing the same to the Greek delegation once their country had been overrun. Playing in the background and reenforcing Stalin's belief that Hitler would not attack in 1941 were the signals displayed to him by the German ambassador to Moscow, Friedrich-Werner Graf von der Schulenburg, who genuinely fostered a cordial relationship with the dictator. As tensions built in June 1940, the Kremlin received daily reports from agents in Berlin and from border troops on the frontier detailing massed German and Axis troop movements, as well as the continual infringements by the Luftwaffe into Soviet airspace. The Soviet leader, however, convinced himself that the advantageous trade agreements that favored Germany would guarantee the peace for many more months, and that the German troop concentrations on the new border carved out of Poland were preparing in secret for the invasion of Great Britain.[18] Weeks before the invasion began, British code breakers cracked the German Enigma code at Bletchley Park, and their results coroborated reports from the Polish resistance of German troops movements. Winston Churchill's ambassador to Moscow, Sir Stafford Cripps, was ordered to inform the Kremlin of British fears a German attack was likely. Stalin was not convinced. The warnings from American intelligence were given equally short shrift.

The performance of the Red Army in the Winter War with the Finns in 1940 had highlighted the poor training of many front-line Soviet formations, their tactical backwardness, poor communications, and inability to handle modern technology. Only overwhelming numbers and armored brigades had managed to overpower the resilient Finns, who lacked antitank weapons and had resorted to improving the basic petrol bomb forever known as the Molotov cocktail.[19] The consequence of such a poor showing was that German planners believed the time to fight the Red Army had come, and that within the Kremlin there was a debate on how bad the Red Army actually was. Stalin's favorite Bolshevik, the hapless Marshal S. M. Budyonny, struck a chord with his brutal takedown of the Red Army's uncoordinated leadership at all levels: "At times we wander around on a great operational-strategic scale, but how will we conduct operations if the company is no good, the platoon is no good, or the squad is no good?"[20]

Stalin's infamous purge of the Red Army officer class in the latter half of the 1930s had caused untold systemic damage to the military's ability to function as a modern armed force. During the brutal elimination, 45 percent of the senior officers and political officials of not only the army but also the navy were executed or sacked, including 720 out of the 837 commanders, from colonel to marshal, appointed under the new table of ranks established in 1935. Out of 85 senior officers on the Military Council, 71 were dead by 1941.[21] The lower ranks suffered less severely in terms of imprisonment or execution, but nevertheless by the time of Barbarossa more than ten thousand officers had been thrown out of the Red Army. Added to this was Stalin's root-and-branch overhaul of the Red Army's organization and command structure in the summer of 1941, creating strategic commands (or "fronts") that controlled a number of armies and had responsibility for a major geographical sector of the front ranging in places for hundreds or thousands of kilometers. Like a German army group, each Soviet front had an overall commander, supported by a political equivalent,[22] and had responsibility for all arms—including air forces.

Within its first weeks, Operation Babarossa yielded incredible results for all three German army groups. Army Group Center surged into western Russia, encircling Stalin's western armies around the key transport hubs of Bialystok-Minsk, taking more than four hundred thousand prisoners and destroying twenty-five hundred tanks.[23] The Luftwaffe achieved air superiority, destroying more than sixty Soviet airfields and four thousand planes for the loss of just under four hundred aircraft. With enemy skies cleared, the Luftwaffe ground strikes supported Panzer formations to blunt Soviet counterattacks. Phase One of Barbarossa—the destruction of the Red Army's forces close to the border—had been achieved. On July 3, German General Franz Halder was scathing about the enemy's lack of coordination, saying he found their tactics employed in these attacks singularly poor. Riflemen on trucks abreast with tanks drive against our firing line, and the inevitable result are very heavy losses to the enemy. Such desultory attacks cannot be regarded as a threat to our operations.[24]

The incredible successes and the seeming collapse of the Red Army across the whole front led ordinary German troops of the Sixth Army to proclaim, "*Russland ist kaput!*" and for Halder back at Army High Command to triumphantly conclude: "It is . . . no overstatement to say that the Russian Campaign has been won in the space of two weeks."[25]

For the residents of the city of Stalingrad in southwestern Russia, hundreds of miles away from the fighting, the shock of the German attack was only matched by the belief that their city was safe situated by the Volga, as sixteen-year-old schoolboy Nikolai Vasilievich Orlov recalled:

> We were told that Kiev had been bombed and the war had begun. To be honest, I cannot speak for the entire city, as I don't know everything, but we lived with two thoughts: that the Germans would never come here—this is the first—and the second that we would win![26]

Debate now raged at Supreme Headquarters. Hitler wanted the original goals of Barbarossa to be achieved: to capture Leningrad, along with Southern Russia's oil and mineral wealth, and subjugate the Crimea, which threatened German oil supplies from Romania. His field commanders, supported by Halder, on the other hand, sought a decisive victory over the Red Army. On July 19, at the height of the ferocious fighting around Smolensk, which guarded the route to Moscow, the Fuhrer ordered that Army Group Center's infantry would continue its drive toward Moscow, but its armored formations would now reroute, with some units heading north to assist with the capture of Leningrad, while others turned south to support the drive into the Ukraine. His Fuhrer Directive No. 34 stated:

> The most important aim to be achieved before the onset of winter is not the capture of Moscow but, rather, the occupation of the Crimea,

of . . . The Donets Basin, the cutting of the Russian supply routes from the Caucasus oil fields.

Stalin's initial response had been to rapidly organize the poor defenses he himself had created, but his response to the looming catastrophe in late July was to single out his commanders for arrest and execution, most notably General Dimitri Pavlov, who led the Western Front, replacing him with a talented officer who would play a major part in the battle on the Volga for the following year—General Andrey I. Yeremenko.

By early September, more than four million Russian troops had been killed, wounded, or captured, Leningrad was under siege, Smolensk and Kiev had been overrun after much bitter fighting, and Moscow desperately constructed concentric waves of defenses. German troops, exhausted but elated, marched east in the heat and dust as columns of ragged Soviet prisoners passed in the opposite direction. In Southern Russia, the German Army Group South was tasked to move toward the Caucasus, capture the main city of Rostov, and move on past the Don River toward Stalingrad. The capture of the oil fields and Moscow was given priority before winter set in, despite the heavy fighting that had severely slowed the army's advance by the end of the autumn. Though nothing like the Red Army's, German losses were substantial—by the end of the summer they had lost more than 180,000 men, greater than the total number of casualties from all their campaigning the previous year. With its armor returned from the fighting in the south by late September, Army Group Center pressed toward the Soviet capital. The Battle of Moscow, commencing in early October, would involve 70 Wehrmacht divisions, totaling a million men, supported by 1,700 tanks, 14,000 artillery pieces, and almost 1,000 aircraft to capture the capital. Once again, the offensive took Stalin by surprise. He was convinced that the German Army was too exhausted and ignored his own intelligence telling him otherwise.

However, by attacking on such a broad front of more than one thousand miles and delaying Barbarossa's launch until so late in the summer, Hitler had failed to take into account not only the worsening weather conditions but equally the Soviets' fighting spirit. More surprising, even though Army Group Center had taken 650,000 Russian prisoners, were reports of yet more fresh Soviet divisions appearing at the next line of defense on the road to Moscow. But despite their own increasing losses in men and machines,[27] by mid-October Army Group Center commander Fedor von Bock's army was less than forty miles from Moscow. The population and civil authorities of the capital panicked, with thousands fleeing to the east on trains and buses and in cars. The second week of October brought some respite, however, as the cold rain ushered in the seasonal *"Rasputitsa."*[28] Unpaved dirt roads now became impassable quagmires. The dazzling daily advances of thirty miles dropped to a plodding two to five miles per day. The momentum had been lost, as had the morale of the German troops doing the fighting. Heavy casualties reduced units to skeleton formations, and several hundred vehicles littered the semi-destroyed highways leading to Moscow. Colonel General Halder bemoaned the losses on November 22: "The troops . . . are finished (e.g., in my old Seventh Division, one regiment is commanded by a First Lieutenant, the battalions are commanded by Second Lieutenants)."[29]

The German commanders' frustration at the weather was compounded by their intense anger at the increased supply problems of ammunition and fuel, which were piling up in depots in Poland, ready to be shipped to the front-line units but not getting there. One issue was a lack of specialized engineer units to transform the smaller gauge Russian railway to allow for German trains, to rebuild bridges and viaducts, and to restore destroyed lines. The crisis was not just confined to provisions for the tanks, but also for the troops' ability to survive and fight in the harsh conditions. Temperatures dropped significantly in November—on some days to well below freezing. Another issue was that tons of adequate winter clothing was stranded in the warehouses back farther west in Poland and East Prussia, unable to be distributed in time due to the transport of ammunition and food taking priority on what rolling stock was actually running. All life seemed to come to a standstill as German tanks and motor vehicles ceased to function and the men operating them sought the shelter to simply stay alive.

This scenario of poor logistics had been analyzed by Paulus's department at Army Headquarters prior to Barbarossa being signed off on. The memo had brought Hitler to a furious tirade:

> I won't hear any more nonsense about the hardships of our troops in winter. . . . There is not going to be a winter campaign. All the Army has to do is to hit the Russians a few hard cracks. Then you'll see that the Russia giant has feet of clay!

He ordered no one within his military circle to utter the phrase "winter campaign" again.

The Red Army around Moscow was now assessed as a spent force: the elimination of the bulk of their professional forces and the destruction of twenty thousand tanks and fourteen thousand airplanes had German intelligence presenting an optimistic picture as Army Group Center contemplated going into winter quarters. In the north, Leningrad was besieged and its capitulation thought imminent.[30] Moscow itself was now protected by a militia force of thirty-one thousand men, strengthened by two divisions of NKVD (the forerunner of the KGB) and reinforced by Stalin's decision to remain and fight. Troops and tanks daily paraded past the Kremlin and through Red Square in a public show of strength as they made their way to the front line. The atmosphere within the city was grim but defiant, as one foreign correspondent witnessed:

> A Moscow face was a haggard face. While children, bundled against the cold, played in the snow, the men and women, the boys and the girls, had pushed themselves and been pushed to the limits of human endurance. Some two million out of a population of four and a half million left for the army or for the Urals and beyond as factories and shops were transferred to safe areas. Ambulances brought the wounded straight from the front to the city's hospitals and clinics. Children who died accidentally or of malnutrition or disease were taken through the streets on sleds to the crematorium.[31]

The Soviet command, however, steeled by the fantastical defense that had saved the capital even if German bombers were sporadically flying over Moscow, now feverishly mobilized whatever forces they could muster to mount a serious counteroffensive. General Georgy Zhukov had taken command of the Western Front since October 10. A talented, abrasive, and somewhat ruthless commander, quite willing to expend men's lives in reckless attacks if ordered to by the Kremlin, he had become over time Stalin's "fireman." He had risen rapidly through the officer ranks since the revolution, survived the purge of the Red Army, and made a name for himself in the Far East by defeating the Japanese in a localized frontier battle.

On December 5, Zhukov launched a ferocious attack with T-34s and ski troops through the freezing morning mist. Though low in the number of tanks they could deploy, all three armies took the Germans by complete surprise. Within a week along the whole front, hundreds of thousands of German troops had been pushed back fifty miles through rain, sleet, and snow. The temperature fluctuating on either side of zero degrees often forced the Germans to seek shelter as a new freeze enveloped them, thus allowing the Soviets to gain the momentum on the battlefield. By December 19, a complete disaster was only averted through Hitler's dogged refusal to retreat, issuing his armies Fuhrer Directive No. 39 to adopt a "hedgehog" defense of existing positions and fight for their lives where they stood.

Though the Soviet winter offensive had saved Moscow, inflicting more than 110,000 German casualties,[32] Army Group Center had not been destroyed, and by the opening of 1942, it was still a strategic threat to Moscow. Significantly the Red Army had stopped a German offensive for the first time and forced them to retreat. Stalin had escaped the catastrophe brought on by his own policies. He believed the momentum was now with the Red Army. On January 5 he announced to the commanders of his military council, the Stavka, the conclusions he had taken from the recent victory: "The Germans are taken aback after their defeat. . . . Now is the time to take the general offensive. The enemy expects to hold up until the spring, to gather his forces and again launch active operations." The new objective for Zhukov was to "deny the Germans any breathing space, to drive them westward without let-up."[33]

When the Soviet general offensive was launched in an uncoordinated fashion of individual mini assaults, as Zhukov had feared, Stalin's great masterstroke met stubborn German resistance, bringing the fighting to an end by the beginning of March 1942. Though the Red Army had seized the initiative, achieved territorial gains, inflicted heavy casualties on the Germans, and secured Moscow, Stalin had ultimately failed to achieve a decisive reversal of the strategic situation. Though the Wehrmacht at certain points along the Eastern Front crumbled and retreated, and at many points suffered Soviet incursions into its rear and flanks, their line had managed to stay together. German losses had been heavy, in men and machines. Some units had been cut off and surrounded, such as the 16th Army south of Leningrad at Demyansk.[34]

With this stalemate, the Kremlin pondered what the next move would be for 1942. How strong were the Germans now? Intelligence reports had confirmed fresh units arriving from the west. With casualty rates soaring, Hitler still had available more than nine hundred thousand fresh troops stationed idly along the French Channel ports awaiting a potential attack from Britain. A continued German thrust to capture Leningrad, or one against the capital? Would they strike south once more with renewed vigor to take the Crimea and the Caucasus?

Feeding this debate was the knowledge of the catastrophic losses Russia's infrastructure and armed forces had endured. Millions of Red Army soldiers had died or walked into German captivity (itself a living death for many). Thousands of towns and villages were now under occupation. The process to train and arm the fresh millions of Russians enlisting would take time they didn't have. Though the Red Army now had the best tanks in the war to take on the Panzer divisions, the tactics to employ them on the battlefield and the communications to coordinate attacks lagged behind the Germans. The Russian state had now succeeded in relocating its heavy industry to the safety of the Urals.[35]

For Hitler an unexpected and crushing defeat had been avoided. Army Group Center had halted Zhukov's counteroffensive with elements now occupying a long salient near Rzhev, more than one hundred kilometers (more than sixty miles) from Moscow.[36] To Stalin's Stavka it represented a serious strategic distraction from their efforts to predict Hitler's spring and summer campaigns. Compounding the setbacks outside of Moscow, and though his armies had been saved from destruction, was the Fuhrer's nagging fear of Germany running out of the raw materials it required to continue waging and winning this war. The setbacks in Southern Russia now made this concern very real indeed. Though not as deadly as Stalin's earlier purges, Hitler took an axe to the German General Staff, including Field Marshal von Bock and several other army- and corps-level leaders.[37] The mistakes in logistics and in the stockpiling of munitions and supplies were rectified to a degree, too, though not completely overhauled successfully by the time of the following year's summer campaign.

In any given situation the Fuhrer would justify his insistence on holding a position by harking back to the bitter fighting outside of Moscow, Leningrad, and Kiev,[38] a thought process that would manifest throughout the early months of the summer campaign as his plans stalled and momentum was lost. It would have dire consequences by the autumn of 1942. For both dictators during that spring, their opinions of what the fighting of the previous year had revealed to them about each other, what their enemy's next move would be, how strong their own forces were, and their own military ability would have dramatic consequences for the coming decisive campaign.

CHAPTER TWO

History Repeating Itself—
March 15–May 28, 1942

Next winter, no matter where it finds us, will find us better
prepared.

—Adolf Hitler, April 26, 1942[1]

I n his address to the German people broadcast on national radio on
March 15, 1942, the Fuhrer outlined the scale of the intense fighting
of the past few months. The Soviet winter offensive had been "defeated,"
and both sides were now settled behind their lines amid the spring
downpours. While the three German army groups attempted to reorga-
nize, refit, and replenish their respective units, at home the Nazi regime
politically sought to take stock, too. Hitler needed to not only justify the
colossal losses to the nation but also explain the failure of Barbarossa
and now prepare his people for the continuing war in the east in 1942.
His speech at the Memorial Day Address in Berlin was an opportunity
to justify the struggle, both to the home front and his armed forces:

> We know one thing already today: The Bolshevist masses which were
> not able to conquer the German and allied soldier in the winter, will
> be beaten in every direction in the summer. . . . Aware of the great
> year which is behind us, which will be followed by one at least equally
> as great, we think of our heroes, and of those of our brave allies, past
> and present, determined to see to it that these sacrifices were not in
> vain and will not be in vain.[2]

Hitler eyed fresh conquests for his forthcoming summer campaign. It was one he was determined would deal a significant blow to the Red Army and potentially knock Russia out of the war, or at the very least cripple it effectively enough for Germany to turn its full attention to deal with Stalin's allies, Britain and America. With Hitler's declaration of war on the United States in December 1941, the Third Reich now found itself in a global economic war of attrition, one it could only win by ensuring it had the industrial strength to compete and defeat the Allies. To achieve that goal, Germany needed a decisive, strategic victory in the eastern theater while their enemy was in a perceived weakened state. Hitler confided to his propaganda minister, Joseph Goebbels, that this offensive would be one of three targets for the year. Once the Caucasus was captured, the focus would switch for Army Group North to capture Leningrad and for Army Group Center to then finish the job of taking Moscow. His ambition far outweighed reality.

This self-belief was powered by the losses Barbarossa had inflicted on the Red Army—more than 3.1 million killed and 3 million prisoners of war.[3] Hitler's optimism for a final reckoning may have been artificially high in the spring of 1942, a view reinforced by his military advisers. The destruction wrought on the Soviet Union since June 22, 1941, had almost succeeded in the elimination of the western half of the Red Army (or at least the formations German intelligence was aware of) and the occupation of the whole of European Russia.

Despite the winter counteroffensive, by the end of the campaigning in March 1942, Stalin looked westward upon a devastated country. Tangible support—an invasion of Western Europe—from his new allies Britain and the United States of America would be slow in coming. Raw materials, fuel, and armaments were arriving into the country via the quickest route, the Baltic shipping lanes to Murmansk, but confirmation on a date for a "Second Front" in Europe would frustrate the Soviet leader of the whole of 1942. German and Axis forces now occupied large swaths of Russia. In the south, the breadbasket of the fertile Ukraine, German occupation had reduced by 50 percent bread and meat supplies to the remaining 130 million Soviet citizens living outside of occupied territory. One-third of Russia's rail network was now lying behind occupied German lines. The best roads had been in western Russia, and the Germans now used them. Production of coal, steel, and iron ore dropped by two-thirds over the next six months, resulting in a significant drop in armaments production.

By the beginning of May 1942, Hitler had taken complete control of the armed forces as their commander in chief by sacking the incumbent Field Marshal Walther von Brauchitsch.[4] The planning for the coming offensive that summer would emphasize how the balance of power had turned in his favor versus the opinion of the traditional German military establishment. He was reluctant to let his military and economic advisers confer, preferring to keep the departments separate lest they discuss the Fuhrer's goals for further campaigns.

The losses suffered by German armed forces in the ten months of continual fighting, though but a portion of the Red Army's, were still staggering to an army used to winning. At the Fuhrer's headquarters (the "Wolf's Lair") in East Prussia, a report drafted by General Franz Halder provided a reality check for the German armed forces operational ability in the coming spring and summer campaigns. From a combined force of more than three million personnel that had invaded European Russia the previous year almost a third were now casualties, with the Wehrmacht short by at least thirty divisions, approximately 625,000 men. The majority of rifle companies were now reduced to between 50 and 60 combatants, with little hope of being reinforced by the limited pool of replacements in Germany.[5] Unlike Stalin, Hitler had not yet set the country's economy for total war, nor conscription to the full quota of German males, which would only begin in the first months of 1943.

As the needs of the war effort for Germany's other theaters evolved, production stepped up for the construction of U-boats for the Atlantic War in 1942,[6] but German workers were not yet as expendable as the hundreds of thousands of Russian workers and prisoners in the Gulag system who were pressed into working in the country's weapons industry.

Halder informed Hitler that of the 3,700 Panzers allocated to the sixteen Panzer divisions of the three army groups in 1941, only 140 serviceable armored vehicles now remained on the whole front (the equivalent of just one full-strength division). More than 13,600 artillery pieces and mortars had been lost, 80,000 vehicles, and well over 180,000 horses.[7] Only the Luftwaffe had been able to partly replace the losses of its planes and pilots that had provided remarkable support to the army. They were, however, now struggling to cover not only the Eastern Front but also their commitments in Western Europe and now Field Marshal Erwin Rommel's North Africa campaign and its operation to destroy the British naval base at Malta, which threatened Rommel's supply lines from Italy.

Processing new conscripts, Halder continued, could be speeded up,[8] but the critical weakness was the irreplaceable losses of junior and non-commissioned officers—essential for any effective combat battalions to operate successfully. To acquire and train such men would take more time, only increasing the structural weaknesses of many already understrength divisions. Morale and discipline, too, had fallen off sharply before, during, and after the winter battles. Many unit commanders reporting flagrant breaches by the rank and file, and the regime's assessment of letters sent back from the front found that soldiers complained of poor rations, living conditions, and the progress of the war. Hitler accepted Halder's sober conclusion that the Wehrmacht was no longer capable of repeating 1941. But it was at this point that the men's proposals for strategy in 1942 diverged, as had been made clear by Hitler's discussions with Goebbels the previous month.

Conducting a war on two fronts Halder and his chief of operations, Major General Adolf Heusinger, now argued for a conservative, defense-based strategy.[9] The Wehrmacht should be allowed to rebuild its shattered infantry and armored divisions behind a solid, fortified line that would repulse any offensive the Red Army might launch. If that was agreed, then limited operations should be the main objective for the coming summer's campaign, such as capturing the Crimea and establishing a base to then launch a major offensive in 1943. Frustrated at Halder's lack of ambition perhaps, Hitler questioned his plan for a defensive front in '42, arguing it would ultimately hand the initiative back to the Red Army, who would be gaining in strength, too.

Arguably the Red Army had the tank of the Second World War, the T-34, but they still needed to work out how to use it properly in terms of formations, tactics, and radio communications—all which the Germans excelled in. But as one German general who inspected a captured T-34 concluded: "If the Russians ever produce it on an assembly line, we will have lost the war."[10] Halder's presentation of the latest intelligence reports, of the Russian factories now operational in the Urals producing six to seven hundred T-34 tanks a month, were dismissed by the Fuhrer as Soviet propaganda. And concerns as to what remained of the vast manpower reserves the Stavka could call upon were silenced, too. Six million were dead on the battlefield or now rotting in German cages, so how could there possibly be fresh armies out there?

The brutal conditions of the Russian winter had caught out the Germans both physically and technologically. The Russian fighting man was well used to the temperature drop, was insulated from the freezing cold with a padded cotton jacket called a *telogreika* (body warmer), a warm hat (*ushanka*), and felt boots and gloves to keep frostbite to a minimum. His weapons, artillery, vehicles, and tanks were better designed and lubricated to combat the arctic conditions, too, thus keeping him mobile and fighting effectively. Facing him by the spring of 1942 was a German infantryman who had barely survived the plunging temperatures, been frustrated by freezing equipment, and subjected to a sporadic supply of food and fuel. He was desperate not to suffer the same fate again, though the rank and file still held faith in Hitler as their military leader.

The spring of 1942 heralded further disruption as the extreme conditions of the Russian Winter now gave way to the clawing mud of the springtime thaw. The daily struggle to simply survive and stabilize the fronts was hard for both sides, as the Soviet war correspondent Vasily Grossman recorded: "Certainly no one has seen such filth: rain; snow; grain; a liquid bottomless swamp; a black dough kneaded by thousands of boots, wheels and tracks."

Hitler was confronted with a variety of opinions about where the next summer offensive should be conducted: A major offensive in the north to finally capture Leningrad, or try to finish the job of taking Moscow and knock out Stalin's communication hub? He realized that the Red Army would fiercely defend the Soviet capital and that the German losses would be great and deliver only a local victory, which would not now affect the overall progression of the war, made more consequential by the entry of the USA. He was fully aware that Germany required the resources to fight on several fronts and survive, so the priority had to be to cripple the Red Army in the south in order to acquire these resources. On April 5, 1942, he made his fateful decision, and his Fuhrer Directive No. 41 set out his goals in the east for 1942:

> All available forces will be concentrated on the main operations in the Southern sector, with the aim of destroying the enemy before the Don, in order to secure the Caucasian oil fields and the passes through the Caucasian mountains themselves.

As yet, Stalingrad was simply a name on a strategic map for the Fuhrer:

> Every effort will be made to reach Stalingrad itself, or at least bring the city under fire from heavy artillery so that it may no longer be of any use as an industrial or communications centre.

For the command of the Army Group South offensive, Field Marshal von Bock, methodical but reliable, was installed on January 20—a mere month after departing his position as commander of Army Group Center. His pathway to the post had been fortuitous and unexpected. The sudden death of Army Group South's recent commander, Field Marshal Walther von Reichenau, originally of the Sixth Army, had to be resolved. Arguably Hitler's most talented operational commander, and a hard-nosed, charismatic Nazi, Reichenau had enforced the regime's "Commissar Order" during Barbarossa and offered logistical support to *Einsatzgruppen* units (paramilitary death squads)[11] liquidating Jewish communities in his area—such as at Babi Yar outside of Kiev, where more than thirty-three thousand Jews were murdered in two days.[12] His promotion to command an army group that December had enabled him to

promote a staff officer he believed would make a solid operational commander of the Sixth Army—General Friedrich Paulus. The men were
a study in contrasts. Paulus was studious, not prone to the explosions
of temper or the tactical brilliance of his commander. Though Paulus
lacked leadership experience in combat, Reichenau predicted his protégé
would rise to the challenge, despite other senior commanders' concerns.

The new partnership barely lasted a month. A fitness fanatic, after
returning from a run near his headquarters on January 14, Reichenau
suddenly collapsed in front of his shocked senior staff:

> The once so strong and active Field Marshal hung slackly between
> two orderly-officers, his eyes staring into nothingness. He appeared
> to have lost consciousness. . . . Reichenau's right arm was drooping,
> as was the right side of his face.[13]

Reichenau had suffered a catastrophic stroke. His medical team
requested the field marshal's personal doctor be flown down from his
unit based with Army Group North. The forty-eight hours travel time
proved costly. Reichenau would be dead soon after the doctor arrived.
To compound the drama, the plane ferrying him back for burial in
Germany crashed outside of Lviv. A shocked Hitler awarded him a
state funeral in Berlin while then ordering Field Marshal von Bock to
assume command of the coming offensive.

Army Group South would first eliminate the Russian forces occupying
the final portion of the Crimea and capture the besieged naval base at
Sevastopol, with its sizeable garrison of Red Army, naval, and air force
units capable of causing havoc to Axis shipping and transportation of
oil supplies. Once this had been achieved, Axis forces would launch
a full-scale two-pronged offensive: pushing as far as the Volga before
advancing down to the Caucasus. The twin goals were to encircle and
destroy Red Army forces and capture Maikop and Grosny to secure
their oil refineries.[14]

It was assumed as an article of faith by Hitler and his military retinue that Russian forces were now in defensive mode, limited by their immense losses and struggling to replace them. German military intelligence had attempted to assess this by studying casualty reports, interrogating prisoners of war, and conducting reconnaissance flights. Halder's intelligence department—Foreign Army East ("FHO"),[15] led by Lieutenant Colonel Ebehard Kinzel—was working on an assumption that Stalin was indeed husbanding his reserves—between thirty and sixty divisions—to protect Moscow. In front of Army Group South, however, along the main front protecting the Caucasus to the south and east toward the Volga, was anything up to one million troops, spread across more than fifteen hundred kilometers (more than nine hundred miles) of terrain.

On April 1, 1942, Kinzel was replaced by one of Halder's own intelligence officers who had assisted him prior to Barbarossa in 1941: Lieutenant Colonel Reinhardt Gehlen. Though the military command had a faith in his methods, in reality he had no clear idea of the troop buildup deeper inside unoccupied Russia. With the fuel they carried, Luftwaffe reconnaissance flights could not possibly venture so far into enemy territory and hope to make it back. In the vastness of the open steppe of Southern Russia it was a challenge to discover new formations, and snatching front-line prisoners only provided limited information on local troop movements.

The Stavka had been building up a huge reserve of manpower since the end of the winter campaign. More than eight hundred thousand troops from the new levees of reservists had been called up after June 22, 1941, plus powerful tank armies were fielding the T-34, which was coming off the production line in the numbers Halder had warned Hitler about. These fresh reserves were busy training and equipping some way behind the existing front line, their positions stretching from northeast of Moscow down as far south as Stalingrad. Their combined strength numbered at least 50 percent of the entire German force on the Eastern Front.

With such resources being assembled and falling for the deception campaign implemented by Army Group Center that Moscow was indeed the target for 1942,[16] the Stavka's new formation for the western armies became lopsided, restructured into eight "fronts" that would stretch along the entire line from the Baltic to the Caucasus. Three fronts protected Moscow itself and comprised 50 percent of the forces, with the southern flank protecting the far weaker frontier of the Caucasus. General Zhukov would command the northern fronts protecting Leningrad and Moscow while Marshal Semyon Timoshenko would oversee the southern fronts.

Hitler's dream was of Ukrainian wheat and Caucasian oil; Stalin's was to drive out all German forces from western Russia by the end of the year, a strategy that had been discussed at length since the end of the winter battles, with offensives mapped out along the length of the Eastern Front. The Soviet leader had informed Winston Churchill on March 14: "I feel entirely confident that the combined efforts of our troops, occasional setbacks notwithstanding, will culminate in crushing the common enemy and that the year 1942 will see a decisive turn on the anti-Hitler front."[17]

One such eye-catching "localized" offensive was proposed by Marshal Timoshenko: to retake the crucial transportation hub of Kharkov, attack Army Group South's forces, thought to be thinly spread to the north and south, and encircle them in a pincer movement around the city. The industrial center of the Ukraine that had built the T-34 until the tank's factories were shipped east, was the fourth largest city in Russia with a population of nine hundred thousand. Its capture and occupation by Army Group South had been one of the German successes during the bitter fighting of the Red Army's winter offensives. The Stavka authorized Timoshenko to make plans for the Kharkov offensive with all the reserves the Southwestern Front could muster. Whether Hitler and the German High Command believed the Red Army capable of such a feat had been discussed at length, but amid his preparations for his own offensive, Field Marshal von Bock's diary for May 8 was telling: "My great concern that the Russians might pre-empt us with their own attack has not diminished."[18]

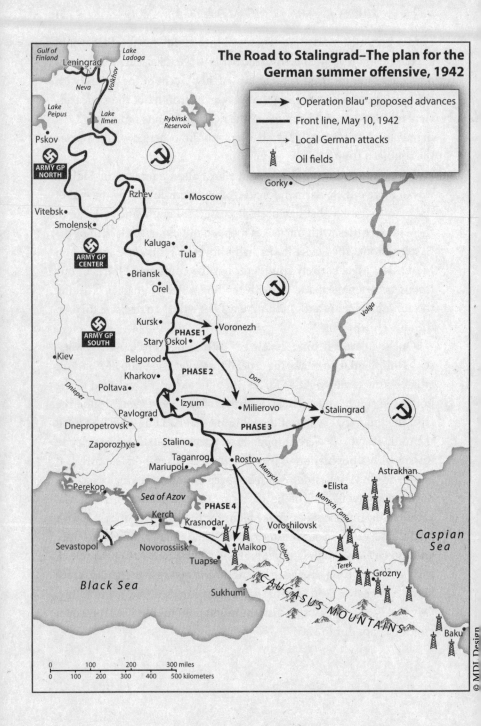

The Road to Stalingrad–The plan for the German summer offensive, 1942

→ "Operation Blau" proposed advances

▬ Front line, May 10, 1942

→ Local German attacks

Oil fields

Gulf of Finland
Leningrad
Lake Ladoga
Neva
Volkhov
Lake Ilmen
Lake Peipus
Pskov
ARMY GP NORTH
Rybinsk Reservoir
Gorky
Rzhev
Moscow
Vitebsk
Smolensk
ARMY GP CENTER
Kaluga
Tula
Briansk
Orel
Kursk
Voronezh
PHASE 1
Stary Oskol
Belgorod
ARMY GP SOUTH
Kiev
Kharkov
PHASE 2
Don
Poltava
Izyum
Milierovo
Stalingrad
Volga
Dnieper
Pavlograd
Dnepropetrovsk
PHASE 3
Zaporozhye
Stalino
Taganrog
Rostov
Mariupol
Manych
Astrakhan
Perekop
Sea of Azov
Elista
PHASE 4
Manych Canal
Kerch
Krasnodar
Voroshilovsk
Caspian Sea
Sevastopol
Novorossiisk
Maikop
Kuban
Tuapse
Terek
Grozny
Black Sea
Sukhumi
CAUCASUS MOUNTAINS
Baku

0   100   200   300 miles
0 100 200 300 400 500 kilometers

© MDL Design

CHAPTER THREE

The Move South

The Red Army's task is to liberate our Soviet territory from the German invaders!
—Joseph Stalin[1]

Marshal Timoshenko was no fool when it came to understanding what was required to defeat the German forces arrayed against his Southwestern Front. To crush Army Group South's premier Sixth Army, take back the city, and drive westward toward the Dnieper River, he would need 640,000 troops, supported by 1,200 tanks and more than 1,000 artillery pieces. Stalin was impressed yet concerned at what was required for just one offensive such as this. Hamstrung by the needs of other fronts, he watered down Timoshenko's offensive to only capture Kharkov and stabilize the line. The Kharkov offensive, however, was a failure in planning and preparation. Logistical logjams forced the Soviet offensive's launch date to be delayed as German forces continued to build for their own campaign, meaning the Red Army would confront twice the force their commanders had anticipated.

On May 12, Timoshenko launched his ground assault against Army Group South but encountered tough German resistance almost immediately, stalling progress as fierce fighting erupted. Within three days, Paulus's Sixth Army had been mauled from multiple directions, losing more than ten thousand men, as Soviet armor vainly attempted to break through his defenses to close their preplanned encirclement. The Wehrmacht's ability to soak up punishment allowed Paulus, with massive air strikes from the Luftwaffe, to tie down the greater portion of the Soviets' northern thrust as the weather turned and Kleist's First Panzer Army then struck the Russian's southern flank.

Intimidated by the speed with which the Germans had counterattacked, Russian military commissar Nikita Khrushchev cabled Moscow to seek permission to withdraw. For a crucial thirty-six hours Stalin refused, until it was too late. By then Paulus's forces were waiting for Kleist's mobile formations to move up from the north to close the door on the hemmed-in Soviet forces. As the weather turned humid in the early summer sun, more than 250,000 Red Army troops were squeezed into an ever-decreasing pocket as German armor, artillery, and bombers picked off retreating Soviet columns of tanks and decimated whole battalions at a time, many Russian soldiers linking arms and marching toward their doom rather than be taken alive. For Lieutenant J. M. Yampolsky, manning a 45mm antitank gun and retreating as the German encirclement grew tighter, there was no cover to find:

> I was one of the four hundred men in the covering force spontaneously set up by some infantry colonel. We took up the defensive, as we were told to give the chance for two field hospitals, chock full of wounded, to move to the rear. The German infantry showed up in the morning. Our defensive line faced the advancing Germans with gunfire. A few minutes later German dive bombers arrived. It was an outrageous bombing.... This was repeated several times.... The Germans did not have to spend their tanks or motorized infantry on us. They just gave their airmen a chance to frolic. In the evening only 19 of us crawled out of that hell alive.[2]

More than 240,000 prisoners were taken, alongside the bulk of the Southwestern Front's artillery park and armor. It was a disaster as bad as anything the previous summer, while German losses had been thirty thousand casualties. Both sides would take valuable lessons away from Kharkov that would come to fruition during the coming winter fighting around Stalingrad. For stragglers who did escape the German encirclement, the official Soviet response as decreed by Stalin would be execution or a penal battalion. A wounded Lieutenant Yampolsky would spend ten days making it back to friendly lines, and be shocked to find upon his arrival that he was still in danger:

> It turned out that such poor fellows like me were sent to the filtration control point located on premises of the commissar's office of the division.[3] I was walking there with high spirit, happy that I finally had reached my countrymen, not even thinking about what torture would be in store for me there. . . . Suddenly someone accosted me:
>
> "Yampolsky, what are you doing here?"
>
> I looked around. There was the food provision officer from my old unit in a 1.5-ton truck. I explain to him:
>
> "I've just come out of the encirclement and am going for verification."
>
> He said to me: "Don't go there! Your arrival in uniform and with identity papers will not impress them and you will be in trouble. I am here on my duty to deliver bread for the brigade from the army bakery. The brigade is stationed thirty kilometers away from here. We have broken out of the encirclement in an organized formation with our banner. One hundred and twenty of us have made it. Wait for me here for about an hour and I'll pick you up on the way back. Just sew your collar insignia back on your tunic [so Russian forces would recognise him] and don't leave this place. Wait for us!"[4]

On June 1, Hitler flew down to Poltava to decide next steps with von Bock. The Fuhrer agreed the Eleventh Army commanded by Colonel General Erich von Manstein would reduce the Sevastopol garrison and von Bock would clear out the salient before the new summer offensive would be launched on June 20 (Operation Wilhelm). With the Luftwaffe dominating the skies and virtually wiping out what Soviet air forces there were in the theater, von Bock's Fourth Panzer Army would break through to the city of Voronezh, a key center of transport and communications, on July 2.

As the fighting for Voronezh began, Sergeant Albert Wittenberg headed south toward Sevastopol to join up with the 50th Infantry Division. He was part of a shock formation harking back to the days of the storm troops of the Great War. In the early 1940s he had been employed as a blacksmith near Cottbus, a university city situated 125 kilometers (about 80 miles) southeast of Berlin, in Lower Silesia. His foreman had managed to postpone his drafting for military service as the blacksmith's profession was deemed an essential service for the economy and logistics on the home front. After the losses suffered from Barbarossa, Wittenberg was one of hundreds of thousands of replacements to receive their call-up papers, and he completed his basic training and was then assigned for further training in a pioneer company. It was known that this was a kind of elite unit, and there was a rumor that especially young, single men and men without relatives were being integrated into these units. The basic training was very tough, with some recruits being killed while training: "An incident occurred during training on hand grenades. One recruit did not throw the grenade but held it in his hand. He was petrified and so were we. An instructor with presence of mind pushed the soldier into a trench. The recruit was killed."[5]

On the other hand, for the first time in his life, Wittenberg had regular working hours, three good meals a day, and a decent pay packet to spend in his free time in occupied Prague. These were all unknown to him until then, and he liked having them. He was employed at first in the blacksmith's center where the wagons of the Wehrmacht—which was still largely a horse-drawn army—shipped wagons, carts, and vehicles back from the front in Russia to be repaired. Thousands of horses were shipped back, too, to recover from their wounds or frostbite from the severe Russian winter conditions. Wittenberg found the suffering of the animals too much to bear and requested a transfer to the division's armory, where he remained until he was deployed to Army Group South in 1942.

As Sevastopol was captured, the soldiers of Wittenberg's unit were transported east by rail to reinforce the losses the 50th Division had suffered capturing the Crimea's main naval port. The fight the Russians had put up would be a precursor of what awaited the Germans along the Volga.[6] Wittenberg described the journey as a relatively pleasant trip, with the new formation being supplied with plenty of rations and cigarettes and the recruits singing songs to maintain morale as the days ticked by.

Well, I'd never been on a vacation trip, and certainly not by train. It felt good though. After a while, some of the soldiers noticed that the train was heading in a southeast direction. It was rumoured amongst the men that the destination of the trip might be Crimea where Manstein's Eleventh Army was battering the garrison holding out at Sevastopol. In the course of the trip this was confirmed by our officers, so I went to Sevastopol.[7]

The unit arrived in the Crimea, and the men were unloaded miles away from the port, their locomotive unable to take them farther as the line was wrecked by bombing. They would march to the coast instead.

We had to gather at a small train station, pick up weapons and luggage, and then march off. I had experienced hot summers in Germany, but I had never endured such heat before. We marched for days, I don't know exactly how long, but that could have been a week. The unit making its way through endless grain fields, now and then interrupted only by a small village. We also often stopped at tomato fields, so we picked some. They were sweet as sugar.

In the evenings we would drop out of the march and move into any billets we could find, in small but also larger villages. You have to imagine that we walked in boots ("Knobelbecher," they were called by my compatriots) in midsummer. We didn't have socks (I sourced some for myself later) in that sense, but rather wraps [puttees]. You had to tie them properly, otherwise you would get your feet sore very quickly, which could be very painful. There was no infirmary.

As had been seen before the previous year, the German invaders were seen by many Ukrainians as liberators, as Wittenberg recalls:

What I noticed was that the civilian population was very friendly towards us, even though we were the attackers, we were already aware of that. So, we behaved in a friendly manner and even got into conversation with some of them. Well, we were young men and of course we wanted girls too. We never had any contact with the enemy, and we didn't see a single Russian soldier. There was also no sign of partisan activities that we had heard of. That should change soon, however.[8]

The boredom of their continuing march in the relentless Crimean summer sunshine was now being interrupted by the increase in flights of the Luftwaffe overhead. The troops began to encounter other German units either dug into foxholes, working in supply stations, or coming back from Sevastopol itself, some marching in formation, many others wounded, aboard wagons and in trucks. Wittenberg and his comrades now began to catch sight of the reality of the Eastern Front.

At some point we reached the suburbs of a city and the further we went, the greater the destruction. I had never seen such chaos in my life. No stone was left unturned. Sevastopol was completely destroyed, only smoking ruins, almost apocalyptic, I was horrified. I think that's when I got scared for the first time.

The reinforcements now encountered their enemy for the first time.

And there they were, endless columns of Red Army soldiers marching west. They looked just like us, only in a different uniform. Some of us said, "if this goes on like this, the war will be over before we even fired a shot." How wrong can you be?

In Sevastopol we had contact for the first time with German soldiers from the front who had taken part in the capture of the city. One in particular got talking to us as we gave him what cigarettes we had. He looked completely done in but warned us: "Don't be fooled, we won't defeat them anytime soon. The Russians fought incredibly bravely. I've never seen anything like it. We had to level the whole damn town until they gave up."

This conversation would come back to haunt Wittenberg amid the fighting for Stalingrad.

At Voronezh the fighting to capture the city dragged on for days as more Soviet forces engaged von Bock's Fourth Panzer Army from the north while Timoshenko's beaten-up armies retreated in their path back toward the Don River. Paulus, fresh from winning his first major battle as a field commander, was now, on June 30, leading the Sixth Army from their base northeast of Kharkov to protect Fourth Panzer's southern flank as they headed east. Paulus's confidence during this period jumps off the pages of his letters home to friends and family:

> We've advanced quite a bit and have left Kharkov 500 kilometres behind us. The great thing now is to hit the Russian so hard a crack that he won't recover for a very long time.[9]

On July 12, Stalin was convinced of the threat to the Volga and established the new Stalingrad Front, consisting of thirty-eight divisions of mixed quality and strength, which broke down into three of Stavka's reserve armies: the 62nd, 63rd, and 64th. Their combined force, making up approximately 160,000 troops, was commanded by Generals Anton Lopatin, Chuikov, and Mikhail Shumilov respectively. The latter two would go on to play a hugely significant part in the Stalingrad story. A week later Stalin telephoned Aleksey Chuyanov, chairman of the Stalingrad *Gorodskoi Komitet Oborony* (City Defense Committee), ordering him to place it on an immediate war footing. On July 20, as German formations of the 17th Army and the First Panzer Army closed on the key city of Rostov to the south, Chuyanov reported back to the Kremlin of his plans to turn Stalingrad into a fortress. The civilian population was now marching out into the hinterland to construct a series of defensive lines comprising miles of tank traps, hundreds of concrete pillboxes, and thousands of yards of barbed wire entanglements. As in the previous year, heavy industry within the city was now being dismantled and shipped eastward to safety, and militia battalions from the industrial sector to the north were being formed. Stalin refused Chuyanov permission to evacuate the population; four hundred thousand civilians would remain in a "live city" his troops would fight harder to defend.[10] Reconnaissance planes of the Luftwaffe were now spotted in the skies above Stalingrad by Soviet antiaircraft crews.

As the two prongs of the German offensive continued to chase the retreating Soviets back down to the Caucasus and eastward toward the Don Bend, the lack of prisoners taken reinforced Hitler's suspicion that the Red Army was teetering on the brink of final collapse. Now he made the fatal decision to split his operations on July 23 and go for broke, issuing Fuhrer Directive No. 45, which summarized the situation this way: "In campaign which has lasted little more than three weeks, the broad objectives outlined by me for the southern flank of the Eastern front have been largely achieved."

Army Group South would be divided into two: Army Group A and B. The former was to engage and destroy Russian forces situated south of Rostov and then "to occupy the entire Eastern coastline of the Black Sea."[11] With von Manstein's successful subjugation of the Crimea, his 11th Army would cross the Kerch Strait onto the mainland, if necessary, and support Army Group A as it progressed south to occupy the oil centers based at Maikop, Grozny, and Baku. Army Group B, divorced for the time being from its armor of Fourth Panzer Army, would direct Paulus's Sixth Army with the assistance of its Hungarian, Italian, and Romanian allies to "thrust forward to Stalingrad, to smash the enemy forces concentrated there, to occupy the town, and to block the land communications between the Don and the Volga."[12]

On July 24, the summer offensive reached a crisis point for Stalin as Rostov was recaptured by the German Army Group A in a matter of a few days, without much of a fight. The Caucasus were now in very real danger of being lost. Little did Stalin know that Hitler's fateful decision was causing undue stress as Army Group B's armor diverted south to aid Army Group A's push to the oil fields. The roads separating the two formations now became mired in confused and clogged-up columns of vehicles and tanks, many stalling due to a lack of fuel. As Rostov fell, the German Sixth Army's infantry reached the Don River, and was now only fifty kilometers from the Volga and Stalingrad. Stalin blanched at the news, fully realizing Russia was on the precipice of losing the campaign before the summer was even halfway through. He needed to act.

CHAPTER FOUR

"Not One Step Back!"

For the first time I saw a clear representation of the city, which
was marked only by a small cross on our maps. It extended
for more than 60 kilometers in a four to seven-kilometer-wide
strip along the western bank of the Volga. I had not realised
how big it was until now. The question immediately arose:
"Will we be able to take this vast city in the first attempt?"
—Colonel Wilhelm Adam, aide-de-camp
to General Paulus[1]

Senior Sergeant Ivan Vladimirovich Maslov had been a regular tankman before the outbreak of the war, having fought against the Poles
in 1939 and in the Winter War with the Finns. He then served with the
44th Army during the disastrous campaign in the Crimea and had been
fortunate to escape back to the mainland. Now he was with the 125th
Special Tank Battalion, where he commanded a T-34 at the Stalingrad
Front as the Russians tried to thwart the German push toward the Volga:

Our resistance in the Don steppes was more tenacious. Yes, we did
incur enormous casualties, but the troops did fight. Once, after a
number of our unsuccessful and bloody attacks, the remainder of
our battalion came over to the Don River crossing near the Cossack
village named Morozovskaya. There was an avalanche of advancing
German tanks and other vehicles. The whole sky was swarming with
German aircraft. . . . Our infantry proceeded to retreat in disorder.

The battalion commander Major Danilov ordered us to recede from the crossing without fighting. He realized that none and nothing of us would exist in a minute.[2]

On July 25, Soviet forces of the 62nd Army withdrew behind the Don Bend as the German Army Group B rolled forward behind their formidable air shield to outflank the Russians' new positions. The hastily put together Russian force was a mixture of new recruits, surviving veterans, and in some cases obsolete artillery and tanks put into service due to the enormous losses suffered at Kharkov. The Stavka now split its four-hundred-mile area of operations into two more manageable theaters of operation: the Stalingrad Front and the new Southeastern Front. The latter would have to contend with the Fourth Panzer Army, now headed back northeast in an about-face Hitler had just ordered, frustrated at his enemy retreating and seeing his Army Group A stalling in the Caucasus. The need for one success focused his mind now on capturing Stalin's city.

By July 28, aware of the need to focus minds, Stalin made the fateful decision to issue a proclamation that instructed his armed forces of what was expected of them for the coming fight: Order Number 227. It was not printed but issued to all units and read aloud. One line in particular grabbed the imagination of the Soviet press to create a slogan with which to galvanize the people. Signed by Stalin as the people's commissar of defense, "Not a step back!" ("*Ni shagu nazad!*") declared his intention for his commanders at all levels to implement a stricter discipline on the army as "it is necessary to defend to the last drop of blood every position, every meter of Soviet territory, to cling to every shred of Soviet earth and defend it to the end." Those officers or attached political commissars who allowed their units to retreat or left their own positions would be severely dealt with: "The panic-mongers and cowards should be exterminated in place." With the Sixth and Fourth German armies now bearing down on Stalingrad, the decree revealed that the Soviet leader was preparing his own troops psychologically to fight to the death.

To implement Order No. 227, Stalin ordered the NKVD to create "blocking detachments" that would monitor front-line troops as well as guard against any unauthorized withdrawals by positioning themselves at all crossings and bridges behind the lines, with the authority to open fire on anyone who retreated without orders. One report of a special section acting along the Stalingrad Front during this period showed that, from August 1 to October 15, these new units detained 139,224 soldiers who withdrew from the fighting. Out of this number, 3,980 were arrested, 1,189 shot, and 2,961 sent to penal companies and battalions, while 131,094 servicemen were returned to their units or sent to transit locations to await further instructions.[3] That each division was supposed to muster their own blocking troops at such a time was sensible but still impractical. These units might well be a few hundred men ordered to instill discipline in a division that might number thousands.

In any case, the vast majority of retreating Russian troops that summer were still conscious of their patriotic duty to defend their homeland. As war correspondent Vasily Grossmann recorded when he traveled with one regiment:

> The meeting began and the enormous crowd as one surged forward toward the truck where the speakers were standing. It was as if the forest clearing was occupied by one enormous warrior with one enormous heart who stood, breathing calm and even.
>
> The meeting was dominated by the sense that a great battle was to take place. Every word spoken by the sergeants, privates, and commanders was about war and designed for war. Those who spoke from the truck, which was camouflaged amongst the foliage, were united in thoughts and feelings.
>
> One of the speakers held out his arms to his comrades and said, "The fate of the nation is in these very hands, in our hands." Every last soldier glanced down at their own hands, and a light breeze rippled through the heaving crowd. Their responsibility is great, and their lot difficult! . . . "We must resist. We must be victorious. The fate of the nation is in our hands."[4]

* * *

While Stalin's order was in the process of being implemented, on the German side of the line, planners had finalized the proposed advance to capture Stalingrad. Army Group B now comprised the German Second and Sixth Armies, the Fourth Panzer Army was now coming back up from the south, and Germany's Axis allies' numbers were increasing, with the Hungarian Second Army being joined by the newly arrived and somewhat fresh troops of the Italian Eighth Army. The bulk of aircraft were placed at Army Group B's service for the next series of operations, guaranteeing the advancing columns the powerful air support it would need to take the city.

The fighting for the Don Bend had by August 2 reached an impasse after heavy fighting, with both sides settling behind their defenses and taking stock. In Moscow Stalin reappointed Colonel General Yeremenko,[5] offering him the job of commander of the Southeastern Front, with the express order to stop the Fourth Panzer Army progressing toward the city. As they talked, German tanks ground northeastwards toward southern Stalingrad, forcing the Russian 64th Army to extend its line of defense to counter it, but at the cost of weakening the line to its north, where the Russian 62nd Army was holding against Paulus's Sixth Army. The Russian formation was now in disrepair, having sustained thousands of casualties and with most of its heavy equipment left destroyed or abandoned.

Upon taking command, Yeremenko immediately reinforced the 64th Army with whatever tanks and antitank guns he could muster, to blunt Fourth Panzer's advance, but still they were pulling back under the weight of armored and aerial assaults. To many retreating Soviet units coming up from the south and southwest of the city, the fortunes of war were all too real. Senior Sergeant Vladimirovich Maslov looked on as some of the local Don Cossack villagers quickly rationalized who their new masters might be:

> We went retreating across the Cossack farmsteads and saw there that the locals were already laying white cloths on the tables and setting out food and drink, preparing a warm welcome for the Germans.... We socked those tables with machine gun fire and saw chips and splinters spewing about.[6]

Down in the Caucasus, with the city of Maikop captured on August 9, and the oil centers blown up, German Army Group A's progress was now butting heads against hardened Soviet defense as its infantry divisions reached the mountain range that stretched from the Caspian to the Black Sea. Local Red Army troops used knowledge of the terrain to their advantage as Private Christian B., of the German 198th Infantry Division, bemoaned:

> We're right among the mountains now. They're certainly steep, but not terribly high yet. But as we advance further in this sector, we'll really come up against the mountain ranges proper. . . . Here there are lots of snipers, for the Russians can hide themselves very well in this brushwood, and it's very difficult for our infantry to comb these forests.[7]

With the German Sixth Army getting the fuel it needed to continue, the recent deadlock was broken with Paulus making a concerted effort to surround and destroy Lopatin's 62nd Army, one German Panzer division also cutting through from the south to encircle the bulk of Lopatin's command around the transport hub of Kalach: twelve rifle and ten tank brigades totaling more than fifty thousand men. Paulus was now free to push toward crossing the Don River, only fifty kilometers (about thirty miles) from Stalingrad. His Sixth Army's spearhead formation of LI Corps ordered two of its infantry divisions to cross the river's shortest stretch of two hundred and fifty meters (about eight hundred feet) opposite the village of Vertyachi, catching by surprise Lopatin's 62th Army, who had prepared for them at Kalach. With his pioneers who were constructing two pontoon bridges once his vanguard units had consolidated the bridgehead, Paulus managed to get a portion of his forces across. All the while Luftwaffe outnumbered the Soviet air force two to one, dominating the skies and supporting Sixth Army and the approaching Fourth Panzer Army to establish a firm base nineteen miles to the south of the city. The remnants of the Russian defense on the steppe were driven back remorselessly by German firepower as the local Soviet commanders prepared themselves for the fight of their lives.

PART II

ALL ROADS LEAD
TO THE VOLGA

The bank of the river was covered in dead fish mixed with human heads, arms, and legs, all lying on the beach. They were the remains of people who were being evacuated across the Volga, when they were bombed.

—Konstanin Duvanov, 62nd Army,
Stalingrad[1]

CHAPTER FIVE

A City of Revolution—
The Birth of Stalingrad

Oh Volga! . . . My cradle
Has anyone loved you as I have
Alone in the morning half light
When all the world is still asleep
When the scarlet gleam just glides
Over the dark blue waves
I escaped back to the river of my birth.

—Nikolai Nekrasov, "On the Volga"[1]

Of course, Stalingrad had been named after the Soviet leader in 1925, but its history had been one of quiet evolution under the rule of the old Russian empire, as its original name—Tsaritsyn—reflected. It was one of many towns and trading posts that had been constructed over the centuries along the Volga, one of Europe's greatest rivers, which flowed from the hills of the northwest outside of Moscow, through dense forests, then the great expanse of open steppe in Southern Russia, across its parched landscape of summertime before emptying out into the Caspian Sea. A journey of more than two thousand miles, with more than five hundred smaller rivers and streams pouring into it. The Volga was a source of natural wonder, rich in fish stocks, including its famous beluga sturgeon. The Slavic word *volga* means "wetness" but to the many tribes of early Turkics who settled along its southern shores it was known as the "big river."[2] Tsaritsyn derives from the Tartar word for the "town" on the Tsaritsa River.

The provinces and settlements of Southern Russia had been used to invaders for centuries; the great exploring Vikings had navigated the river's length in the eleventh century, and had been supplanted by the Mongols and Tartars in the 1200s, who in turn would be conquered by Tsar Ivan IV[3] (the "Terrible") in the sixteenth century, who united the country under the governance of the growing Christian empire emanating from Moscow and Novgorod.

By the late nineteenth century and the arrival of the railways, just as it would in the United States of America, and Continental Europe, this new faster and all-weather transportation link radically increased the trading potential for the Volga as railway hubs turned once small, sleepy settlements into boom towns. The trading post of Tsaritsyn was one such success story as a railway terminal built in 1871 to export the grain brought to it from the vast fields of the steppe, to Moscow and St. Petersburg eleven hundred miles to the north, and Astrakan two hundred and fifty miles to the south. By the time Tsar Nicholas II took the country into the Great War, the town was a city with a population of 131,000 inhabitants. Though its main districts, streets, and squares were constructed of paving and granite steps, that connected a central core of stone buildings housing administrative, judicial, and religious centers, the majority of the new city was navigated by muddy paths much like the industrial cities of America's Midwest at the time.[4]

Warehouses were constructed along its high western bluffs close to the railway terminal, and adding to the city's shipyards, fisheries, sawmills, and oil storage facility, foreign investment in 1898 developed heavier industry. The town was growing into the city that the German invaders peered at through their view finders in their Panzers in 1942.

The coming of the Great War (1914–18) brought disaster for the Russian monarchy and the ruling order as it was overthrown by social upheaval and revolution in 1917, spreading from St. Petersburg to all corners of the country by the time the Bolsheviks seized power from the provisional government. What followed was a vicious and prolonged civil war (1917–23), which arguably in a small way put Tsaritsyn on the map outside of its locality due to its position as a transport link and the fight for its ownership. The town, along with others along the Volga, played a crucial role in building support bases and feeding the Red Army of the Bolsheviks fighting the White forces in the south.[5]

This was a period of large independent armies living off the land as they attempted to win control in the key agricultural and industrial parts of the country—a situation made worse once Germany controlled the breadbasket of the Ukraine after the peace treaty of 1917. The large population of workers employed in the metalwork factories of Tsaritsyn were radicalized by events in St. Petersburg and Moscow, joining with the local garrisons to establish Bolshevik bases of supply. Tsaritsyn would change hands a few times before finally coming under the leadership of a ruthless Bolshevik from Georgia whom the Moscow leadership had sent to run the Party's militia in 1919—Joseph Stalin.

Although in the precarious position of being surrounded by superior forces, Stalin refused to pull out of the city and ordered the residents to dig trenches to prepare for a siege. The Soviet defenders spoke of Tsaritsyn as a "Red Verdun" that would never surrender to the White Russians and the foreign meddlers who backed them.[6] Against orders, Stalin called up reinforcements fighting in the south to attack the unprotected rear of the besieging White forces in October 1918. Once the threat of the Whites had been resolved, Stalin set about restoring governance through terror, executing suspected collaborators and setting aflame whole villages thought to be against the new regime.[7] Such stubbornness to not abandon his position and instead implement ruthless martial law on the city's inhabitants would be his guiding principle once he took control of the country and in Stalingrad twenty years later. By January 1920, the Battle of Tsaritsyn had been won and Stalin's position was ascendent.

By 1925, with Lenin dead, Stalin was in the process of a three-year struggle to wrest control of the Supreme Soviet at the cost of his rivals such as Leon Trotsky. It was at this time, when he was general secretary of the Party that the legend of his defense of Tsaritsyn took on greater significance for him. In order to boost his profile further among the Party faithful and the Russian public in general, his supporters running the city requested Moscow to change its name in his honor. It was now not the "city of the tsar" but rather the "city of Stalin," and as such, Stalingrad would reflect all that was modern and industrial in the "Five-Year Plans" Stalin now directed the country must adopt to modernize in ten years. The city would become a showcase of modern socialism to the country and to the world.

The land to its north had been developed to create an enormous manufacturing and engineering base titled the Factory District. City leaders set about redeveloping the heart of the city itself from its nineteenth-century (still in some places feudal) design to a modern, futuristic, open-spaced series of squares, boulevards, parks, and embankments. Housing for the population working in the nearby heavy industry would be modern apartment blocks incorporating the latest technology of electric lighting and gas fittings.

The central section of the city was transformed and resembled many of the new cities springing up in North America such as Chicago and Detroit. Central Stalingrad now contained more than one hundred blocks on a rough grid system, with department stores, schools, technical colleges, libraries, and apartments.[8] Looking north from the Krutoy Gully and dominating the city as you looked upon the industrial plants lay the open grassy park where Stalingraders picnicked in the summertime, an old Tartar burial ground—the Mamayev Kurgan. It was the highest point in the area, with a wonderful panoramic view for miles in all directions.

The city planners were still aware they needed housing to accommodate the work force that had achieved this modernization and would continue to construct and expand these new sections of Stalingrad, as well as housing to retain the large numbers of local agricultural workers who had lived there for generations. The southern districts would hardly change, primarily still one- and two-storey dwellings constructed of wood, with stone chimneys, and the streets were still little more than bare frozen, muddy, dried earth, depending on the season.

Stalingrad was only one part of the grand strategy that Stalin's State

Planning Committee (*Gosplan*) had devised for the country to take a giant industrial leap forward. Part of the Communist Party's New Economic Policy, set in motion by Lenin, was to prepare the country for an attack from the west that Lenin seemed certain would come. Stalin described this metamorphosis as a "revolution from above."[9] The human cost would be enormous in terms of mass deportations of peasants to Siberia if they protested, lives lost to subsequent famines brought about by ill-prepared policies, and the heavy toll of increased working hours in highly dangerous construction and mining jobs inflicted on a badly trained workforce.[10] As a model Soviet city, Stalingrad would be a benefactor, its population rocketing from 151,000 to 450,476[11] citizens by the start of the Second World War.

The industrial expansion not only increased the workforce but equally made Stalingrad and its key landmarks a pivotal target for any enemy. The Tractor Factory Plant began operations on June 17, 1930, manufacturing US-designed tractors, with a maximum of 144 vehicles rolling off the line per day.[12] By the first full year of the Second World War the factory had been retooled practically overnight to produce artillery tractors, shells, mines, and above all the pivotal weapon of the war, the T-34 tank. Shipyards by the river were churning out submarines and armored launches, while other factories were producing motor-sleighs (for winter warfare), the Il-2 strike bomber, weapons, and uniforms of all descriptions—all destined for the front. Surrounding the giant factories stood large areas of housing for the workers of the Factory District as well as administrative buildings. Approximately 80 percent of the city's adult population by the summer of 1942 worked in one form or another for the war industry. In addition, the volunteer corps, which the head of the City Defense Committee, Aleksey Chuyanov, had ordered be mustered the previous winter, now numbered 13,600 men and women, 11,000 of whom belonged to the Party. In the whole region this number swelled to more than 50,000 volunteers.[13]

Among other landmarks that emphasized the modernization of the city was the five-storey Univermag Department Store—the showpiece building near Railway Station No. 1 in Red Square.[14] To the south of Red Square was the easily recognized Grain Elevator. The famous monolithic construction was built from steel-reinforced concrete, which dominated the skyline, thirty-five meters (more than one hundred feet) high, and almost one hundred meters (more than three hundred feet) in length. Well to the south of that the coal-fired StalGRES Power Station provided electricity to the city and its environs but would not come under direct ground attack. When the fighting began, the steel-reinforced concrete structures would not only provide shelter but also prove excellent defensive positions for the Russians as the Sixth Army pushed into the city.

Stalin valued the city not only because of his personal connection to it but also because of its industrial output for the war effort. Strategically, Moscow had earmarked the area of the southern Volga as a safe haven should the Germans break through to capture the capital. Samara, eight hunded kilometers (about five hundred miles) northeast of Stalingrad, had been studied by the government as the fallback position to set up the government, safe enough behind Russian lines to thwart enemy bombers, but close enough to be in contact with Red Army front-line formations. But now in August 1942, as the Sixth Army approached from the northwest, the Fourth Panzer Army suddenly appeared on the horizon as its armored formations swept up from the south, catching Yeremenko off-guard. Tens of thousands of refugees fled the steppe, swelling Stalingrad's population to approximately 850,000 as German reconnaissance planes flew high overhead. It looked to Stalin as though history were repeating itself. A new defense of the old Tsaritsyn was called for, forged from the spirit of the revolution.

As he had done in 1919, the Russian leader issued orders prohibiting the evacuation of civilians, ordering the quick construction of the defensive works that had already begun to be speeded up. The surviving units of the Soviet 62nd and 64th Armies—or what was left of them—would fortify the factories to thwart the enemy thrust to the Volga. Holding the line would be imperative while reinforcements ordered by the Stavka from the reserve[15] were dispatched to the north of Stalingrad for a forthcoming counteroffensive. The Bolshevik mindset of self-sacrifice was paramount, with Aleksey Chuyanov,[16] the head of the Stalingrad Civil Defense Committee, taking control of all districts, setting up checkpoints manned by men of the 10th Division of the NKVD—a mixture of regular Red Army troops, border guards, and more than three thousand civilians and Party workers.[17] Martial law was enforced,[18] the city authorities decreeing:

> Like 24 years ago, our city is again experiencing hard times. . . . In the momentous 1918 our fathers held Red Tsaritsyn against the onslaught of the gangs of German hirelings. And we ourselves shall hold Red Stalingrad in 1942. We shall hold it so that then we may drive back and destroy the bloodthirsty gang of German occupiers. . . . Everybody to the construction of barricades! Everybody capable of bearing arms to the barricades, to the defense of the native city, the native home![19]

Chuyanov had kept the civilian workforce busy for the past year, commandeering more than 250,000 people, 1,000 vehicles, 200,000 cubic meters of timber, and 1,000 tons of cement to construct over 3,000 kilometers of defensive lines—including hundreds of artillery emplacements. Adhering to government guidelines in preparing a major Russian city for attack—which had partially helped the defenders of Sevastopol—Stalingrad would be surrounded by three defensive belts of various depths. The farthest was the Outer Defense Belt or "O-Line," stretching out one hundred kilometers (about sixty miles) into the steppe. The Red Army would then retreat to the Central Defense Belt or "K-Line," which had more intensive firepower, with well-sited fortifications, tank traps, and minefields guarding the main roadways into the city. Finally, with both the Sixth Army and Fourth Panzer Army being worn down by the attrition of their respective advances, a final Inner Defense Belt or "S-Line" was constructed just on the city perimeter, making good use of the terrain and protecting of what civilian housing was in the suburbs.

The one area of defense the city authorities fell short on was the mass construction of bomb shelters for the civilian population—which had almost doubled by August due to the flood of refugees. At the time such preparations were not deemed necessary, but the destruction that would be meted out on the city from the air, on the eve of battle, would be unparalleled on the Eastern Front.

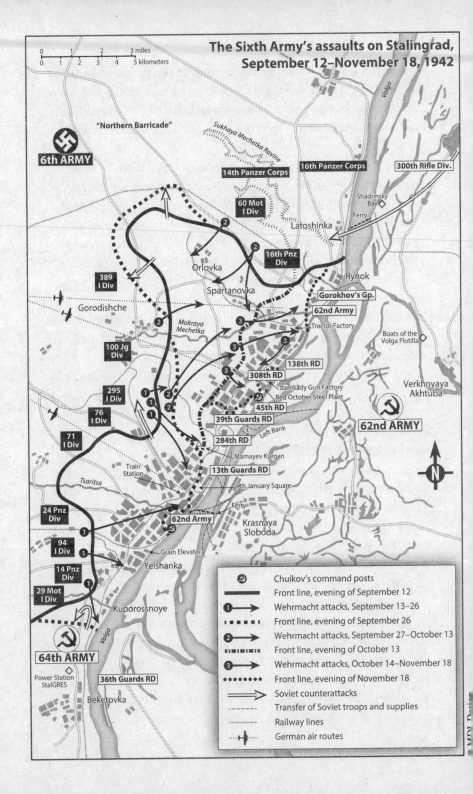

The Sixth Army's assaults on Stalingrad,
September 12–November 18, 1942

6th ARMY

"Northern Barricade"

Sukhaya Mechetka Ravine

14th Panzer Corps

16th Panzer Corps

300th Rifle Div.

Volga

Shadrinsky
Bay ◇

**60 Mot
I Div**

Ferry

Latoshinka

**389
I Div**

Orlovka

**16th Pnz
Div**

Rynok

Spartanovka

Gorokhov's Gp.

Gorodishche

62nd Army

Mokraya
Mechetka

Tractor Factory

Boats of the
Volga Flotilla ◇

**100 Jg
Div**

138th RD

308th RD

Verkhnyaya
Akhtuba

**295
I Div**

Barrikády Gun Factory
Red October Steel Plant

45th RD

**76
I Div**

39th Guards RD

62nd ARMY

**71
I Div**

Left Bank

284th RD

Mamayev Kurgan

Train
Station

13th Guards RD

Tsaritsa

9th January Square

**24 Pnz
Div**

Ferry

Krasnaya
Sloboda

62nd Army

**94
I Div**

Grain Elevator

**14 Pnz
Div**

Yelshanka

**29 Mot
I Div**

Volga

64th ARMY

Kuporossnoye

Power Station
StalGRES ◇

36th Guards RD

Beketovka

0   1   2   3 miles
0   1   2   3   4   5 kilometers

☭	Chuikov's command posts
────	Front line, evening of September 12
➊➤	Wehrmacht attacks, September 13–26
▪▪▪▪▪	Front line, evening of September 26
➋➤	Wehrmacht attacks, September 27–October 13
▬▪▬▪▬	Front line, evening of October 13
➌➤	Wehrmacht attacks, October 14–November 18
●●●●●	Front line, evening of November 18
➤	Soviet counterattacks
─·─·─	Transfer of Soviet troops and supplies
────	Railway lines
··✈··	German air routes

© MDV Design

CHAPTER SIX

Rain of Fire

Stalingrad burning. A fantastic picture in the moonlight.
—Major General Wolfgang Pickert,
Luftwaffe 9th Flak Division[1]

General Paulus sat atop his command vehicle, cast aside the binoculars hanging around his neck, and impatiently squinted up at the clear azure-blue sky as yet another Fieseler Storch reconnaissance plane flew overhead. The activity by the Luftwaffe was rapidly increasing as the Sixth Army pushed forward from its previous position by the Don Bend. Though the day promised much, such was the nature of the man that he still fretted about the haphazard nature of the Germans' apparent success in breaking the Red Army's previous front line. As had happened before that scorching hot summer, shortages of fuel and supplies were hampering the German advance, while the strength of resistance from the Soviets to Paulus's front and northern flank was increasing. The feeling was one of impotence, as the chance to capture Stalin's city and deliver a killer blow to the Red Army was palpably slipping away. The stop-start pattern of supply was a sore point not only to the commander of the Sixth Army. Chief of the General Staff Halder, present at headquarters with the Fuhrer, witnessed on a daily basis how the chaos of Hitler's unrealistic ambition was now mirrored on the front line. German forces were only stuttering toward their operational goals down south in the Caucasus and on the Don steppe, their lines of supply lengthening every day. Halder bitterly recorded in his diary: "Our attack can't proceed because of fuel and ammunition shortages."[2]

Despite the continued malaise in logistical support, by August 22 the Army High Command's directive to the Luftwaffe's *Fliegerkorps* VIII to provide air cover to the Sixth Army would pay dividends in a fresh and daring advance. Paulus, acting somewhat against type, seized the initiative by ordering General Gustav von Wietersheim's 14th Panzer Corps to break out from their bridgeheads on the Don Bend toward the Volga. This startling advance would bring consternation to the Soviet high command. Paulus's strategy of focusing his point of attack with all formations at his disposal—*Schwerpunktbildung*—was not innovative, but it was the first time he could implement such an operation that summer. The ambition of the overall plan stretched Axis units across several hundred miles of Russian steppe that summer, negating their ability to coalesce a major attack on one point of the enemy's defensive line and achieve the kind of rewards their encirclements of the previous summer had yielded. Only in the last two weeks had incisive drives at given points around the town of Kalach brought the first tangible success for the Sixth Army, more than eleven hundred tanks destroyed and fifty thousand Soviet troops of the 62nd Army captured.

With his forces replenished to an operational level, Paulus's situation on the Don Bend now forced him to make a decision. Digging in and accepting an increase in casualties as the Red Army continued to counterattack was not an option, especially as he was repeatedly being urged by the Army High Command to advance toward the Volga. He needed to hit the enemy to his front and smash a way through to Stalingrad. This calculated gamble would be led by the tanks of the 16th Panzer Division with the 3rd and 60th Motorized Divisions following in the wake of the hole the Panzers would punch in the Soviet defenses. Air cover would be provided by the fighters of *Fliegerkorps* VIII while its bomber groups would blast everything in the 16th Panzer Division's path to smithereens. Paulus knew his army was overextended and his divisions depleted after six weeks of intense fighting, but the timetable set by Hitler's directive was unforgiving. The attack was a roll of the dice he had to make.

*   *   *

That morning, in more than sixteen hundred sorties, the German Bf 109F fighters cleared the skies over the battlefield, allowing Heinkel 111 and Ju 88 bombers, and several Stuka groups, to rain down more than a thousand tons of high-explosive death and metal-cased destruction prior to the advance of General Hans Hube's 16th Panzer Division. Since the beginning of the Second World War, the Luftwaffe had successfully evolved its air-to-ground coordination systems, and thus by August 1942 the infantry and armored units, such as Hube's formation, could enjoy the benefit of close air support in a timely fashion—in many cases during this advance in a matter of fifteen to twenty minutes. A pathway established, the German armor now stormed out of its traps from the bridgehead, smashing into the survivors of the 62nd Army's secondary defensive line and opening up a seven-kilometer-wide corridor (about four miles).

Hube's plan was now for two regimental-sized battle groups to speed toward the wide-open spaces of the steppe and push toward the Volga until they encountered resistance. The 8th and 16th Soviet Air Armies put up as many planes as they could muster, in a vain attempt to support their beleaguered infantry and armor being massacred by the onrushing German blitzkrieg.[3] Though Soviet air forces were now taking ownership of the latest fighters and bombers, albeit in small numbers that summer, the inexperience of pilots combined with rudimentary communications systems made it an uneven match. The Soviet losses were heavy and would have drastic consequences for the coming air defense of the city itself. These consequences began in a matter of a few hours, one German fighter pilot observing:

> We flew at low level above the roads on which our troops advanced. Everywhere the soldiers on the ground acted crazy with joy. The summer was dry and as we flew over the spearheads, the dust clouds from the tank formations reached high above the ground into the clear sky.[4]

*   *   *

For Yeremenko, contemplating this latest enemy attack back at Russian front headquarters, such a catastrophic loss of planes and pilots left him blind, with no idea of where the enemy was headed, or the size of the force he was facing. Compounding this crisis, further reports from the Southeastern Front revealed the advance of Fourth Panzer now coming up from the south. The consequence of a repeat of the 1941 summer encirclements were too terrible to imagine. Hoth's tanks were now fueled up and only seventy kilometers (about forty miles) from the city, in all likelihood to link with Paulus's divisions now coming from the north, outnumbering, encircling, and destroying both the 64th and 62nd Soviet Armies, ultimately giving the Germans control of the Volga.

By midday of August 23, Hube's tanks were motoring unopposed toward the northern suburbs of Stalingrad, some units reaching Gumrak, several miles southwest of the city. Their presence was spotted by a unit of the worker's militia, who quickly drifted back toward Stalingrad. The only real resistance now came from several batteries of 85mm anti-aircraft guns of the 1077th Anti-Aircraft Regiment, manned primarily by civilian and female crews. The inexperienced gunners were forced to lower their sights to engage the German armor. Lacking armor-piercing rounds, their only ammunition of high-explosive shells proved useless. Some reports stated that the amateur gunners' heroic defense inflicted significant German losses, but the reality was that within a few hours Hube's tankers had swatted aside the hastily put-together force, destroying thirty-seven guns and killing more than five hundred personnel. The Panzer crews were reported to be shocked to find they had been fighting and killing women. Reconnaissance vehicles then sped the last few kilometers to the Volga and arrived at the suburb of Rynok, situated to the north of Stalingrad, by the evening. Since he had commenced his advance, it had taken Hube just fourteen hours to cover the sixty kilometers to Stalin's city.

All across the northern front, the demoralized Russians were falling back to a new defensive perimeter before realizing that it, too, was in danger of becoming encircled by the sudden appearance of yet more

German tanks, and thus a new evacuation of men and materiel to a new line continued afresh. The Soviet battlefield correspondent Vasily Grossman described the Red Army retreat into Stalingrad:

> Men's faces were gloomy. Dust covered their clothes and weapons; dust fell on the barrels of guns, on the canvas covering the boxes full of headquarters documents . . . and on the . . . sacks and rifles piled chaotically on the carts. The dry, grey dust got into people's nostrils and throats. It made one's lips dry and cracked.
>
> This was terrible dust, the dust of retreat. It ate up the men's faith, it extinguished the warmth of people's hearts. . . . The first units of the retreating army entered Stalingrad. Trucks with grey-faced wounded men, front vehicles with crumpled wings, with holes from bullets and shells. . . . And the war's breath entered the city and scorched it.[5]

It was an audacious, arguably foolhardy, but remarkable achievement. General von Wietersheim's forward Panzer units were now parked up on the high bluffs overlooking the Volga, his men gawping at its wide expanse and the spectacular views of the wild Asiatic lands beyond. Some of the jubilant tank men stripped off, laughing as they dived into the cold water to cool off from their dazzling success that day, basking in the evening sunset over a thousand miles from the Fatherland. Taking photographs of one another, they could be forgiven for believing that the end of the war might now be in sight.

Though they, and the Fourth Panzer Army coming from the south, had indeed enjoyed a seemingly victorious advance and were pushing Yeremenko's forces back toward the Volga and the confines of the city, to the north the Germans themselves were now in a precarious position. General von Wietersheim's corps were now strung out along the sixty-kilometer corridor they had created, without the necessary support to expand or reinforce it. Each of the three divisions were separated by approximately fifteen kilometers (almost ten miles) of hostile territory and in great need of re-forming to establish a solid bridgehead from the Volga back toward the Sixth Army. With the vast bulk of the infantry still some way behind, it would need time to catch up to establish the breakthrough and stabilize the new front. In the meantime, a Soviet counterattack to the rear of Hube's forces now isolated him from the bulk of the Sixth Army—still making their way on the dusty Russian roads, trucks and armor in their hundreds stacked up in vast columns, all impatient to catch up. Hube's Panzers had expended the majority of their precious fuel just to reach the Volga and more now parked in the evening sunshine. And yet still, almost suicidal infantry and armored attacks were being launched by the "beaten" enemy, all around them.

Reassured to a degree by the Luftwaffe beginning to dominate the skies above the city, Hube ordered units of motorized infantry to probe the Soviet defenses to establish how strong they actually were, one regiment of grenadiers entering the suburb of Rynok. As had happened outside the gates of Moscow the year before, the Germans now encountered the local tram lines that ferried commuters into Stalingrad. Some of the carriages still had passengers, their surprise at encountering troops in field-gray uniforms turning to terror once they realized who they were. Elements of the Sixth Army now progressed forward into the corridor, all around them the grisly remains of the fierce battle that had and still was taking place, as one eyewitness from the 71st Division recounted:

> During the night we moved forward through a narrow corridor in the direction of Stalingrad which had been opened by our panzer divisions. Along the road we saw German columns which had been shot to pieces, still with many unburied bodies. The muzzle flashes of guns to our left and right showed that the corridor could not be very wide. The impact of enemy shells never came close to us.[6]

German units were now little more than two miles away from the Tractor Factory, whose director, K. A. Zadorozhni, called the city's Party headquarters to inform them.[7] The reports of Germans so close to the city sent Yeremenko's command (now joined by Nikita Khrushchev as front commissar) into controlled panic. The front commander, robbed of aerial intelligence, had been caught unprepared for the German thrust so far east. He now gave the fateful order, possibly in panic, certainly in haste, for the pontoon bridge his engineers had painstakingly constructed across the Volga to be blown up. One can sympathize with his dilemma. But in the coming weeks and months of fighting, and the precariousness of the 62nd Army's supply route to its troops across the Volga, any bridge would have been invaluable. Now it was gone, its charred pieces floating downstream. But for Yeremenko, the fear of providing the advancing Panzers the gift of an easy route across the Volga had been too much to contemplate.[8]

Stalin, shaken by the German successes, spat cold fury down the line at Khrushchev and Yeremenko for allowing the enemy to finally reach the Volga and to be subsequently now shelling river traffic and the city. His city! He demanded an immediate response. The front commander now gathered what units he had to counterattack from both north and south of the corridor and destroy von Wietersheim's vanguard. Within the city itself Yeremenko hurriedly pulled together a disparate group of worker's militia units, two dozen T-34 tanks driven straight off the production line, and two regiments of NKVD to rush to the western outskirts and block Hube's advance. That night and into the following day the attacks on the fifty-kilometer corridor Hube had opened were repulsed. Despite the Russians' numerical advantage against an over-extended enemy, the accuracy of the German antitank gunners and supporting airstrikes took its toll. The Russian losses in armor were significant, with 224 of 340 tanks destroyed in the attack from the north, while their southern advance met a similar fate.[9] To make matters worse, Panzers positioned outside the city and supported by the Luftwaffe now began to target civilian and military shipping along the Volga, causing mayhem to those trying to escape the city. Within the city itself, the main train station (Stalingrad-1) and the streets surrounding it were crammed with an influx of more than 150,000 retreating soldiers and terrified refugees desperate for escape.

Unknown to Yeremenko and Khrushchev, Hube had halted his advance less than two miles from the Factory District. Arguably he could have seized the opportunity to storm the city and take the Factory District there and then with only a threadbare Russian defense to his front. But although a gambler by nature, he was mindful of the precariousness of his division's position at the sharp end of Sixth Army's advance. The reckless Soviet armored counterattacks and incessant artillery barrages had certainly spooked him. The enemy may have fallen back to the city, but to the north and south he was well aware of a Soviet counterattack actually succeeding. Without sufficient supplies of fuel and ammunition, his division would be a sitting duck. As the days ticked by with no sign of reinforcements following in his wake, Hube began to question the sense of his division remaining in position even if they were the first German troops to reach the Volga. With casualties in his own division reaching five hundred a day, he discussed with his senior officers the plan for a breakout west back to Sixth Army's lines. The proposal was dismissed out of hand by his superiors at Vinnitsa following explicit orders from Hitler to hold the position they had fought so hard to win.

The increased activity of the Luftwaffe in the skies rekindled Hube's confidence enough for him to finally decide to remain in position and await resupply. He ordered his men to dig in and for his armored units to set up a "hedgehog" defense. They would ride out the storm and await rescue. Hube, ever the pragmatist, now busied himself constructing his sleeping quarters using straw in a gun pit under his own tank. But the bombing of Stalingrad would now begin in earnest—the fiercest bombing on the whole of the Eastern Front.

Luftwaffe commander *Generaloberst* Wolfram von Richthofen more than lived up to his famous cousin's reputation from the Great War. An ex-infantry officer from the first war, he had switched to become a pilot and by the 1930s had been brought into the Luftwaffe by Hermann Göring. Ruthless, driven, and a brilliant tactician, he was arguably one of the ablest leaders on the Eastern Front and the finest air force commander in the Second World War. The skills of close air support he had pioneered in the Spanish Civil War he had then perfected in the conquest of France and the Low Countries. By 1942 he was recognized as the premier combat leader to augment the southern offensive with the combined air strength of a reinforced *Fliegerkorps* VIII. It had thus far dominated the skies as Army Group B advanced on the city, its tank-killing Stukas enjoying unparalleled success against Soviet armored formations either stranded where they'd stopped due to lack of fuel, or desperately trying to thwart the advance of Paulus's armor-tipped spear. Either way, they were sitting ducks and knocked out. One Stuka pilot recorded: "Since early morning we were constantly over the . . . spearheads, helping them forward with our bombs and machine guns."[10]

By August 23, von Richthofen had assembled the force he wanted for the coming attack on Stalingrad. Though no official communiqués or entries from the War Diary of Supreme Headquarters exist today, one can imagine this massive operation of men and machines must have been authorized, or at least verbally acknowledged, by Hitler. The aerial attack was simply the first stage in Army Group B's approach to capturing a large city, improved upon since the attack on Guernica during the Spanish Civil War. Massive aerial assault was followed by artillery barrages which would silence all opposition, thus allowing the Wehrmacht to move in and occupy what remained without incurring significant losses themselves. Richthofen had taken his first trial run in 1937 in Spain, and with the subsequent campaigns in the Low Countries, the Balkans, and during Barbarossa he had perfected his tactics to quickly reduce the Sevastopol fortress.[11] Now Stalingrad would surpass anything his air corps had thus far achieved. It would also write his name in infamy.

The planners of *Fliegerkorps* VIII had been busy that June and July combing the entire Eastern Front to monopolize sufficient air-worthy planes and experienced pilots for just such a task as the reduction of Stalingrad's ability to defend itself. Approximately four hundred Ju 88s and He 111 bombers were made available. On that first afternoon, they would fly more than sixteen hundred sorties alone, dropping more than one thousand tons of bombs, high-explosive and incendiary, in what Richthofen later described in his war diary as his "second great attack of the day."

*   *   *

Stalingrad air defenses had the firepower neither on the ground nor in the air to prevent the attack. The 8th Soviet Air Fleet was otherwise engaged in the north tackling the German armored encroachments. The Party authorities and NKVD security leaders, though aware of an impending air assault, were caught out by its size and ferocity.

The city's population had been through air raid drills and warnings before. The Luftwaffe had even attacked as early as October 1941, though their missions had been mainly reconnaissance, with only sporadic bombing. Still, for many days, as the fear of attack grew ever closer in August, the authorities had staged numerous warnings and instituted checkpoints. Many Stalingraders had grown weary of the false alarms. So as the sirens wailed, and loudspeakers announced again, "Attention. Attention. Citizens, we have an air raid! We have an air raid!,"[12] many either ignored the message or remained calm. Only the unfamiliar sound of live firing from the city's antiaircraft units broke the spell of disbelief, as people shaded their eyes from the late afternoon sun to spot the black spots in the distance growing ever bigger as the enemy approached from the west.

Children and teenagers caught up in the terror and excitement of spotting the great armada flying toward their city were soon witness to the maelstrom of flying metal and flesh, as fourteen-year-old Albert Burkovski recalled:

> When the bombing began, it was really horrible. I can still remember the planes, the noise they were making, and it became real hell. I don't know how people managed to bear it. It was one big fire. We climbed to the roof, and we could hear the moaning, groaning from down below.[13]

German bombers came in waves, some thirty to forty strong, others of between seventy and ninety aircraft. The heavier-ladened planes came in on a low altitude of six thousand feet to drop their payloads. The flights of Stukas, in contrast, peeled off to screech down toward their targets and ensure pinpoint accuracy. As they flew over the city, German pilots were guided by detailed maps supplied by the Luftwaffe's air intelligence, pinpointing Stalingrad's major industrial sites in the northern sector as well as military and naval installations along the Volga.

Civilians of the city and those refugees cramming streets tried to find any protection from the storm being dropped from the sky. "People were writhing around on the ground, bleeding heavily or already burned black. Others suffocated from smoke trying to escape the fire in sewers. Those who managed to get out carrying children, throwing off smoldering clothes until they were half-naked were running toward yet more fires on the Volga. Everything there was on fire too. The quays, steamers, warehouses, and barges were all in flames."[14]

The industrial district was struck heavily in particular, all three main plants taking severe punishment over the coming days and weeks. In the first raid, however, the direct strikes on the oil refinery quickly set it ablaze, black clouds of thick, choking smoke rising more than three thousand meters (about 10,000 feet) into the air. The scenes of destruction ran the length of the Volga, and even the river itself was ablaze with burning oil. The hundreds of wooden houses in the old southern districts were as well ablaze and would soon be charred ruins, only their stone chimneys giving a clue as to what had originally stood there. From the air the German pilots now could see only large square patches of bare earth bordered by streets. The central districts had been hard hit, too, their large apartment blocks, administrative buildings, theaters, and schools providing excellent trigger points for increased accuracy.

Hour after hour, the Luftwaffe reigned supreme over the beleaguered inhabitants, dropping their loads with impunity, driving the civic leaders underground for protection and to attempt to reassert some vestige of control over who and what remained. Militia units still had the presence of mind to keep to their posts amid the smoldering ruins and the masses of people blindly running in panic. Orders from Yeremenko's headquarters were for Red Army personnel still alive to assist the militia to now dig in for an expected attack from the north and south. That evening, as von Richthofen congratulated himself in his war diary, "We simply paralysed the Russians," Khrushchev and Yeremenko, crammed into their underground cellar, with concussive blasts shaking its foundations, took orders from Stalin. The local Party consensus to give up the city was forbidden: "The evacuation and mining of the plants will be interpreted as a decision to surrender Stalingrad." Stalin now ordered the city be defended—soldiers would fight for a living city rather than a deserted one. The Stalingrad Defense Committee issued the following proclamation: "We will not abandon our city to the Germans! All of you, organize brigades, go to build barricades. Barricade every street . . . quickly in such a way so that the soldiers defending Stalingrad will destroy the enemy without mercy!"

All efforts now had to be preparative to attack Hube's armor to the north and make ready defensive works for the Fourth Panzer Army coming from the south. Clearly the Germans were attempting another classic pincer strategy to cut off the city's defenders from support farther east. All were aware that the aerial blitz was likely to recommence the following day. On August 24 German bombers were less random in their assault, targeting once again the industrial plants, the Central Landing area, and the river traffic attempting to move supplies into the city while evacuating the wounded. The southern districts and outlying suburbs were now heaps of ash, forcing the defenders to move back into the city, where stone buildings and ruins offered more protection from the advance they knew would come. The central water supply system had been taken out, critically denying the city's firefighters water to do their job as all around them buildings in the central district were blown to pieces.

The death toll on August 23–24, 1942, has been hotly contested for many years. Forty thousand deaths is the most popular figure, the single most deadly day of aerial assault in history before the atomic bomb was dropped on Hiroshima on August 6, 1945.[15] The report from the local Soviet air defense authorities for August matter-of-factly states: "Starting from mid-August the city experienced non-stop air bombing by large groups of enemy planes."

The actual figure for that first day of carpet-bombing will probably never be known, because the catastrophic air raid struck just when the city was packed with refugees waiting for transportation eastward by train or vehicle. The city's population of more than four hundred thousand had swelled to almost double that number. With few air raid shelters to be found, the refugees were fish in a barrel for the Luftwaffe bombers. Although this was not on the scale of an Allied raid on Dresden or Cologne, it is hard not to believe that many thousands would have perished from indirect bombing and from being deliberately attacked as they fled across the Volga.[16]

For Anatoly Grigoryevich Merezhko, a young lieutenant born in Novocherkassk in the Rostov area, his baptism of warfare that summer had been hellish. Called up for service into the Red Army before the war in 1939, his period of study at officer's college had been cut short due to the crisis on the southern front in Crimea. Transported to Crimea, his unit was evacuated before Sevastopol fell, and now like thousands of other troops falling back from the onrushing German assault, they found themselves on the road east to Stalingrad, where they would be amalgamated into a cadet's regiment.[17] Merezhko and his comrades had suffered in the summer heat as they traveled on the parched steppe, choking on the dust of countless vehicles that passed by taking the wounded and the fleeing civilians to the safety of the city. They had frequently been buzzed by reconnaissance planes of the Luftwaffe, and in some instances forced to find shelter as the odd Messerschmitt strafed a column.

His column was still some way from their destination even as the sky seemed full of black dots, waves of enemy bombers now making their way to Stalingrad. Within an hour, plumes of smoke filled the horizon to the east. An air of dismay and anger spread through the soldiers and civilians alike as they watched the awesome display of firepower continue until the late evening:

> After it got dark . . . we saw this endless burning wall. A fire of such magnitude that the flames could be seen from 40 kilometers away, and the whole sky was lit up by it. The planes . . . coming low to bomb Stalingrad and returning back high. Those pilots did three or four bombing sorties. So that's why 23 August was the day when our hatred for the invaders reached its peak.[18]

*   *   *

After the first day's attack, emergency services attempted as best they could to tackle the conflagration in the Factory District, as well as the destruction wrought in the center of the city. Hundreds of houses, dozens of apartments blocks, and many government buildings and businesses had been badly damaged. The subsequent raids over the coming days would completely destroy a great many more. The city's open spaces and parks now resembled moonscapes, littered with debris, the dead, and bomb craters. Stalingrad was engulfed in smoke as fires raged, especially in the Factory District, where chemical and oil facilities, which had been deliberately targeted by the German bombers, spewed out their flammable liquids and materials.

By midnight, the City Defense Committee had declared a state of siege. Party workers, militiamen, and NKVD police pasted up posters around every district: "Anyone caught disturbing social order and peace will be shot at scene of crime without enquiry or trial, and all other malicious persons violating public order and security in city will be hauled before military tribunal." The river crossing points had already been closed off for some hours as the police and militia set up checkpoints, allowing only essential workers to travel to the relative safety of the eastern shore. By the time the second attack came on Monday, the City Defense Committee finally relented and allowed all women and children to leave the burning city, with the authorities struggling to police the panicked crowds making their way to the Central Landing.[19]

Harking back to the successful defense of the city during the 1917 revolution and the civil war itself, the Defense Committee continued through broadcasts, posters, and pamphlets to call for more volunteers to repair the damaged utilities and support the ongoing construction of defenses. The water system and electricity supply were partially restored, damage control parties were sent out to subdue and extinguish some of the major fires, and the grisly task of collecting the dead for burial went forward. Yeremenko continued to arm and organize as many worker's brigades as possible to transform the buildings and ruins of the Factory District into fortresses. Teams set to work to block the main thoroughfares and streets, setting up makeshift tank traps and building barricades in the hope of blocking the Germans. Very few had any military training, even fewer had weapons. Yet thousands poured toward the front lines. All the while above them the Luftwaffe continued to rain destruction on the survivors. The Mamayev Kurgan, the great hill dominating the center of the city, was now fortified and housed the command post of the 62nd Army. The battered formation had only twenty-five thousand survivors from which Yeremenko had to construct a workable defensive perimeter to hold off Paulus's main thrust, which would come soon.

On August 25, as the bulk of Paulus's infantry now crossed the Don and began their march toward Stalingrad, the Volga River was used, belatedly, to evacuate women and children from the city, despite attacks on steamers by German aircraft. In all, between 200,000 and 280,000 civilians were evacuated across the river.[20] One witness to the attacks on the river craft was Shustov Vladimir Konstantinovich,[21] a Stalingrader by birth in 1929 who had grown up in the new industrial districts. By the time of the Sixth Army's approach to the city, he was twelve years old. He recalled the stunned silence of his classmates as they listened to the radio announcement by the secretary of the regional committee, Comrade Chuyanov, on July 15, informing the city's residents of the impending attack and the need to now assist with defensive works.

> We schoolchildren gathered at the school and went to the construction of defensive lines (in the people's militia). At first, I joined the 327th Army Engineering Battalion of the 62nd Army; they were directing the pontoons near to the water pumping station. Soldiers going to the frontline stopped for supplies, descending from the embankment to the shore, where we had our communal kitchen. They received thermoses of cooked food or tea, and we gave out canned food, too.

Organized into a Komsomol cell,[22] a Leninist group of young Communists, Shustov and other young volunteers were headed by one of his school friends and supported one of the medical battalions of the 62nd Army, primarily staffed by female Red Army medics. Shustov's battalion was near the Tractor Factory as he helped to transport the many wounded soldiers coming back from the fighting on the outskirts of the city, ferrying them to the overstretched medical facilities on the eastern bank of the Volga. At that point, traversing the great river by boat wasn't as straightforward a task as it had been only a few weeks before; the danger of the approaching enemy and possible bombing air raids toward the end of August had been announced by the civic authorities. The twelve-year-old Shustov would soon experience what this meant. "I was ferrying wounded soldiers, a commander and some political workers to the east bank and was accompanied by two nurses (Raya and Nina) both in the late teens."

The young medics realized the need to get one of the badly wounded officers to safety and shouted at Shustov to row as quickly as possible for the far bank. "Water pillars soared up from the breaks, the boat was thrown around, it was hard to row, nothing was visible. Nina, bending over to the groaning commander, noticed that he was deteriorating and we had to move forward."

Shustov tied a rope around his waist and connected the other end to the bow of the boat. He dived into the water, desperately swimming for his life to tow the injured man to safety as the shells landed meters away. Luckily for all of them, the current of the Volga was in their favor and pushed them along to their destination. As they made their way to shore, Shustov flinched as he encountered the dead and parts of bodies floating in the water. With his boat now in the more sheltered part of the riverbank, his wounded were unloaded and more soldiers appeared with boxes of ammunition, ordering him to take them back to the fighting. By the time they stopped packing the wood crates, the boat was just twenty centimeters (eight inches) above the waterline.

As the evacuation of tens of thousands of residents of the city was underway, Shustov witnessed the steamer the *Joseph Stalin* loading with women and children and the elderly on the right bank of the Volga. By dusk it was thought safer to cast off and attempt to sail upriver to

Latoshinka (Latoshinsky Garden). Within minutes German phosphoric candles lit up the Volga, the right and left banks, and the island. The boat's occupants could see everything, as the night turned into day. Three Stukas suddenly appeared and dived down to strafe the terrified passengers. "I remember the screams of women who jump into the water and grab each other in a chain. Screams [could be heard] far across the water: 'Mama save yourself, Mama jump, Mama, Mama . . . ,' and the ship is on fire and turns over."

For both sides, witnessing the destruction of the city left the same impression—Stalingrad looked finished. Nineteen-year-old conscript Konstanin Duvanov had retreated with the Red Army all the way from the Ukraine back to his home city. One of his most vivid memories of those early days was as he marched closer toward the suburbs and saw the Volga itself: "Everything was on fire," but upon closer inspection the river held a more horrific flotsam: "The bank of the river was covered in dead fish mixed with human heads, arms, and legs, all lying on the beach. They were the remains of people who had been being evacuated across the Volga, when they were bombed."[23]

One officer from Paulus's headquarters situated on the steppe ventured outside his map room to grab a cigarette. Looking skyward, he marveled at the flights of German aircraft making their way either to or from their targets: "The whole landscape was bathed in sunlight on this beautiful late summer's day. But from the west, flanked by fighters, came the squadrons of bombers to drop their loads on the city with ear-deafening noise and prominent mushrooms of smoke. 'That's how it goes all day long,' commented an officer of the engineer staff. 'One cannot see much left of the city. One has to accept that the hail of bombs is extinguishing everything alive.'"[24]

General Vasily Chuikov, at that point deputy commander of the severely mauled 64th Army, would be more succinct in his appraisal of the state of the city in the aftermath of the blitz:

The streets of the city are dead. There is not a single green twig on the trees: everything has perished in the flames. All that is left of wooden houses is a pile of ashes and stove chimneys sticking up out of them. The many stone houses are burnt out, their windows and doors missing, and their roofs caved in, pulling out bundles, samovars and crockery, and carrying everything to the landing stage.[25]

By this point war correspondent Vasily Grossman was the first of a steady stream of Soviet writers working for the Red Army newspaper *Krasnaya Zvezda* (*Red Star*) who were sent into the battle. His first short story "On the Volga" would be the first piece of written work to bring Stalingrad into the larger public consciousness.[26] His later work would capture the bombing of the city:

What did the strange blaze in the distance portend? Whose defeat? Whose triumph? Radio, telegraph and ocean cables were already promulgating the news of the Germans' massive strike. Politicians in London, Washington, Tokyo and Ankara worked all through the night. Ordinary labourers of every race were studying newspapers. There was a new word on the front pages: Stalingrad.

The next few weeks would now determine if the city could be captured quickly.

PART III

"LIVING CONCRETE"— THE SEPTEMBER BATTLES

The Germans have reached the Volga; the Germans wish to seize us by the throat. But for us there is no "hopeless situation." We have a way out. There is only one way out but it is a trusty one: we must repel the Germans. And repel them we shall.

—Ilya Ehrenburg[1]

CHAPTER SEVEN

The King of Stalingrad!

We were told, "Another hundred metres and you're there!"
But how can you do it if you just don't have the strength left?
—Joachim Stempel, 14th Panzer
Division[1]

Jubilant *Generaloberst* von Richthofen may have been because of the overwhelming destruction his aircrews had inflicted upon the city, but a sense of gloom dominated the thinking of Paulus, now heading toward his destiny at Stalingrad. He was under pressure from Army Group B's commander, Maximilian von Weichs, to relieve the crisis affecting Hube's division in the north. The Army High Command was determined that now German forces were at the Volga, they should remain there. The advances in the south by Army Group A gave fresh impetus to Army Group B's objectives.

Hube's division was increasingly under duress with the counter-attacks from the north and the fierce fighting against the makeshift Russian defenses in the Factory District. The crisis was only averted by the Luftwaffe diverting some squadrons from the bombing of the city to offer ground-support fire and parachute what meager supplies they could accurately deliver. On August 25, as a column of Panzers from the supporting 60th Motorized Division finally battled their way to Hube's position, his men joyously greeted a column of 250 trucks coming in the Panzers' wake, brimming with supplies and precious fuel and ammunition.

The corridor of steel that 16th Panzer Corps now maintained was vital to block off the city from reinforcement, and enabled Paulus to now press forward with the bulk of his army against the survivors of the 62nd and 64th Russian Armies, who were pulling back toward the suburbs. Slowly, the two attacking German armies would strangle the city's defenders. What Paulus hadn't planned on was the fierce defense Yeremenko's mixed bag of miltia, NKVD security police, and Red Army troops would put up to block both assaults. Their suicidal defense bought time for Yeremenko as fresh units began to trickle across the Volga and go straight into the fight, an operation that would be repeated endlessly over the coming months. The Germans may have missed a huge opportunity to seize the city while its defense was in such a shambles.

To the city's north Hube's men quickly realized that the enemy was not so demoralized from the bombing raids and was intent on putting up a fierce fight for the ruins of the suburbs and the Factory District lying behind it. As with their approach to the city itself, German troops were struggling to overcome a tenacious Soviet defense that had been prepared by the city authorities weeks before they arrived. Von Richthofen's delight at reducing Stalingrad to rubble from the air was turning sour for the German troops and armor on the ground. Shocked at the level of firepower still being brought against his units, General von Wietersheim cabled to Paulus that the positions on the Volga might be given up again. He did not believe that this vast city could be taken. Paulus demurred and repeated their orders. The attack would continue and Stalingrad would be taken.

At Army High Command confident with the devastation the Luftwaffe had inflicted on Stalingrad's defenses, Hitler announced to Army Group B's commander, Weichs, that once captured and occupied by Paulus's Sixth Army, the city should be destroyed and its male population exterminated. The viper's nest of Communism would be wiped from the map despite the daily misgivings from his chief of staff Halder about the hard going the army was encountering as it pushed eastward. This was now the pivotal battle that would rescue his whole summer campaign.

Attacking Stalingrad from the south, General Hoth's Fourth Panzer Army ran into similar difficulties. Frontal assaults with combined armor and infantry units were repulsed at great cost, well-dug-in Soviet antitank gunners taking their toll on the advancing Panzers as T-34s undertook suicidal charges into the German armored columns. As one Panzer commander described:

> Fighting other tanks in a tank my own death didn't matter to me. But everyone processes it differently. During our first skirmishes on the advance my tank suddenly stopped. My driver had a panic attack and wanted to get out. He had seen how the Russian T-34s' main gun could cave in our Panzer III and IVs. I managed to bring him back to his senses by kicking him in the neck from above. That was our first encounter with the T-34 tanks, we didn't know the Shilouette. At dusk we were driving towards Stalingrad on the so-called Russian road in a column. Suddenly Soviet tanks appeared in front of us on a broad front. We started to shoot, but our shells ricocheted off, they flew vertically into the night sky. Two of us hit them and they went up in flames. Via my larynx microphone I ordered my troop to fan out and we bypassed the T-34s left and right in order to be able to shoot at them from the side. We destroyed them all. Despite our victory, we were all in shock. Our ammunition was not enough to destroy these tanks from a range that protected us, at least not in direct comparison.[2]

As each topographical point was encountered by the advancing German forces coming from the south and west, Yeremenko's forces, what was left of them, valiantly, somewhat suicidally attempted to stem the enemy's advance toward Stalingrad itself. Their use of the terrain in some cases made up for their lack of men and armor to inflict any telling blow on the advancing enemy. The casualties were, though, becoming too great to ignore, as one Panzer commander observed: "The Russian is using every fold in the ground and not giving up a meter without a fight. Our losses increase every step that we take forwards towards the city."[3]

The continued aerial assaults by the Luftwaffe were the constant rabbit from the hat that Paulus could rely upon to ensure forward momentum as the bitter fighting continued. On September 10 units of the 29th Motorized Infantry Division reached the Volga at Kuporossnoye. Now the city was cut off in all directions except heading east back across the Volga itself. The remnants of Yeremenko's southern front retreated back into the city, the 62nd, commanded by the increasingly erratic Lieutenant General A.I. Lopatin, occupying the city center and the Factory District of the north, while Major General M. S. Shumilov's 64th Army held the southern suburbs. Paulus and Hoth had for now succeeded in splitting the Russian armies apart, but they had yet to completely destroy them or even stop their resupply from across the river at Krasnaya Sloboda. Yeremenko could still rely on the various armored speedboats, tugs, and barges that made up the Volga Flotilla to undertake a perilous transportation of men and material to attempt the impossible and hold on to the western side of the city.

On September 12, as Yeremenko's headquarters withdrew to the far side of the Volga, the Germans made ready for what would be the first battle for the city. The 62nd Army Commander Lopatin's nerves by this stage finally broke as he anxiously requested to withdraw his army out of the city. Very aware of Stalin's express orders, Yeremenko and Khrushchev hastily sacked him. The city defenders now received the leader they needed to attempt to hold Stalingrad against the coming juggernaut. General Vasily Chuikov was about to take his first step into the battle that would make his name.

Summoned to appear before the Southern Front Military Council the morning of September 11, to receive his new command and orders, Chuikov recalled in his memoirs the crisis briefing with Yeremenko and Khrushchev where the command was offered to him:

"How do you, Comrade Chuikov, understand the mission?" I had not expected I would have to answer that question, but I did not have to think long. All was clear, self-explanatory. I immediately replied: "We cannot surrender the city. To us, to all Soviet people, it is very dear. . . . Everything will be done to ensure that the city will not be surrendered. . . . I will take every measure to hold the city and, I swear, I will not leave it. We will hold the city or die there."[4]

He spent the rest of the daylight hours collecting his thoughts, assessing the strength of his command on paper, and sending messages to his new army staff and unit commanders. As darkness fell, Chuikov went quickly across the Volga, heading into the blazing city ruins to land at the Central Landing Stage. From there, forcing his way through the hundreds of civilians and wounded troops desperately trying to board the ferry he'd stepped off of, "wounded were being carried out from trenches, craters and shelters. People with bundles and suitcases appeared. Before the arrival of the ferry, all of them had been taking shelter from the bombing in holes and bomb craters."

The 62nd Army commander now scurried, ducked, and drove rapidly away from German artillery and mortar fire, into the bowels of the city center, searching for his new headquarters located at the Tsaritsa Gorge. Unable to locate anyone from his new staff, Chuikov's party were redirected by a Red Army commissar to the new location on the Mamayev Kurgan.

Stopping the car, we climbed the kurgan on foot, hanging on to bushes and some kind of thorn trees. Finally, we heard the long-awaited cry of the sentry. "Halt! Who goes there?" The command post. A gully, clods of freshly dug earth, dugouts.

His headquarters were well dug in, but as yet the enemy's artillery was not targeting the area but laying down a random barrage. For now they were as safe as it was possible to be in the circumstances. Chuikov immediately conferred with his new team. His chief of staff General Nikolay I. Krylov was a veteran of the siege of Sevastopol that spring and someone Chuikov knew from reputation as a formidable administrator. Supporting both men would be army commissar K. A. Gurov, famous for his shaven head and dark, bushy eyebrows, very much in keeping with his reputation for instilling terror and discipline into the units he oversaw. Chuikov would be grateful for both men's skill and determination over the coming months.

*   *   *

On the same day Chuikov landed in the city, Hitler personally addressed his own leadership team, who he expected would win the city for him. Army Group B's commander Weichs and General Paulus stood at the Fuhrer's situation table in the *Werwolf* headquarters. With his chief of staff Halder looking on, the Fuhrer brushed aside any misgivings either man had about the army's weak flank, the ability of their Axis allies to protect said flanks, and the weakened state of his Sixth Army now charged with taking a city as large as Stalingrad. The only discussion Hitler engaged with his officers in was how long? When could he expect the swastika to fly over Stalin's city and then consolidate the front and prep his forces for winter quarters? Paulus now repeated the timetable he had initially given to Halder upon his arrival at Vinnitsa the previous day: the Sixth Army would need ten days of combat to take the city, followed by two weeks of mopping up operations to regroup and prepare for winter. The assault in the city would commence the next day.

By September 12, the divisions of the Sixth Army though strong on paper, were operating on a shoestring of manpower. Together with Hoth's Fourth Panzer Army, Paulus had twenty-four divisions overall. Due to his concerns for the state of Army Group B's flanks, only thirteen divisions would be spared to attack the city along its forty-mile front (170,000 men, and though 500 tanks and 3,000 artillery pieces are often quoted, in reality they were nowhere near this number due to repairs and breakdowns). The front-line reality, however, painted a different, more worrying picture. The fighting from the start of the campaign to the gates of Stalingrad had cost Paulus forty thousand casualties, with only fifteen thousand arriving to replace them. German tanks, assault guns, and motorized vehicles were coming to the end of their service in many cases, with repair depots and spare parts many miles farther back behind the new front line. Air support was still strong, provided by the Luftwaffe's 8th Air Corps, comprised of almost a thousand planes.

Facing the Germans were 90,000 Red Army troops combining the strength of the 62nd and 64th Armies, supported with 2,000 artillery pieces, 120 tanks, and just under 400 planes. Chuikov's brief for defending the twenty-five-mile front of the city itself allocated him 54,000 men, 900 artillery pieces, and 110 tanks. What was not obvious was the imbalance the Soviets enjoyed in manpower across the region. Along the whole Stalingrad Front, Yeremenko commanded three armies of 130,000 men for the city's defense and to protect its southern flank, while to the north a much larger force, consisting of more than 335,000 men, would offer continual attacks on Army Group B's flank. Added to this ratio of 3 to 1 in his army's favor, Stalin would now begin the steady release of tens of thousands of fresh troops from the Stavka Reserve held back for any assault on Moscow.

The fighting for the city's hinterland, even before the battle reached its center, had been horrific for the German Sixth Army. Mobile warfare, successful in Western Europe, had worked for the Army Groups A and B in forging the path to Stalingrad and rapid advance into the Caucasus. Aerial bombing led to focused artillery bombardments followed by Panzer divisions pushing through shattered, demoralized defenses, for the infantry to be last in the queue, to mop up. But as the Sixth Army from the north and the Fourth Panzer Army from the south soon realized, once they reached the Stalingrad's suburbs a different, more intimate fight was now on their hands, which the Soviets used to their advantage as Lieutenant Anatoly Merezko of Chuikov's headquarters staff recalled:

> They had to deal with high-rise buildings, solid brick . . . [which for all their armored strength,] powerful as it was, broke down into rivulets. The buildings, like wave-breakers, broke them; they had to take the streets where they were shot at from every building. And, what's important is that the tanks were afraid to go deeper. And the infantry wouldn't advance without them.[5]

The urban fighting now amid the rubble-strewn landscape had not only caused a stream of casualties in Paulus's infantry, but clearly affected the soldiers' confidence in coordinating movements to fight alongside their armor. German tanks and mobile assault guns found the going tough amid the wasteland of brick, rubble, burned timber, and twisted steel that covered what had once been the city streets. As more casualties were inflicted upon LI Corps spearheads advancing into Stalingrad, as well as from the north, Paulus's commanders became more reliant on any infantry they could muster to fill the gaps in their depleted formations. This led to his armored units fighting alongside troops inexperienced in mechanized support, resulting in failed, uncoordinated assaults. Their ability in open country ceased to be a factor in the confines of city streets where the enemy could be above you, behind you, or coming up from the sewers. The reinforcements sent in to replace these devasted units had little training with armor, making progress even slower.

Equally, with the enemy now deploying more antitank methods (satchel bombs, mines, Molotov cocktails, and antitank armor-piercing rifles) to knock out the unwieldy Panzers, Paulus became more reliant on his infantry to pave a way toward the Volga. *Hauptfeldwebel* Friedrich Hundertmark recalled the trauma a tank crew would face when navigating the terrain:

> It was different here in Stalingrad. We hardly fought against tanks, the Russian combat units had such small PAKs [anti-tank guns] that were very light and manoeuvrable. Such a thing almost became our undoing. I saw an anti-tank gun being fired through the armored mirror and dropped down directly onto my driver. The shell hit the turret and my ass and back were full of splinters. My driver hadn't received anything, everyone else was dead or wounded.[6]

For Paulus's initial assault on the city itself, on September 13, the task to quickly capture the central districts, split in two Yeremenko's front, and encircle and destroy them was allocated to General Walther von Seydlitz-Kurzbach's LI Corps. He would have a sizable force (across the 389th, 295th, and 71st Infantry Divisions), all operating at almost 60 percent of their actual strength, each having suffered significant losses, with their regiments now comprised of six instead of the requisite nine battalions. Compounding this manpower shortage, all units now lacked experienced combat leaders and NCOs who had been killed or wounded in the campaign thus far. To support LI Corps from the south were Hoth's Fourth Panzer Army, which like Paulus's units had incurred heavy casualties in men and machines on their way to the city.[7]

In the vanguard of LI Corps would be the 71st Infantry Division under Major General Alexander von Hartmann. Their attack route into the city was deemed by Paulus the shortest and quickest to pierce the inner defensive ring of Stalingrad. As part of a general assault the division had previously captured Gumrak airfield on September 3 and pushed hard to be established along the Mamayev Hills before advancing toward the Tsaritza River and along the main road leading from Gumrak into the city's suburbs, dominated by hilly terrain that gave excellent views into the city and the Volga beyond. This had given Paulus a tactical advantage as the Russian forces fled into Stalingrad behind the city's final ring of defenses and precipitated General Lopatin's mental disintegration, leading to Chuikov replacing him.

Along with other units, von Hartmann's 71st Division was now tasked with assaulting and capturing the central section of the city, defended by the remnants of the 62nd Army bottled up within the key administrative centers, Railway Station No. 1 and the NKVD complex, and protecting the strategically vital Mamayev Kurgan and the Central Ferry Crossing overlooking the Volga. The German depleated divisions designated for the assult would be supported by heavy aerial bombardments to clear their path to their respective objectives. On September 13 LI Corps began its main attack into Stalingrad, suffering casualties every step of the way as the Russians, lacking infantry strength, resorted to mobile Katyusha rockets and heavy artillery to attempt to dent the German momentum.

After a brief artillery barrage, backed up by salvos of different calibre Nebelwerfers [German multi-barreled rocket launchers], our infantry, escorted by numerous assault guns, went on the offensive. When the soldiers reached the city outskirts and disappeared between the wooden houses and gardens, a real inferno from salvos of Stalin Organ rockets caused the whole suburban settlement to disappear in a wall of fire and smoke.[8]

Major General von Hartmann would now attempt to advance into the central districts with Infantry Regiment 194 leading the way. Along with the rest of the 71st Division, it was now positioned on the incline overlooking Railway Station No. 1 in the distance. The aim was for this central assault to strike at the same time the XXXXVIII Panzerkorps would push up from the south. Maintaining close radio contact, both would meet and thus trap remaining Soviet forces still in the city. For such a tough operation going into formidable terrain, von Hartmann was relieved he had the right man to lead his key regiment. Like his divisional commander, Colonel Friedrich Roske was a combat veteran from the Great War. He had trained as a structural engineer in the 1920s and had for a while worked for an architectural company based on Madison Avenue in New York. He had enlisted again in 1934, been promoted to major by the outbreak of fighting in 1939, and fought in the campaign for France in 1940. By June 1941, with increasing losses of infantry officers across the whole Eastern Front, Roske—now a lieutenant colonel—had been taken from the officer reserve to serve wherever he was needed across the front line, leading battalions. As winter arrived, he had then been placed back in the officer pool and was reassigned that December to teaching tactics at the Army School in Dresden. In a quirk of fate, he had taught von Hartmann's own battalion commanders once the 71st Infantry Division had been taken out of the front line. The general would remember him. Born to lead troops, Roske volunteered for a new combat command by August 1942, as Sixth Army's need for replacements intensified that summer.

A man's fortune can turn on a conversation or phone call, and so it was for Roske. He was standing in the Military Personnel Office discussing a future post when a call came through, as Roske recounted:

> I could tell from what Colonel Marx was saying that the person at the other end of the line was the Adjutant of the Sixth Army Lieutenant Colonel Adam from the Army Headquarters at Poltava. Adam was asking for a substitute for the previous commander who had been

promoted to Major General. These were the troops I had been using to teach tactics. A first-class regiment who had knowledge of me as a tactical instructor. After the end of the phone call Colonel Marx asked me,

"Well, what do you think of having the I.R. 194?"

"That is the Regiment I would choose for myself," I replied.

Marx studied the situation map on the wall. "But I believe that the 71st which was originally going to go to the Caucasus has now been sent to Stalingrad."

"I don't mind. If a thousand others are risking their necks there, I will go too. I'll take I.R. 194."

However, Roske's personal papers reveal that despite his willingness to enter front-line combat, to his wife he had secretly questioned the sense of launching Barbarossa in the first place, as well as the German's chances of overall victory. But he was still set on achieving his ultimate goal: to lead a new combat formation where the fighting was fiercest. By September 4 he had arrived, from Dresden via Breslau, at von Hartmann's headquarters with his orderly (Private Berndl), the general himself greeting him as he stepped off his command coach: "Thank God, the right one!"[9]

The 71st Infantry Division hailed from Lower Saxony, comprised of three infantry regiments (the 191, 194, and 211), an artillery arm, and various supporting elements. All told it mustered approximately fifteen thousand officers and other ranks. From its successes at Verdun in the French campaign in 1940 it had earned the sobriquet of the "Lucky Division." Its current commander, von Hartmann, was a Prussian, a highly experienced and hard-nosed combat leader who had led a regiment in the French campaign and now been promoted to command a division. He carried his Great War service in the form of a limp from a severe leg wound suffered at Verdun in 1916, but he drove his men hard and fairly and led by example, as one of his officers (Captain Ernest-August Deppe) recalled his early leadership years:

As regimental commander Colonel von Hartmann tirelessly encouraged the continued education of his officers, especially in peacetime. He found it important to broaden one's very narrow military horizon through speeches or lectures, musical performances, and discussion in the arts. He was the typical multifaceted representative of a well-educated Prussian officer, who had a love of music. In the mobilisation of 1939, Hartmann made a speech in which he bade farewell to those officers who had to be placed into newly created regiments. Without any illusion he saw the tragedy of the war approaching—and, as though he foresaw his own death, he requested that a memorial to the fallen of the I.R. 37 be erected at the wall of the barracks in Osnabrück-Haste in the future. When he gave orders, he was precise, exact and circumspect. In the nighttime battles crossing the Seine, south of Rouen, he led I.R. 37 from the front line.[10]

Promoted, Major General von Hartmann had taken command of the 71st Division once it was refitting in Germany, and by June of 1941 he was part of the invasion of Russia, heading into the fierce fighting in the Ukraine with Army Group South. The division had endured the conditions and privations in the bitter winter fighting before being transferred back to France for rest and resupply. Like many of his officers, von Hartmann took the time to get a precious period of leave, when Captain Deppe met with him one final time:

I was on a recovery holiday in 1942 when he invited me to his daughter's wedding. It was a very small do, in Osnabrück. I was able to report to him about his old regiment in Russia. Then he spoke in a very personal manner to me about the military situation. His constantly sharp, sober mind prevented him from succumbing to the propaganda. He foresaw the desperate tragedy of the trapped troops in Russia in advance and knew that since the USA had entered the war, Germany's military situation was hopeless in the long run. On the other hand, he was convinced that the West would not accept the bolshevism of Germany—and therefore of Europe—

which meant to him that there was a chance of a ceasefire, albeit
a small chance. He was hoping for a change of political leadership
through that.[11]

Despite his private misgivings, von Hartmann had returned to the
east by April 1942 for his division's participation in the fighting around
Kharkov prior to Paulus's Sixth Army marching east that summer. Like
many of his sister divisions in LI Corps, von Hartmann's had suffered
heavily in the seven weeks of combat that had taken them the six hundred kilometers from the Don Bend to the gates of Stalingrad.[12]

Getting up to speed on the strengths and weaknesses of his new command, Lieutenant Colonel Roske had quickly set about reorganizing a
badly mauled regiment, reconfiguring as best he could to rebuild its
combat strength, though many new recruits were not pleased, as one
of the division's artillery officers recalled:

> The infantry had to regroup. They desperately needed a break. . . .
> Oberst Roske, newly arrived at the division, was the only one to
> draw the logical conclusion: he disbanded one battalion and several
> companies and formed two new almost up-to-strength battalions into
> which he incorporated the mounted platoon, telephonists and pio-
> neers. Prior to the regrouping, the companies had already been below
> platoon strength. Only the supply trains had been up to their original
> strength. They were oversized in proportion and reinforcements
> could therefore be gained from them for the front. Those affected
> were not all thrilled. . . . The best thing that could happen to them
> was to get a "Heimatschuss" [literally meaning "home wound"].[13]

Now, after a week of fighting through the final outer ring of the
city's defenses, the capture of Gumrak airfield, and into the suburbs,
Roske stood with von Hartmann by a semi-destroyed brickworks, gazing
toward the center of the city and Railway Station No. 1—his regiment's
new objective. Plumes of black smoke ascended in dozens of places where

the Luftwaffe had bombed targets. He took his binoculars and studied the mess of abandoned trains, wrecked locomotives, and semi-destroyed T-34 tanks now marooned in and outside the vast station complex. The square around it looked as if some giant had careered through it smashing everything in sight. Roske informed von Hartmann that he would not send in his men in a stretched-out frontal attack. He had already seen what Russian artillery and snipers did to that. Instead, he would utilize what strength still remained in I.R. 194 and send down two "shock" columns, a block apart and supported with heavy artillery. Though von Hartmann displayed concern for the division's weakness on the flank, Roske was adamant he could take the station and push on to the river, but they must act decisively and be closely supported by the Luftwaffe.

Roske marched off to his regiment's positions and gathered his battalion and company commanders selected for the attack: Major Dr. Fritz Dobberkau would lead the II Battalion on the right, while Captain Gerhard Münch's III Battalion would take the left. Both would advance down the steep embankment into the tangle of train wagons below and on into the built-up streets toward the river beyond. They would have 88mm flak artillery as well as StuG III assault guns should they encounter any KV-1s or T-34s still active in the city environs.[14] Their right flank would be protected by their sister regiment, the 191. Units of the 295th Division were some distance to the left of Roske's own northern flank, heading toward their own objective atop the Mamayev Kurgan, though one unit (I.R. 518) would advance in parallel to Roske's battalions. Speed would be the key for success. Major General von Hartmann, though exasperated at the quantity of troops his colonel would have for such a crucial assault, nevertheless bade him good luck and jumped into his staff car and sped off back to the division's headquarters.

Both divisions would advance in concentric waves, assaulting the Soviet positions in a wedge-like formation to pierce the final defensive line of the 62nd Army and cut it in two at the river's edge, rolling up both its flanks and bringing about its ultimate destruction. Both of Roske's battalions would have artillery support to blast out any resistance met in the houses lined along their routes toward the embankment. Roske and his staff and communications would follow up close behind to coordinate fire support. Though fretful of sporadic air attacks, he was more concerned as to the strength of the force his men faced below and the intensity of the fighting that was to come.

Before the attack commenced, Roske again instilled in his officers the need for the men to press ahead, not wait for the wounded, and for the battalions and regiment itself to seize this initiative offered by the enemy's weak lines of defense due to the speed of the German advance. It might pave the way for a final victory over the Red Army. His memo read to his officers stated:

> We stand in this phase of the struggle, which is of exceptional impor-
> tance for the war and especially for the Eastern campaign. The whole
> world looks at the troops from Stalingrad and besides, the quick and
> victorious conclusion of the battle with the reaching of the Volga also
> means a conclusion for the regiment. The troops are to be informed
> of this. I expect the whole regiment to exert a great deal of strength,
> which will be worthy of the achievements of IR 194 so far.[15]

As the afternoon wore on, the regiment watched as airstrikes from waves of at least sixty Stukas pounded suspected Red Army positions. That morning regimental scouts had reported from the parked train carriages of sniper activity that had already inflicted some casualties. These carriages were by now being systematically destroyed from the air. With his elevated position looking down on the center of town, the scene below Roske was now one of fire, smoke, burning wagons, and streets strewn with rubble. The sky was now devoid of friendly planes and the objective ahead looked desolate, with the Russians nowhere to be seen. Captain Münch took his chance and ordered the III Battalion forward:

> I decided, if we wanted something, we needed to do it ourselves. It
> wasn't far from the railway station to the water—just 600–700 meters.
> If we wanted to do it, then we would have to do it now.[16]

Roske quickly ordered his regimental team and radiomen to follow him as they got in behind the battalions now double-timing down the incline, their flak guns being towed behind.

I can still see myself at the very moment of approaching the front slopes, accompanying our soldiers . . . and calling out encouragements to them—that today, on reaching the Volga, the war would be won.[17]

Then disaster struck. As Münch's battalion reached the burned-out wagons in front of the railway station, his lead units now urgently tore at their backpacks to find and ignite smoke-recognition cannisters, their purple trail becoming visible as they drifted above the black smoke of the fires below. With sirens wailing overhead, however, Münch instinctively knew they were about to be attacked. A few hundred yards behind them, looking on, Roske winced as he recognized the wailing siren of an incoming Stuka, the cluster of bombs landing squarely among a company of III Battalion. It was bloody mayhem. The ground shook violently as the concussive force threw the German attackers to the ground, blinding dust and clouds of purple smoke shrouding the screams of the wounded that now broke the initial concussive silence.

Münch survived, but one of his nearby companies had been virtually wiped out, only four men now fit for combat, and they were preoccupied administering first aid to their wounded or dying comrades, who lay all around the scorched impact area. Body parts, weapons, and rubble now littered the street as Münch's next company advanced farther through the grisly scene and on to the station. The enemy still had to be located and destroyed. It was then that the Germans enjoyed one piece of luck. Despite their losses and lack of armored support, they managed to capture the northern railyards of Railway Station No. 1. The Soviet defenders had been so bludgeoned for hours by aerial and artillery bombardment that the survivors crammed into the cellars gladly surrendered to the remnants of III Battalion as they entered the ruined buildings.

*   *   *

With so few men now under his command, and with Dobberkau's II Battalion pushing on to the river on his right flank, Roske urged his men on and to ignore occupying the buildings still standing along the streets they were advancing down. He now lacked the numbers required to storm the buildings and root out the defenders floor by floor; other units behind him would do that. For now they would take their chances and push on to the riverbank—only a matter of a few hundred meters away. He could see the Volga glistening in the distance. Three impressively large buildings near to the Central Landing pier were now occupied by the survivors of the battalion's assault: the State Bank, the House of Specialists, and the Brewery. These buildings would be the scene of savage fighting back and forth for the next three months. For now, believing victory might well be in sight, Roske was in admiration of his regiment's performance:

> Being able to achieve this success despite being bombed by our own side [Luftwaffe] and facing a determined enemy was a superb performance of both battalions. Only the survivors who experienced such a firestorm can appreciate what the men like old battlers Dobberkau, Münch and their wonderful men did.

Roske set up a regimental command post (CP), urgently needing to assess the threat to his flanks, aware that he had pushed farther than any other German unit. What had happened to the 295th Division protecting his left flank? Had they been as successful on the Mamayev Kurgan? He could not afford to have Dobberkau and Münch's positions dangling in no-man's-land should the Soviets now counterattack. Driving this anxiety were reports of increased activity to his rear from surviving Red Army and NKVD personnel who had been bypassed as I.R. 194 advanced to the river. As he was busy dictating orders for further artillery and infantry support, at 15:15 hours, an official message via the field telephone suddenly came in from Münch's III Battalion: "I have reached the Volga!" Roske immediately called divisional headquarters: "The Grenadier Regiment 194 has reached the Volga at 15:15 hours!"

At the other end of the field telephone line in the divisional operations room, its chief of staff Lieutenant Colonel von Below replied incredulously: "What? I beg your pardon? Please, Lieutenant Colonel, say that again!"

Roske repeated his message, handed his phone back to his operator kneeling beside him, and began to quickly scribble out orders for his battalion commanders to take up a defensive perimeter. The remaining men of I.R. 194 would begin to fortify the House of Specialists and the formidable State Bank complex. Both offered solid protection and gave excellent views across the city center and the Volga. Roske positioned artillery spotters atop each building, to start directing fire onto river traffic and to the far shore, where Katyusha rocket launchers were still sending salvos toward his position and toward the 295th Division on his flank. At the lower levels of both buildings his men rapidly set about creating firing points and fortifying entrenched machine gun positions.[18]

He still had the presence of mind to dispatch his adjutant, First Lieutenant Gerhard Hindenlang, back to the divisional CP in the church on the hill with a hard-won trophy—a bottle of fresh water from the Volga. Gingerly making his way back along the side streets in case he should encounter retreating Russians, Hindenlang crept past the semi-destroyed Railway Station No. 1, navigating his way around the burned-out wrecks of vehicles and destroyed Soviet tanks. Bypassing the medical teams giving aid to the wounded, he ignored the bodies now strewn everywhere from the fighting a few hours before. The Stukas and the Russian Katyushas had both done their worst. The place was more than a war zone, it was a slaughterhouse, worse than anything he had witnessed thus far on the Eastern Front.

Finally, he was at the hill and made his way past the armed sentries into the divisional CP. Triumphant from the news he was bringing, Hindenlang was shocked to find that von Hartmann had company. Ready to receive him was his corps commander General of Artillery Seydlitz-Kurzbach himself, both senior officers standing before him like expectant parents. Hindenlang snapped to attention and reported the regiment's new position on the river. He plunged a hand into his knapsack and withdrew the bottle. Thrilled with the news of Roske's daring, the generals eagerly took turns at taking a swig, toasting Roske and I.R. 194. General von Hartmann mocked Hindenlang that the bottle didn't contain schnapps. Seydlitz-Kurzbach took the bottle back and laughed at the young adjutant's nervousness, joking that he had not brought back any frogs with it. Smiling, Hindenlang still couldn't get the image of the carcasses of the dead lying around the square out his mind.

Meanwhile, back at Dobberkau and Münch's redoubts overlooking the Volga, enemy activity to their front by the Central Landing pier was increasing as the Soviets on the ground realized the Germans had reached the riverbank and were setting up to remain. The situation was made more urgent once both commanders' artillery spotters began to bring down fire onto the river traffic. Those Red Army soldiers who had survived the aerial bombardments at the train station and the fighting withdrawal along the streets toward the Central Landing had found cover beneath the steep river embankment. Having dug foxholes, the survivors directed fire onto the two blockhouses. A sporadic firefight erupted, peppering both German positions with machine gun fire. Roske heard the desperate calls coming in from Münch's undermanned battalion CP and issued a rapid radio call for an airstrike.

The tragedy of friendly fire that had virtually wiped out one of his companies a few hours earlier was almost repeated. Roske recounted:

> Despite my [earlier] protest at our own planes not dropping bombs near my area of operations, a German pilot unloaded too close to the pier, which, although it struck the Russians, also inflicted losses for us. One Stuka strike hit a large house with many storeys, in whose cellar the staff of Münch's battalion was situated. It destroyed the house down to the cellar and only the staff quarters were more or less intact afterwards.[19]

Roske's radioman screamed down the line for the airstrikes to move away from the zone and concentrate on the embankment itself. Within minutes the familiar siren could be heard above as new attacks dived down to dismantle the Soviet earthworks along the riverbank. They caused chaos, mercilessly pounding the defenders, who died where they fought, clawed at the earth in their foxholes, or fled back along the shoreline until out of range as they ducked into the ruins as yet unoccupied by Roske's men.

Roske ordered Dobberkau and Münch to gather what men they had and sweep their front of whatever surviving Russian troops they encountered, which they duly did, setting up defensive positions along the shoreline and taking occupancy within the ruins of the State Bank, the House of Specialists, and the water pumping station, which dominated the Central Landing pier. With the enemy still on the western bank and the distinctive rumble of Soviet tanks in the distance, the fear of a counterattack was uppermost in Roske's mind as the late afternoon made way for the evening darkness that he knew would reduce his men's aerial defensive shield.

> My impulsive decision to push through to the Volga was now starting to trouble me because at any moment the Russians could break into our rear. As a defensive strategy, I ordered up the supporting divisional artillery and placed a field howitzer in every one of the fourteen connecting roads to our rear, flanked by machine guns and the carabiners of the artillery. From sunset onwards, every so often a comforting shot could be heard roaring far behind us.[20]

To the supporting artillery of the 71st Division, Roske's startling success was just the tonic after weeks of hard fighting and heavy losses. As they positioned their guns on the intersections Roske had ordered, the rumble of rogue T-34s could be heard in the distance. Despite the division's flank still being unprotected from the tanks' forward surge, and the threat of whatever remained of the enemy still lurking in neighboring buildings, morale was high. Their objective had seemingly been reached; the enemy appeared to be if not beaten, then certainly unable to offer fierce resistance, and there was the Volga, shining in the evening light, the flames of the shelled buildings reflected on the water amid the acrid smoke. Lieutenant Wigand Wuster captured the atmosphere that evening:

> In the ghostly night, lit by flames, our spirits remained high. . . . Our losses had been relatively few. The neighbouring divisions neglected

to stay on the tails of the retreating Russians beyond their daily objective. The divisions to our south endured the hardest possible fighting before they too could finally reach the Volga, while our neighbouring divisions to the north never made it to the river, despite mounting ever more ferocious attacks.[21]

Roske's concerns as to the overall situation for the south of the city were well placed. The tenacious defense put up by Chuikov's 35th Guards Rifle Division had effectively stopped XXXXVIII Panzerkorps during their northern advance on the center, denying their planned linkup. It was a crucial failure, as one German staff officer would later comment:

The time for conducting large-scale operations was gone forever; from the wide expanses of the steppe land, the war moved into the jagged gullies of the Volga hills with their copses and ravines, into the factory area of Stalingrad, spread out over uneven, pitted, rugged country, covered with iron, concrete and stone buildings. The mile as a measure of distance was replaced by the yard.[22]

Back at his makeshift regimental command post, Roske now sat back on an upturned box, took off his *Stahlhelm* and studied the situational map pinned to a wall. Counter battery fire was coming across from the east bank of the Volga, searching for targets but only causing a nuisance for his men, who were busy digging in. Tired, still calculating the regiment's losses from the fighting, and elated at his men's startling success, he half-jokingly sent a message to the Luftwaffe air controller coordinating the airstrikes: *No more bombs in a wide circumference around my area. But if you have to drop something, make it sausages and chocolate please!*[23] Perhaps after days of constant pressure coordinating multiple ground attacks, the Luftwaffe officer in question reacted badly to the intended gibe: *That's all you can say after we've been working day and night to procure the bombs, drag them into place, flying all hours, constantly, and defending ourselves to the bone!*

*　　*　　*

The regiment had overcome deadly friendly fire from the air, driven out a tenacious enemy in vicious house-to-house combat, and sustained yet more casualties from its own Stuka support just as they reached the Volga. But despite these setbacks, the 71st Division's objective had been achieved and, in Dobberkau and Münch's battalions' case, even exceeded. The men had also now captured a Russian 76mm artillery piece, turned it eastward, and already hit and sunk two Volga ferries. Roske recorded his delight: "We managed to avert a mass panic, and the men retained their good spirits. . . . I was the master of the centre of Stalingrad!"[24]

His success would elicit contrasting reactions a thousand miles from the city. Exclamations of jubilation echoed in the humid operational rooms of Hitler's headquarters at Vinnitsa, whereas consternation stalked the corridors of the Stavka while in the Kremlin Stalin paced around his conference table glaring at Zhukov and Vasilevsky as they updated the Soviet leader. Though Stalin fretted as to the extent of the danger the city would fall into, he was pragmatic enough to give license to his two military strategists to briefly outline a plan they had been discussing: a daring counterstroke aimed at the enemy's overextended flanks that might reverse their fortunes not only in the fight for the city but in the Southern Russian theater itself. Intrigued, Stalin ordered them to draw up detailed plans they would discuss further once the current crisis was stabilized. Looking down toward the Central Landing of the Volga, meanwhile, Lieutenant Colonel Roske's success was not to last for long. Stalin ordered Zhukov to get on a plane to Stalingrad to assess the situation and oversee what counterattacks could be mustered on the German northern flank, to ease the pressure on the city itself. As Zhukov departed for the south, the Soviet leader authorized the Stavka to signal Yeremenko to bring Major General Rodimtsev's 13th Guards Rifle Division across the Volga to Chuikov's aid and retake the city at any cost.

CHAPTER EIGHT

Send for the Guards

There are no miracles in the world. In the art of war, every hour and even minute is precious.

—Colonel Ivan Pavlovich Elin[1]

A day before Roske's men of I.R. 194 were striding down to the Volga embankment, Lieutenant General Chuikov of the 62nd Army had already set to work on a proper defense by ensuring his besieged forces would have supply across the Volga, already hamstrung due to Yeremenko's hasty decision to blow the main bridge days earlier:

> I ordered my deputy for logistics to immediately set up three piers and three river routes: the first pier near Verkhnyaya Akhtuba, the second near Skudri and the third near Tumak. From those piers, cargo could be shipped at night to piers at Krasnyy Oktyabr Metal Works and Spartanovka on the vessels of the Volga Military Flotilla and other boats. There was a pedestrian bridge on iron barrels from the area of Barrikady Gun Factory to Zajtsevskiy Island. From the island the east bank of the Volga could be reached by ferry.
>
> All boats in the army's sector were strictly accounted for and allocated between the divisions and brigades. A ferry landing was set up for each division. They were operated under the exacting control of and according to a schedule established by division commanders. The rifle brigades operating south of the Tsaritsa River were supplied independently, through Golodnyy Island, with the assistance of boats.[2]

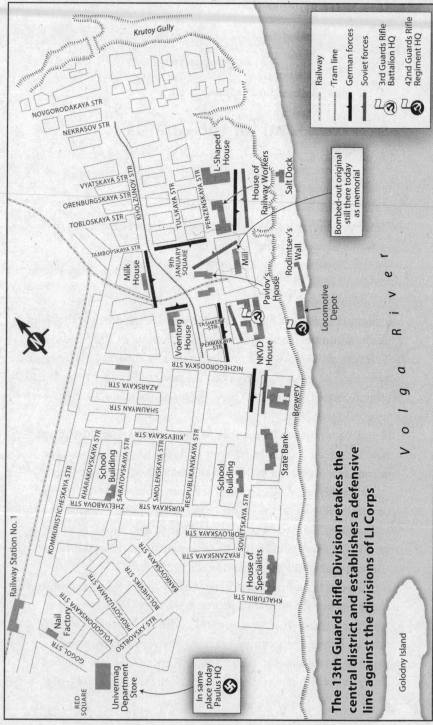

The 13th Guards Rifle Division retakes the central district and establishes a defensive line against the divisions of LI Corps

Map legend:
- Railway
- Tram line
- German forces
- Soviet forces
- 3rd Guards Rifle Battalion HQ
- 42nd Guards Rifle Regiment HQ

Labels on map:

Krutoy Gully

Novgorodakaya Str
Nekrasov Str
Vyatskaya Str
Orenburgskaya Str
Tobloskaya Str
Tambovskaya Str
Kholzunov Str
Tulskaya Str
Penzenskaya Str

L-Shaped House
House of Railway Workers
Salt Dock

Bombed-out original still there today as memorial

Mill
Rodimtsev's Wall

9th January Square
Milk House

Voentorg House
Tashkent Str
Permakaya Str
Nizhnegorodskaya Str
NKVD House

Pavlov's House
Locomotive Depot

Azarskaya Str
Shaumyan Str
Kiievskaya Str

Brewery

Kharakovskaya Str
School Building
Saratovskaya Str
Smolenskaya Str
Republikanskaya Str
Zhelyabova Str
Kurskaya Str

State Bank

School Building

Orlovskaya Str
Sovietskaya Str
Ryazanskaya Str
Bankovskaya Str
House of Specialists

Khalturin Str

Kommunistcheskaya Str
Bolshevik Str
Prosovuznaya Str

Railway Station No. 1

Nail Factory
Gogol Str
Volgodonskaya Str
Ostrovsky Str

Red Square
Univermag Department Store

In same place today Paulus HQ

Volga River

Golodny Island

© MDL Design

What Chuikov brought to the battle was the belief his men so lacked due to the constant pounding they had taken from the enemy. In the spirit of Stalin's Order No. 227 he would defend Stalingrad to the death:

> I had not given any thought to removing myself to the east bank. I considered it inconceivable to even withdraw to one of the islands. That would have had an immediate effect on the morale of unit commanders, their staffs and all the soldiers. . . . We sensed, we knew, that the divisional and regimental staff officers closely observed the behavior of the Army Council. To feel sure that we were all together on the west bank, many subordinate headquarters sent officers and political workers to army headquarters. . . . It was particularly important at the time that the unit commanders and soldiers knew that they were not alone, that the army military council was with them."[3]

With the Germans on the city's embankment, Chuikov had a divisional commander in his own image to help him save the situation. As had the rest of the Red Army in Southern Russia by the summer of 1942, the 13th Guards Division had endured a tough spring campaign. Since its redesignation from the 87th Rifle Division at the beginning of the year, it had been badly mauled in the disastrous Kharkov offensive, only escaping the German encirclement by the skin of its teeth and then conducting a fighting retreat to west of the Don River. The Supreme Command now instructed the commander, Major General Alexander Rodimtsev, that the division would be relieved from front-line duty, replenish lost equipment, and await replacements.[4]

With the look of an academic and a committed Communist, at thirty-seven years of age, Alexander Rodimtsev was in his prime— a skillful, experienced Red Army commander, totally fearless, exceptional in decision making under fire, feared and equally loved by the men under his command. Already awarded the title of Hero of the Soviet Union for his service in the Spanish Civil War in 1937,[5] he was steadily rising through the ranks as war came. He had originally commanded, at the time of Barbarossa, an elite airborne brigade,[6] which had then been turned into an infantry formation (the 87th Rifle Division) and fought in the failure to stop the Germans taking Kiev. Due to its limited successes amid a string of horrendous defeats suffered by the Red Army that summer, it was redesignated in January 1942 to elite status as the 13th Guards Rifle Division. Guards' divisions were in theory allocated the best recruits, the newest weaponry, and better pay. Rodimtsev had led his division well, guaranteeing their survival, but by July 1942 he was keenly aware of the battle that was coming for Stalingrad as the army retreated west of the Don River. Although the Kharkov Offensive had been a disaster, Rodimtsev's reputation had emerged unscathed, with his performance earning him a promotion from colonel.

The division was badly understrength, significantly weak among the junior officer and NCO ranks, and many of the new recruits had come from the republics of Transcaucasia and Central Asia. As Senior Lieutenant Aleksei Efimovic Zhukov of the 3rd Battalion, 42nd Regiment, recalled:

> The division was replenished only with personnel: front-line soldiers discharged from hospitals after recovery, and military cadets who had graduated from the academies in the city of Astrakhan. Many from the Urals and Siberia.[7]

One issue that no amount of physical training could resolve was the language barrier between a great many of the guards whose first language wasn't Russian.[8]

But the core of the old discipline and the ethos of the battered division were retained, with each regiment still containing dozens of combat veterans who had survived and were ready to go into action again once the new intake had been assimilated quickly. This was a recognized policy for the Red Army. As Stalin himself had frequently stated, his troops were "cogs of history"—as with a car, truck, or farm tractor, the engine might fail of the fan belt break, but it could be replaced to allow the vehicle to run again successfully. So it was with Red Army formations who had endured severe losses that summer. Mikhail Kalinin, Stalin's chairman of the Presidium of the Supreme Soviet Union, concurred, telling writer Vasily Grossman: "A regiment

or division can reconstitute itself after any battle as long as its backbone, embodying in itself the highly developed battle traditions of the
unit has survived."[9]

The 13th Guards now comprised their headquarters unit; the 42nd,
39th, 34th Guards Rifle Regiments; the 4th Guards Antitank Regiment;
the 32nd Guards Artillery Regiment; and various support units. Relying
on the backbone of experience that the surviving veterans of his old unit,
the 5th Airborne Brigade, brought to the 13th Guards, Rodimtsev was
impatient while his new soldiers were trained to master the techniques
of accurate shooting and combat tactics. He placed great emphasis on
his men displaying initiative in their own tactical awareness of defensive
and offensive tactics. This brief downtime for refitting would soon be
disturbed by a communiqué from the Headquarters of the Supreme
Command:

> Our Bolshevik Party, our people, our Great Motherland ordered to
> prevent the enemy from reaching the Volga, to defend Stalingrad. The
> defense of Stalingrad is critical. Sparing no effort, despising death, we
> will not allow a German to the Volga, we will not surrender Stalingrad!

The 13th Guards would now come under command of the Stalingrad
Military District, commanded by Colonel General Andrey Yeremenko,
who had taken command of the whole Southeastern Front on August 7.
He had then been given the Stalingrad Front two weeks later, on
August 23. An ex-officer in the Tsar's Imperial Army during the Great
War, he had then swapped sides to fight for the Red Army during the
civil war as a cavalry commander. Surviving the purges in the late 1930s,
he then saw action commanding forces in the campaign in Poland in
1939 before taking command of Russia's Far Eastern armies in Siberia.
Eight days after the German invasion he was recalled to defend against
the German Army Group Center's drive for Moscow in 1941, putting
up a fierce defense of Smolensk and wounded three times over the next
twelve months of bitter fighting. Stalin was keen to have him defending
the city bearing the general secretary's name, even though Yeremenko
arrived at his new post with the aid of a walking stick. Chuikov's 62nd

Army naturally fell under his command. By the time the 13th Guards would reach the east bank of the Volga on September 14, the division would number 9,603, including all ranks,[10] coming to Chuikov's aid just at the crucial moment.

The division reached Kamyshkin by forced march on September 10 and awaited orders for the next designated forming point before they headed into the maelstrom of Stalingrad. By September 12, all units were motorized, moving along bumpy, dust-filled dirt roads in Lend-Lease American-made trucks and cars[11] destined for the town of Srednyaya Akhtuba. Rodimtsev ordered his regimental commanders to ensure the men traveled in small convoys of four vehicles, spaced five hundred to seven hundred meters apart. With yellow-nosed Messerschmitt fighters and Dornier reconnaissance planes already dominating the skies around the Stalingrad hinterland, any Russian column churning up a dust cloud in daylight was easy prey. The battalions arrived sporadically that evening, the dense fog drifting off the river shielding their arrival, allowing time to construct camouflaged positions. Rodimtsev, however, was appalled to be informed by the advance party of his divisional HQ that the bulk of the weapons promised to him by Vasilevsky two days earlier had not arrived, just six hundred rifles to be distributed among thousands of men. More than 50 percent of the division were without arms on the brink of being sent into a major battle. Rodimtsev recalled in his memoirs:

> Our division still hadn't been equipped, but we were supposed to get weapons soon. I objected and said I wouldn't go without weapons. There were times when my men had been unarmed, and we had had to take weapons off deserters. I was called to the direct line. I had a talk with Vasilievsky. He ordered me go there first and then get my weapons. Stalingrad, he said, was in a difficult situation.[12]

Having rested and taken in much-needed rations, the guards, with units of the 42nd Regiment in the lead, set off on a forced night march on their last leg before Stalingrad, as Senior Lieutenant Zhukov of the 3rd Battalion recalled:[13]

The march was not easy, but the soldiers were cheerful. Here and there, jokes and fervent laughter were heard in the column. Before dawn, we arrived in Krasnaya Sloboda, on the shore at the bend of the Volga.[14]

They encountered a large yellow sign in the shape of an arrow, pointing west and simply stating "Ferry."

Senior Lieutenant Zhukov continued:

And immediately, as if on command, the jokes and laughter stopped. The soldiers, shocked by what they saw, even spoke in a whisper: burning islands of oil floated along the entire length of the Volga, and beyond [the river] lay all in ruins, Stalingrad was burning. A genuine alarm appeared on the faces of the soldiers: what will happen to them there, in this fiery hell?![15]

The men's mood was improved with the issue of extra rations of bread, sausage, and even the rarity of sugar, which they eagerly used that evening for their dark tea boiled up in every unit's samovar.[16]

By the next day Yeremenko and Rodimtsev had conferred by radio. The battered units of Chuikov's 62nd Army—a mixture of the 112th Rifle Division, the remnants of the 10th NKVD Division, and a mix of city militia—were all fighting in the central district. The previous day's fighting had taken a toll on Chuikov's forces after a failed counterattack had been heavily repulsed by Luftwaffe aerial attacks. Now it was the Germans' turn to push forward. Behind yet more aerial bombardments, two infantry battalions belonging to Roske's I.R. 194 had surged ahead through the city streets and set up assault guns to control buildings overlooking the Central Crossing Point and begin firing on shipping. Behind this new enemy position were elements of an isolated regiment of NKVD troops who had been defending the Railway Station No. 1 and whatever survivors were left from city militia and 62nd Army stragglers. The 112th Rifle Division had also been pushed off their defensive works atop the Mamayev Kurgan by relentless Stuka attacks and the assaults of the 295th Infantry Division, who had been advancing alongside Roske's 71st Division. By late afternoon, therefore, German infantry controlled fifteen hundred meters (almost a mile) of the central embankment and were only eight hundred meters (half a mile) away from Chuikov's HQ relocated from the Mamayev Kurgan and now dug into the Tsaritsa Gully, with German combat engineers cutting his communications. The whole defensive central line of the Russian 62nd Army was close to collapse and with it possibly the city itself.

The fortunes of war would once again pit Rodimtsev's men against the same German formations they had fought over the past year. Yeremenko informed Rodimtsev that the German domination of the river crossing meant that attempting to take his own artillery across by boat would be extremely difficult. Just getting his soldiers quickly across intact would be a small victory, before they even went into battle—and they would be crossing very soon. Whatever boats the Volga Flotilla could muster would be used. Nevertheless, Rodimtsev still undertook to cross the Volga by barge in broad daylight with his aide, Senior Lieutenant Voitsekhovsky, a reconnaissance officer, and two guards for security.[17] Chuikov and the Front Military Council needed to brief him on the lay of the land he'd be fighting over. After a hair-raising dash across the Volga, the captain cutting back and forth to avoid incoming shells, the party scrambled onto the sandy shoreline and made for Chuikov's headquarters. Several times the men were forced to dive for cover in shell holes and abandoned weapons pits amid a German bombardment. Rodimtsev arrived and was shown down a series of corridors, the air becoming fouler as he went deeper into the tunneled complex. Much to Chuikov's amusement, Rodimtsev appeared disheveled, his uniform covered in dirt, coughing, spluttering, and spitting out dirt onto his staff room floor before presenting himself to his commander.

As the roar of another German artillery barrage dropped around his position, Chuikov ordered that one battalion be turned over to secure his own HQ and then instructed Rodimtsev to brief his regimental commanders of their targets in the central sector. All units fighting would report to him. Leaving their heavy weapons on the eastern bank, and coming across after dusk in waves of rowing dinghies, small tugs, and armored boats, the 42nd and 34th Regiments, commanded by Colonel Ivan Elin and Colonel Dmitry I. Panikhin, respectively, would clear the enemy out of their fortified positions by the State Bank, the House of Specialists, and Railway Station No. 1. The 39th, led by Major Semyon S. Dolgov, meanwhile, would go forward to reinforce the beleaguered 112th and recapture the key elevated position of the Mamayev Kurgan. Chuikov pointed to his situation maps on the table to brief his new arrival how their enemy was now firmly in position, supported with artillery and mortars. As he had just experienced, enemy artillery from the Mamayev could now dominate the central ferry crossing as well as river traffic. It was crucial that Rodimtsev's men cross as soon as possible that evening and drive the Germans back before they could establish artillery at the water's edge, which would wreak havoc on any future crossing of the Volga. At whatever cost, they "must" recapture the Mamayev. They would jump off at 2100 hours with the 1st Battalion of the 42nd Regiment leading the way to establish a bridgehead. From there, Rodimtsev's area of command would stretch from the Mamayev in the north to the Tsaritsa River in the south.

"How do you feel about that?" Chuikov asked, and studied his divisional commander's face.

"I am a Communist," replied Rodimtsev. "I'm at the front and won't withdraw."[18]

As Chuikov later remembered of that critical meeting: "After a bit of thought, he [Rodimtsev] said he would be ashamed to sit at a command post to the rear of the army CP. I reassured him, telling him that as soon as his division had completed its mission, we would let him move his command post forward. I added emphatically, 'We have no right to expect passive operations from the enemy. The enemy are resolved to annihilate us and take the city. Therefore, we cannot just defend ourselves. We must use every opportunity to counter them. We must impose our will on the enemy and disrupt their plans through active operations.'"[19]

Rodimtsev again reported to Chuikov to obtain more weapons for his division. Realizing he might well need him to cross the Volga within hours, the incredulous commander managed to remain calm as he ascertained what could be sent to the troops in the little time they had. "Submachine guns," Rodimtsev announced matter-of-factly. "I need submachine guns."[20] Chuikov promised he would contact his deputy on the east bank, Lieutenant General F. I. Golikov, to ensure the guards had what they required by that evening.

Fully briefed, Rodimtsev left the bunker to return to the river shoreline, ducking and diving as before. Boarding the barge, his team repeated their perilous route to navigate a way through the German barrage. Lost in his thoughts of the coming attack, Rodimtsev seemed unconcerned by the shouts of his fellow passengers as fountains of water erupted all around their boat. He needed to brief his regimental commanders soon if a crossing was to be attempted that night. Stepping quickly off the boat, once more the officers ran from the shallows to take cover as Stukas appeared suddenly overhead looking for the enemy they knew must be among the trees. To his left, two hundred meters downstream, another wooden barge took a direct hit, its bow disintegrating in a ball of flame as the survivors attempted to jump to safety. The burning oil on the water showed what their cargo had been.

Deputy front commander Golikov approached Rodimtsev as he stood by the water's edge studying the opposite shoreline. Concerned for the fate of the men he would send to tackle such impregnable positions, Rodimtsev spoke his mind of the need for more time to prepare fully. Golikov listened intently but then told him what Rodimtsev already knew to be true: the guards had to cross tonight no matter what the cost; otherwise there would be no city left to save by the next day.[21] His good news, however, was that they had located a supply of PPSh-41 submachine guns, factory-new but without the standard two-drum magazines that normally came with them. Golikov promised Rodimtsev he had men sourcing more ammunition which would arrive soon, a fierce weapon for street fighting with a powerful rate of fire. *All well and good with ammunition*, thought Rodimtsev, *but no use at all if you have ambitions to take back a city from the Wehrmacht*. The guns would prove essential.

*   *   *

Having rested in the woods with his men all day to avoid enemy spotters as well as the intense summer heat, Senior Lieutenant Zhukov's dark mood about what lay ahead was lightened as the sound of trucks broke the silence:

> Field kitchens and trucks with weapons and ammunition drove up. After dinner, which was both breakfast and lunch, we received light machine guns, grenades and ammunition for machine guns and rifles. They took ammunition—as much as possible, therefore, anticipating the upcoming battle, we loaded up to order.[22]

Rodimtsev's mood was also brightened by the bonus of two dozen heavy machine guns and at least fifty antitank rifles being delivered. The PTRD-41, requiring a two-man team and firing a single-shot 14.5mm armor-piercing round, had proven successful when tackling German halftracks and the Panzer III—hitting it side-on where its armor was weakest.[23] His biggest fear, that they would encounter enemy armor immediately on landing, was still at the forefront of his mind. He could remember the carnage this had caused for infantry outside of Kiev the previous summer and at Kharkov a few months earlier. Though both Chuikov and Rodimtsev's memoirs do not mention this, the 13th Guards Combat Diary, as well as various testimonies from guards veterans who survived the encounter, state that a battery of 45mm antitank guns did make the crossing in the second wave. What happened to them after the crossing cannot be ascertained.

From the safety of the tree line, observing the Luftwaffe bomb the smoking city in the distance, Colonel Elin called his men together into a wooded clearing. In an attempt to inspire, standing in their center, beneath a Party banner, he passionately invoked his own memories of serving in the Reds' defense of old Tsaritsyn during the civil war and spoke of how it was now his men's turn. He pointed over his shoulder toward the burning city and declared: "Let us give every one of our lives, but the city must be defended!"[24] As he stood with his back to the river, his outline was striking against the black smoke of burning oil floating on the river. It was an unnerving sight for the young guardsmen, many of whom had still to experience actual combat.

The regiment's senior battalion commissar Oleg I. Kokushkin then addressed them with a fiery oration imploring the men to fight for their lives. He eyeballed individuals and gesticulated upstream, across to the Factory District, recalling how he had participated in the actual construction of the Stalingrad Tractor Factory when he was the age they were now, and the pride he'd had working there before the war. Were they going to allow the fascists to take it? Old veterans of the regiment then rose to speak: the scout Popov, Private Glushchenko, the commander of the 2nd Rifle Battalion Major Andriyanov, and division commissar Comrade Vavilov—all declaring their love for the Motherland but also their devotion to the Red Army. All of them at the end of their speeches demanded the men swear the regimental oath: "To defend Stalingrad, and to defeat the enemy!"[25]

As the hubbub died down, the men disbanded to check their equipment one final time. Colonel Elin ordered his battalion commanders to follow him to the river. They broke the cover of the trees and crept to the shoreline to inspect the boats that would ferry them across. German artillery still sporadically landed just yards away in the shallows, searching for victims. Black smoke billowed from the oil refinery upriver to their right, shells landing continuously. In the distance, outlined against the deep blue sky, the black dots of enemy planes could be seen making their way to their next bombing runs. The feeling of impotence among Elin's group was palpable. For their comrades still holding on to the pockets of territory against what they could only suspect were overwhelming odds, it must have been hell.

Pointing to the central ferry area, Elin briefed his commanders as to what should be their ideal angle of approach, where they should lay down their red flares for the Soviet artillery to then zero in on to offer supporting fire, and which units would then press forward to capture strategic buildings by the central ferry crossing as per Rodimtsev's orders. He finished by again stressing the need to keep moving across the Volga at all costs and wait for no one. Casualties would be high. The officers nodded. No one spoke; they turned away toward their men in the trees and waited for darkness.

At 21:00 hours Elin and Rodimtsev stood on the eastern shore, studying the opposite bank through their binoculars. The darkness enveloping their positions was in stark contrast to what they could see ahead: the city ablaze in deep orange and red from the flames engulfing the central districts. Rodimtsev had donned his black Cossack leather coat for concealment. He was impatient to get going. Enemy movement was sporadic, he thought, but he was certain the Germans were there and could inflict murderous fire on the six hundred men of the 1st Battalion under Senior Lieutenant Z. P. Chervyakov.[26] Rodimtsev studied the men that he was about to send into the maelstrom:

> All the soldiers and officers in helmets and cape-tents seem alike, therefore in the dark I [could] hardly recognize Senior Lieutenant Fedoseyev, Chervyakov's deputy; and rifle company commanders Dragan, Koleganov, Kravtsov and others. After Burlakov's antitank gunners with their long antitank rifles resembling museum arquebuses, stand the crews of 45-mm antitank guns. The antitank rifles and 45-mm guns are the only fire assets Chervyakov has against tanks. Yes, and maybe antitank grenades and Molotov cocktails, too. Not much![27]

Silently Chervyakov's men climbed quietly into the K- and R-type motor launches the Volga Flotilla had supplied. Rodimtsev had briefed him down by the water's edge that speed was essential to take the enemy by surprise, and that once on the opposite shore, he should mark his landing positions and where his flank would be, in order for the next waves to land safely and for support artillery to provide covering fire if required. Chervyakov was nervous about what reception the first wave could expect from the Germans, dreading the thought that German armor would be close to the riverbank, too. If that was the case, they were as good as dead already. He hoped the handful of T-34 tanks Chuikov had promised would move to support them would appear. The boat's engines spluttered into life, breaking the silence at last. Chervyakov led the way in the first armored boat, immediately followed by several others, all soon disappearing from their commander's view as yet more boats came alongside his position to take the next wave.

Now Rodimtsev would have to nervously sit and listen for events to unfold.

When the boats were halfway across, the Volga was bathed in brilliant white light. A volley of several parachute flares had been launched from the far shore. Sharp-eared German pickets now clearly saw what they had suspected. Surprised that the enemy was now dug in right on the Volga, Rodimtsev could clearly hear shouts on the opposite embankment. His blood turned cold as he tried to focus his binoculars on where he thought Chervyakov's boat was by now. The silence was shattered as tracers of MG-34 machine guns tore into the water. Within seconds the Volga erupted as German mortar and artillery rounds started to fall among the boats.

The spray of a near miss soaked the terrified guardsmen, who prayed they would at least make it to solid ground. One boat received a direct hit and was sunk, the dozen survivors either swimming back to shore, drowning due to the weight of their packs, or, the more lucky ones, picked up by the next boat behind. The first wave now raced for the shore, though at least one boat turned tail and tried to get back to safety.

Chervyakov's boat was raked with fire, killing two of his men. His second in command, Lieutenant Fedor G. Fedoseyev, shouted above the din for the boat's captain to ram the shoreline at full speed. As they neared the shallows, the smoke of the flares combined with the German barrage impaired the visibility of the guardsmen, who became disorientated. Where were the docks of the Central Crossing, which had been their primary target to secure for the following battalions of Elin's regiment? Many didn't wait to find out and leapt into the water, unslinging their submachine guns and firing in the direction of the incoming tracers as they waded onto the sandy shore.

*　　*　　*

Once the firefights began, the initiative instilled in the 13th Guards in the weeks of training leading up to Stalingrad overrode the panic of the first minutes of the intense firefight. Chervyakov realized that the enemy (Roske's battalions) were strongly entrenched directly ahead of him, one hundred meters (a little more than three hundred feet) distant, and he made the critical decision not to wait for reinforcements but rather to skirt past the Germans and push westward into the central district, toward the Univermag Department Store and the Nail Factory.[28] As they did so under heavy fire, the guardsmen, with grenades and sub-machine guns, cleared out the German positions they encountered. The fighting was ferocious as their stunned enemy fell back in alarm. The guardsmen hooked up at this point with the three T-34 tanks Chuikov had promised Rodimtsev and headed toward Railway Station No. 1. Colonel Elin's regiment from the second wave would mop up behind them. Indeed, the 71st Infantry Division's commander von Hartmann was now concerned that Roske's battalions were out on a limb ahead and could be surrounded. Arriving in the second wave, Colonel Elin's boat took direct hits, which killed several guardsmen, and directed fire on the shoreline at Roske's III Battalion holding the Brewery. More guard units were arriving and tackling Roske's men who were also holed up in the State Bank.

Double-timing along the darkened, ruined streets, the guardsmen encountered survivors of the 10th NKVD regiment who had been defending their own complex of buildings as well as fighting under the direct command of Chuikov's 62nd Army. That the enemy was so close to the shoreline had come as a major surprise and only increased Chervyakov's impatience to reach the center of the city before the Germans might counterattack. One could understand his reasoning as the situation on the ground in Stalingrad changed by the hour, by the minute—every leader had to react according to what he was presented with.

By the time Elin's 1st Battalion began crossing the Volga, German forces now held Railway Station No. 1, the State Bank, the House of Specialists, and the Univermag Department Store, as well as the main thoroughfairs

connecting them—many running through the large expanse of Red
Square. As Chervyakov's men advanced away from the shore, Chuikov
in his HQ was informed about the loss of these buildings and the need
to react quickly. (Rodimtsev on the far shore, yet to cross over, was
oblivious.) Chuikov's staff managed to find Chervyakov in the city and
took him to the 62nd Army commander's bunker in the Tsaritsa Gully.
Chuikov now ordered the senior lieutenant to push the attack with all
speed, with the aim of taking possession of Railway Station No. 1 and
blocking the roads and buildings skirting Red Square's perimeter. This
was an extraordinary measure, of countermanding Rodimtsev's original
orders to secure the bridgehead for the whole division, but the situation
was now critical as Chuikov realized he needed to capture these strategic
points quickly or be in danger of being driven back into the Volga as a
consequence of the Germans counterattacking in strength once they
realized the magnitude of the Soviet's assault.

Chuikov now made contact with Colonel Elin once he had established his position on the shoreline:

> A few minutes later I was met by three officers from the operations
> department of the headquarters of the 62nd Army with a map ordered
> by the army commander, Lieutenant General Chuikov. This order
> set the regiment's task: two battalions with the remnants of the 112th
> Infantry Division to capture the height 102.0 and hold it until the
> arrival of the 39th Infantry Regiment.[29]

Watching from afar, stranded on the east bank, unaware of Chuikov's situation, the divisional commander was more concerned with
the incoming fire on his men still crossing the Volga:

> I had no idea that the enemy had already reached the riverbank, but
> in the first two waves 1st and 2nd Battalions had to be left to establish
> a beachhead. We heard that the enemy was on the shore, that the
> battalion had already engaged them, fighting from the moment they
> reached dry land. I realized we had to move faster. We were literally
> giving out ammunition on the barges.

He was further shocked to now hear in the distance the familiar single shots from his men's antitank rifles—*Surely the enemy's armor couldn't be that close?* he thought. More boats, with the second and third waves, were now landing on the west bank, with more heading across as the hours ticked past midnight. The 2nd and 3rd Battalions of the 42nd Guards Regiment had now landed and were engaging Roske's battalions situated by the shore. Farther upstream of Rodimtsev's positions, the 39th Regiment prepared themselves for the task of crossing toward the Red October Steel Plant area. Their orders were to make for the base of Height 102, where they hoped to make contact with the survivors of the 10th NKVD and the 112th Rifle Division, who had by now lost contact with Chuikov's HQ. Together they would then storm the Mamayev to recapture the heights. More units were lined up on the eastern shoreline to be fed into the battle as Rodimtsev described:

> Throughout the night, lorries and carts loaded with various cargoes kept arriving at the Volga. The troops immediately picked up bread, crackers, tinned food, packets with condensed rations, boxes of ammunition, grenades, Molotov cocktails, tobacco and sugar; and used sagging gangways to board the landing craft.[30]

By daylight on the first day of operations Rodimtsev had succeeded in getting five battalions across the Volga to engage the enemy. Quite a feat. Casualties had been relatively light, though certainly not the figures described in the Soviet press afterward, which were created to emphasize the heroic sacrifice for Stalin's city.[31] One boat had turned back, and its captain was shot as a result. Records from the Ministry of Defense's own "Memorial" database show that on that first nighttime crossing eleven guardsmen were killed and eight were listed as missing in action.[32] Casualties would increase dramatically, however, once the Germans counterattacked the following morning.

By 4 a.m., amid intense fighting, the Russian 1st Battalion had made their way toward the Univermag Department Store, where they set up their HQ and continued on to the Nail Factory bordering the expanse of Red Square. They now looked to take Railway Station No. 1. Lieutenant Anton Kuzmich Dragan led the 1st Company toward the station. To his right and left were the 2nd and 3rd Companies occupying the Univermag and neighboring buildings. Lieutenant Dragan, seeing enemy machine gun fire coming from the front of the station, set his squads up for the coming attack:

> As soon as we approached the station from the rear, the company took up battle formation, heavy machine guns took their places in the corners on all sides of the station building. At the set signal, the company moved into the attack, throwing grenades, machine guns opening a hurricane of fire, killing the fleeing Germans and those who were trying to come to their rescue.[33]

German radio in Berlin had announced to the world the previous day the capture of Railway Station No. 1, hubristically proclaiming that the Berlin-Tsaritsyn express service would soon be running. Rodimtsev therefore received the news of the station's recapture by the 1st Battalion with a huge grin. But he knew they would pay a price to keep it: "It was a great victory for us. After Mamayev Kurgan the station was considered practically the second most important tactical asset in the city. I realized what it would cost now to hold it."[34]

But with the element of surprise gone, von Hartmann's 71st Division also realized they now faced a serious assault on their recently won positions, and Roske's battalions, situated farther forward on the Volga embankment, were in peril of being isolated and destroyed, too. Infantry reinforcements rushed up to stem the tide and eliminate the Soviet threat. Soon Elin's 1st Battalion encountered several companies of German infantry, supported by Stug assault guns, coming up from the south of the city. The fighting was fierce and unrelenting as men grappled and died in the dark—across the station platforms, in train carriages, and running through the rooms of the Univermag Department Store, advancing and retreating floor by floor. Burning vehicles littered Red Square and the streets surrounding it; dead bodies and the screaming wounded were strewn in corridors, throughout the station concourse and across the square. Piles of weapons, spent cartridges and shell casings lay amid the rubble, shell holes, and the dead.

German and Soviet artillery now competed for dominance throughout the central district. General von Hartmann briefed his commanders to recapture lost ground, rescue Roske's battalions, drive the 13th Guards back to the river, and link up with the neighboring division coming up from the southwest of the city, who were fighting for the Grain Elevator.[35] He ordered up StuG III assault guns to support a new thrust that morning once the Luftwaffe had softened up the Soviet defenders.

Many narratives have described the 1st Company of the 1st Battalion's defense of Railway Station No. 1 lasting for days, a feat similar to their comrades defending the Grain Elevator farther south. In reality they held the station for less than forty-eight hours. Much as they fought to keep ahold of it due to its significance, the next few days would be a series of counterattacks and mini firefights to defend the neighboring Univermag Department Store, the Nail Factory, and the houses nearby and in the open green spaces and gardens bordering the area where the guards had dug in. As Rodimtsev later concluded in his memoirs, urban warfare like this was just as tricky for his men as it was for the enemy:

> One can get used to local terrain, advancing through the city's cluttered courtyards, sheds with household belongings, through the gardens with roses and dahlias, or, finally, across an area paved with asphalt where enemy riflemen or machine gunners would even cut off the grass if it grew there. But it is fiendishly hard to do it in a maze of flats, corridors and staircases; in the complete darkness of nocturnal basements, cellars and attics; without knowing where the enemy is, and at times confusing in the dark friend and foe.[36]

After the seizure of part of the station, the survivors of the company strengthened their defenses by bricking up the windows and digging out embrasures for firing holes. The Germans twice attempted to storm the position at various points simultaneously but were driven off with counterattacks led by 1st Battalion commander Chervyakov himself. Though the Russians held out, the casualties incurred were significant—almost a third of 1st Battalion's strength was gone by the morning of the 17th. The German firepower could not be withstood forever without tanks or air support. Constructed of reinforced steel and concrete and 150 meters in length, it was a formidable structure. The flights of Stukas struck their designated target at will with savage accuracy, thus ensuring that the guardsmen's defense was tenuous, as Dragan recounted:

> At dawn, the Germans pulled up artillery to the station and began firing into [our positions]. It was impossible to stay in the station, but nevertheless, suffering heavy losses, we continued to hold. The situation was [becoming] terribly difficult. When the bombs began to explode in the station building, we were forced to leave it and fight on the square and on the railroad tracks. The Germans began to surround [our positions] and seized the corner building in front of the station square [the Nail Factory].[37]

It would be in the Krasnaya Zastava Nail Factory, constructed of brick and mortar, with a basement for cover, that the prolonged defense would actually take place once Dragan's men were reinforced with what remained of a machine gun company sent to his aid by Colonel Elin:

> The position of our battalion was dire. Chervyakov was wounded and then disorientated with shellshock and somehow carried back to the river, the battalion command now passed onto Lieutenant Fedoseyev. The battalion headquarters set up in the department store.[38]

They were now surrounded on three sides:

> The Germans were pressing everywhere. The position with ammunition was serious and there was no question of food or sleep. The

worst part was the thirst. In our search for water we fired at pipes to see if any dripped out. The fighting would die down and flare up anew. In short skirmishes we used knives, spades and the butts of our rifles. . . . Small groups of German snipers and machine gunners began to penetrate our rear. They hid in the ruins and sewer pipes and proceeded to fire at us.[39]

Lulls in the fighting would be sporadic, each time the Germans gathered themselves to launch another attack amid further Stuka airstrikes. Still Dragan's men held out. The whole of the central district was now unrecognizable—a heap of rubble and burned-out vehicles. Bizarrely the Barmaley Fountain outside the station remained intact.[40] To complete this local offensive, the intensity of fire increased significantly upon the guards being ferried across the river to support the bridgehead, several barges being forced to scatter and seek the city shoreline wherever the enemy fire was less deadly. Other units suffered amid the confusion of battle, with their boats failing to reach the shore. Machine gunner Ilya Vasilievich Voronov of the 3rd Battalion recounted:

The barge was overflowing with soldiers. There was a command to sail away from the shore. We were already 15 meters from the shore when suddenly the engine broke down. The NKVD policing the barge wanted to shoot the mechanic, but he turned out to be innocent. The commander gave the order to unload from the barge as best we could. By the time the gangway was brought up, almost all the soldiers had already jumped into the Volga. Enemy planes swooped down to strafe us, wounding nine and killing three soldiers.[41]

As a result, those units or groups of survivors who did make it across the Volga now found themselves spread along the shoreline many hundreds of yards wide, operating in pockets in the central district. The 1st Battalion was out on its own now without any chance of support, but they were continuing to stymie the advance of the enemy.

*   *   *

Rodimtsev had moved his own divisional headquarters over the Volga to set up by the embankment the day before, directing more battalions into battle. As he recalled:

> I could see that we needed to get the entire division across. I called to get permission from Yeremenko. That day our headquarters staff made the crossing aboard a cutter. That was about 10:00 a.m. We came under heavy enemy fire, and Colonel Uzky, the chief of our engineering team, was wounded by a mortar. But we got across. The Stalingrad regional NKVD had some men there. They had a tunnel. I put my command post there because they had a direct line with Yeremenko. We had no contact of any kind with Chuikov.[42]

Rodimtsev's command center had belonged to the NKVD and was in fact a large shaft tunnel one entered via a logwood extension that had been covered with iron sheeting. Reminiscent of the trenches from the Great War, the walls of the tunnel were reinforced with wooden planks, top and bottom. The wide cracks between the planks were visible in the ceiling, from which earth fell from time to time. Three-tier bunks lined the entrance on both sides, separated by an aisle, too narrow for two persons to pass. The whole enterprise was makeshift and claustrophobic, with a constant smell of stale air, but it was safe from enemy shelling. The chaotic nature made for a very intimate battle, as Rodimtsev observed later in his memoirs:

> The main axis of attack from our own troops and the enemy changed several times a day on some occasions. Buildings and whole streets changed hands with similar frequency. The entire depth of our divisional formations was exposed to rifle, machine gun as well as submachine gun fire. Quite often, the forward edge ran across a hallway, a flat, a stairwell landing. On some occasions, our troops were separated from the enemy by just a wall or a ceiling. Sometimes staff officers struggled to mark the forward edge on maps because it kept shifting.[43]

*   *   *

As battle raged around Red Square, most certainly the greatest feat of arms on the 16th was performed a mile or so away, on the key topographical position of Stalingrad itself, as Soviet infantry, supported by the 62nd Army's last ten KV-1 tanks, were tasked by Chuikov to recapture it. They assembled near where the survivors of an NKVD rifle regiment had managed to dig in, ironically for all concerned close to a meat processing plant. The assault was to destroy the two companies of the German 295th Division that sat atop Height 102.

The German defenders were firmly entrenched, with well-sited lines of fire and supported with artillery and aerial support. Their artillery spotters were now raining down accurate fire on the 13th Guards fighting around Railway Station No. 1 and the Central Landing Stage, the latter guardsmen losing the battle to bring Chuikov's supplies safely across from the eastern shore. Though facing a tough assignment, the men assembled were under no illusions that they had to achieve the impossible.

The Soviets jumped off at 3 p.m. that afternoon after a short preliminary artillery barrage. The guardsmen followed behind, taking the first line of the German positions on the southeastern slope, before working their way up to capture the summit. Just as it was with the battle at Railway Station No. 1 and indeed right throughout the city, the fight for who controlled the Mamayev would critically sway back and forth over the next hours, changing hands several times. Before the war, Height 102 had been a popular beauty spot for Stalingraders, its lush grass-covered fields a romantic setting where hundreds of couples could gather. Now, after three weeks of fighting, it resembled a burned-out moonscape, pockmarked with shell craters and littered with shell fragments, spent cartridges, and corpses. The fighting for its occupancy was savage and reminiscent of the worst trench fighting of the Great War.

Rodimtsev's guardsmen used machine guns, rifles, grenades, and where necessary, as a last resort, Molotov cocktails. When they ran out, fists, bayonets, and entrenching tools made do. One 13th Guards regiment worked its way up to capture the German positions on the northern slopes while another unit, from the 112th Division, at great cost—a platoon of thirty reduced to six survivors—won the summit, driving off the German defenders. Counterattacks were repulsed, with the guardsmen knocking out two Panzers in the process. For now, the Mamayev was in Russian hands, but the battle for this strategically vital spot would continue for months as both sides launched repeated attacks and churned up the ground with relentless artillery barrages. Writer Vasily Grossman described their destructive power on the ground: "These clouds of earth then passed through the sieve of gravity, the heavier lumps falling straight to the ground, the dust rising to the sky."[44]

While battle raged on the Mamayev, the fighting had now escalated around Railway Station No. 1, the Nail Factory, and the Univermag Department Store. Two rifle companies arrived to shore up Dragan's command in and around the Nail Factory and those still holding foxholes outside Railway Station No. 1. The Germans constantly probed for weak points in both guard redoubts, supported by assault guns. For the armored units this kind of inner-city fight was chaotic and highly dangerous compared to the good times of rolling across the open steppe. In the ruins of Stalingrad, simply managing to navigate one's tank, assault gun, or armored personnel carrier across the rubble-strewn streets was a deadly business. The ruins of high-rise buildings made perfect terrain for an enemy attack by sniper rifle, or an ambush using grenades or Molotov cocktails. By the end of the battle the Sixth Army would have lost over one thousand armored vehicles in conquering the city. Around the positions of the three surviving companies of the Russian 42nd Regiment lay the wreckage of German assault guns and armored cars. Their crews had either burned to death inside or were otherwise corpses lying in the street. The stench was indescribable.

Now von Hartmann's commanders tried a new approach. Sappers of his 71st Division punched a hole in the wall of the Nail Factory and then lobbed grenades in, killing four guardsmen. Again, quick reactions saved the day as the attackers were driven off by automatic fire. But the position of the Russian 1st Battalion was worsening every hour, as their food, medical supplies, ammunition, and grenades began to run out. The wounded had to make do where they lay. The men, desperately thirsty, hunted through rooms and cellars for any water to drink. Dragan had begun the fight with almost a full company; he was now down to fewer than thirty-five active combatants.

The survivors still held one workshop in the Nail Factory and their positions by the fountain[45] in order to protect their escape route out of the building and back toward the river. Dragan reported his position to Acting Battalion Commander Fedoseyev, situated two hundred yards away in the Univermag. Aware the cross streets between them was being swept by German machine gun and mortar fire, Fedoseyev still dispatched what was left of the 3rd Rifle Company of Lieutenant Koleganov to support the garrison. Amid withering enemy fire, only twenty men made it safely across. A disheveled but jubilant Koleganov reported: "Arrived at Nail Factory. Situation difficult, but while I am alive no bastard will get through."[46]

By that evening of the 17th, as darkness began to settle upon the city, and the temperature dropped sharply for the first time that autumn, Chuikov again was forced to make the decision to abandon his position in the Tsaritsa Gully. The danger of the encroaching German infantry of the XXXXVIII Panzerkorps, who had bypassed the fight for Railway Station No. 1, threatened his position, their mortar and artillery fire coming too close for comfort. With agreement from Khrushchev and Yeremenko at Front HQ, he and his staff took an armored boat back across to the east bank, drove along its length until almost opposite the Factory District, and then recrossed the Volga to set up shop east of the Barrikady Gun Factory, near to what they believed to be empty fuel storage tanks.

The fighting intensified yet again the next day. The 13th Guards Combat Log daily report offers a glimpse of how savage the fighting was and how precarious any given moment in the city could be. This is the entry for September 18, 1942:

> During the street battles, our guardsman units operated in small groups. These groups infiltrated to the rear of the enemy where they destroyed the crews of artillery guns and machine guns.

For example, Guards Senior Sergeant Dynkin made his way to a street occupied by the enemy and climbed into the attic of a house from where he shot and killed the crews of two machine guns. The section of men under Guards Senior Sergeant Ustyugov, shooting from the windows of houses, destroyed an enemy group of 23 soldiers and officers. The mortar crew, consisting of the guardsmen Kizlyakov, Kepin and Korostyshev, advanced behind the infantry; a German tank accompanied by 16 submachine gunners suddenly appeared from around the corner of the building. The Mortar teams let the German kampfgroup close to 100 meters and with a quick fire destroyed all the submachine gunners and knocked out the tank with anti-tank grenades.

That same day the 13th Guards main ammunition dump exploded near to the shore when a German shell struck, killing several guardsmen and dozens of civilians waiting for escape on a barge. Chuikov ordered for all future supplies of munitions and rations to be buried in trenches away from the shoreline.

The NKVD report of the fighting at the same time, however, focused on the intensity of the enemy's firepower and the chaotic consequences it had for the men trying to hold the bridgehead:

Today the enemy was conducting particularly intense artillery fire, bombing the city center and the Central Ferry Crossing from the air. Two central docks have burnt down. There are many victims. At the pier on the right bank of the Volga, disorganization continues. Ammunition transported at night by representatives of the command of the 62nd Army and formations is not supplied in a timely manner, in connection with which they are unloaded ashore and during the day are often destroyed by enemy fire. The wounded are not taken out until evening. The seriously wounded do not receive help—they die. Their corpses are not removed. . . . There are no doctors. Local women are helping the wounded.

For the next twenty-four hours, as the fighting in the north and south of the city intensified, Dragan and Fedoseyev's isolated commands continued to thwart the German assaults to overrun their positions. The losses for both sides were heavy. But the Germans still retained the initiative. They managed to capture Railway Station No. 1 and gained entry to the Univermag. Mini firefights were now erupting along the length of the building, on every floor and in the basement, as the Germans fought Fedoseyev's men room by room and up and down stairwells, as one writer described:

> The "Univermag" was just an empty ruin. Mannequins riddled with bullets lay all over the place. Dead Germans and Russians, as they had fallen, lay side by side in the corridors. The whole department store had become a morgue.[47]

The survivors of the 1st Battalion were being worn down. In and around the Nail Factory Dragan's reduced garrison was almost finished. He now called for a dozen volunteers to covertly get behind the rear of the German positions to cause havoc. Issued with five days of rations, they waited until nightfall to crawl through the debris and bodies toward German lines. Within a short while Dragan could hear in the distance the sound of explosions and machine gun fire taking their toll. He never saw the men again. The siege continued.

While the fight for the Univermag and the Nail Factory continued, the Germans had been busy transforming other key buildings in the area, such as the NKVD complex, the State Bank, the Houses of Specialists, and the House of Railway Workers, into fortresses. Aware of this development, Chuikov, at his new HQ by the Barrikady Gun Factory, ordered the 13th Guards to be aggressive and look to recapture these positions with the limited resources they had. He relocated more troops from the Mamayev Kurgan to supplement Rodimtsev's losses. Colonel Elin's 42nd Regiment (including a Junior Sergeant Pavlov) were ordered to capture two key German fortifications that dominated the flank: the Railwayman's House and the larger, six-storey L-Shaped Building. This was the first time the Soviets attempted the use of small, powerfully armed groups of assault squads to rush a defended position using submachine guns and grenades. This, it could be argued, was more a plan made "on the hoof," due to their losses, than the commanders on the ground realizing they had developed a whole new method of urban fighting. As we shall see later, these two operations would soon develop into a doctrine of attack.

The massed Soviet counterattack along the whole Stalingrad Front ordered by General Zhukov on the 18th proved a costly failure in terms of lost tanks and heavy casualties. From Zhukov down through the chain of command to front commander Yeremenko, then to Chuikov at the Barrikady Gun Factory and finally to Rodimtsev commanding what was left of his division, the Stalingrad Front leadership was under pressure from an impatient Stavka to not sit passively behind its fortifications. Stalin made clear to General Zhukov that the fight for "his" (Stalin's) city meant continued counterattacks wherever necessary, even if the cost to the 62nd and 64th Armies was enormous.

For Paulus and the German Sixth Army these local operations might have been irritating, but their purpose of gradually wearing down the effectiveness of the German divisions trying to capture Stalingrad was also beginning to tell. As one artillery officer of the German 71st Division commented:

> The Russians doggedly held on to the ruins of the city with a stubbornness that was beyond their already impressive fighting spirit and morale. They did this so effectively that we could barely make any further headway. Their system of political officers could not account for this. How could it have had any effect on their close-quarter fighting? Only now did we realise how fortunate we had been to push deep into the city centre on our first attempt and to have taken a broad stretch of the Volga bank.[48]

At the Nail Factory, by September 20, Dragan had received a message from a local civilian, Maria Vedeneeva, who had thus far survived the carnage. Sharing with the men what food she had saved for herself, she reported what she had recently witnessed, that the Germans were bringing fresh artillery and tanks to their position and massing for a concerted attack. Dragan gave the order they must retreat to set up a new line of defense. Their casualties were enormous and reflected the cost all Red Army units had suffered in the two weeks of fighting for the city districts.

Since Rodimtsev's division had come ashore on the 14th through to the major counterattack launched by the Germans on September 22, the combined cost for the attacking 71st and 295th Divisions had been 370 killed, 1,555 wounded, and 29 missing in action. The Russian 13th Guards Division's losses were an estimated 1,896 killed and missing in action. Though the two German divisions suffered more losses than any other Sixth Army division in that period of fighting (a combined total of approximately 20 percent of their combat strength), the 13th Guards' losses were significantly higher (a ratio of 4 to 1), with Fedoyesev's 1st Battalion's position in the leading wave bearing the brunt.[49] When one factors in the other units that fought alongside the 13th Guards in this crucial week, then the overall losses ratio to their opponents jumps to a staggering 16 to 1.[50]

This enormous sacrifice of his "One-Man Fortresses,"[51] as Chuikov called them, bought him valuable time to dilute the power of the German assault through the center of Stalingrad and to save the Central Crossing from capture. He had also denied the enemy the summit of the Mamayev Kurgan. Despite repeated infantry and aerial assaults, the German 295th Division attempts to recapture it were running out of energy and soldiers—some of its companies were now down to as few as fifteen men apiece. Yet more experienced battalion and company commanders had been killed by snipers, causing a further drain on the Germans' operational ability. This would be a theme in the whole battle as the weeks progressed.[52] By September 19, the 71st Infantry Division had suffered the heaviest losses within the Sixth Army. I.R. 211 had lost 392 officers and all other ranks, I.R. 191 had lost 377, and in Lieutenant Colonel Roske's own I.R. 194 the total was 304 men killed or wounded. Across the four infantry divisions Paulus had ordered into the city, it was their fighting companies that had suffered the greatest casualties.

The struggle of the German armor attempting to support the troops was equally concerning. More protection was needed for these units, from hidden Soviet antitank crews, squads with armor-piercing rifles, and of course those simply throwing Molotov cocktails. The attrition rate of the constant and confused house-to-house combat was taking its toll on all elements of the German advance.[53]

To the Soviet correspondents on the ground, the mounting German losses and the failure of their tactics was cause to celebrate small victories:

> The battle for Stalingrad has been underway for two weeks. The fighting is brutal. The Germans have decided to attempt to capture the city: they want to slice right across the Volga and suffocate Russia. Dozens of German divisions have been thrown into the fight at Stalingrad. The whole of Germany rages against us, against an indomitable city, in the hot steppe. There are SS, Prussians, and Bavarians; sergeants, tanks and soldiers sent from France; Dutch gendarmes and Egyptian pilots; and veterans and rookies. Here, though, the promised iron crosses are being turned into wooden crosses.[54]

Occupying the summit of Height 102 succeeded in providing some protection to Rodimtsev's line of supplies and manpower being ferried across the Volga from the relative safety of the east bank to the Central Landing. His regiments had been mauled—especially the 42nd—but those survivors still fighting in their pockets a kilometer inland of the central shoreline were ready to continue the fight as long as this lifeline was secure. On September 18, General Zhukov had pressured Chuikov to launch a new counteroffensive in the center in order to appease Stalin in Moscow that the Stalingrad Front was fighting and not sitting passively behind its defenses. Chuikov, though well aware of the firepower his men were up against, was willing to send them in. Rushed to implement, badly coordinated, and lacking firepower in the areas Chuikov chose, each attack was beaten back—including Rodimtsev's 13th Guards' assault on the State Bank, which by now the Germans had converted into an impregnable position. But that, too, failed in its objectives. It was becoming clear to the senior Soviet commanders that the Sixth Army was struggling to impose itself on both Chuikov's and Shumilov's armies. General Paulus's forces, though still dictating events, were now not strong enough to overpower the Russians to take the city in one assault. Not while the Red Army could continue to resupply its beleaguered forces clinging to their strip of land on the west bank.

Emphasizing this point, Rodimtsev's division received its first reinforcements that night to make up for the losses suffered by the failed attacks—nine hundred replacements were dispersed across all three regiments. Meanwhile, opposite their positions, General von Hartmann's division and the neighboring 295th of General Rolf Wuthmann, still occupying the slopes of the Mamyev, were reinforced to a lesser degree, as Paulus scraped the bottom of the barrel for replacements within his rear echelon units. Many lacked basic combat experience and had no idea of the dangers of urban house-to-house fighting. The life expectancy of German troops was dropping significantly. All the while, Rodimtsev urged his regimental commanders to take the fight to the enemy. Supporting them where possible from across the river would be heavy artillery and the Katyushas Chuikov was husbanding to make themselves felt on the enemy—his only real response, as the Soviet air force was still to pose any kind of threat to the Germans. For the Sixth Army, the battle for the city was to now reach a new phase, as Paulus's LI Corps attempted to decapitate the Soviets facing them on the western side of the river. The Russian 13th Guards faced another desperate fight to survive, and right on the front line, by Railway Station No. 1, the survivors of Lieutenant Dragan's unit would pull off a quite audacious escape back to the Volga.

CHAPTER NINE

_____

Success Measured in Meters and Bodies

Every breath of air is worth its weight in gold.

—Major General Alexander Rodimtsev[1]

The writer Vladimir Germanovich Lidin, who had produced reports for *Izvestia* during the first year of the war, wrote for *Pravda* possibly one of the most poignant wartime articles, which encapsulated the life-and-death struggle each Red Army soldier on the front line faced. It was a personal struggle of honor:

> Whether your home is near or far it doesn't matter. At home they will always learn how you are fighting. If you don't write yourself, your comrades will write, or your political instructor (politruk). If the letter does not reach them, they will learn about you from the newspaper. Your mother will read the communique, will shake her head and say: "My dear boy you should do better than this." You are quite wrong if you imagine that the one thing they want at home is to see you come home alive. What they want you to do is drive out the German. They do not want any more shame and terror. If you die while stopping the German from advancing any farther, they will honour your memory for ever. Your heroic death will brighten and warm the lives of your children and grandchildren. If you let the German pass, your own mother will curse you.[2]

*   *   *

After two weeks of fighting, Stalingrad was a wasteland, with more than 90 percent of the city in ruins. For those huddled in semi-destroyed shelters, improvised dugouts, and hastily formed trenches the threat from a sniper's bullet or stray artillery shell was only made worse by the sudden drop in temperature. On September 22, it fell below freezing (minus three) for the first time. Winter would be approaching, with all the terrors that brought to many in the German command and their troops on the front line amid the rubble of the city.

Lieutenant Colonel Roske and his men, however, even so close to the enemy, still found time to create what comfort they could at their base in the abandoned GPU prison—the commander fashioning his own quarters in a basement cell, complete with camp bed, wardrobe, carpet, and stove. With the incessant crump of Soviet mortars dropping around his position, he still found time to update his wife on his position amid the fiercest fighting yet for the city:

Russia, Regimental Prison Stalingrad, on 22nd September 1942

My dear lovely Bärbel,
I want you to receive my warmest greetings and news that I'm very well. I'm sitting here in this fairly tumbledown house, Hindenlang is on the phone, others are negotiating, the lads are coming and going all the time, our own Stukas are throwing off bombs which make everything vibrate, sunshine, cigar (the latter from a top-notch box which the Divisional Commander General Hartmann brought back for me).

Last night a couriered parcel arrived from the Army for me with the attached letter and a bottle of champagne!!! How nice of Adam. So now I want to write to his deputy Hering and add this note to you, my darling whom I love above everything.

Always,
Yours
Fritz

With the advance of Army Group A into the Caucasus frustratingly stalled, Hitler was now consumed by the belief that taking Stalingrad would make up for the costly mistakes of his generals that had wrecked the original objectives of Case Blue (*Fall Blau*). The capture of the city was now essential. Whether or not Paulus had enough men to achieve this was of no consequence for Hitler; he still had the Luftwaffe. Chuikov, on the other hand, was the obstacle to Sixth Army's success, even more so as von Hartmann's 71st Division continued to suffer losses at the hands of Rodimtsev's stubbornly resistant 13th Guards. Another assault would now be launched to finally destroy Rodimtsev's command and to target the commander himself.

While the battle raged north of the city, the Soviet supply line across the Volga came under increasingly deadly attack. Now, Paulus's LI Corps would strike with aerial and mortar bombardments, forcing Chuikov's units to fall back to makeshift defenses, in some places only four hundred meters in distance from the Volga. Across the length of the embankment and the Mamayev Kurgan chaos reigned. Amid this carnage German infantry advanced behind massed armor, toward the fortified Russian positions, the ruined buildings becoming a bloody arena as both sides fought room by room with flamethrowers, grenades, and knives, while suicidal Russians launched Molotov cocktails at advancing German Stugs (assault guns). Teams of mobile tank hunters from Colonel Elin's 42nd Regiment ambushed German armor as it advanced through their positions from three directions to recapture the State Bank and the Central Landing. It was clear to both Elin and Rodimtsev that the German plan was to split the division's line, envelope its units, and take the main crossing point on the river. Elin ordered his 2nd Battalion to counter the threat:

> An avalanche of German tanks appeared on Sovetskaya Street. Some of my men were nervous, only calmed by their commander of my 2nd Rifle Battalion, Major Andriyanov. Immediately the message was sent

out via radio: "Let the enemy tanks pass along Sovetskaya Street into our defenses to within one hundred meters, then at my signal, the [green rocket], the artillery will open fire on the sides of the tanks, and the submachine gunners fire on the enemy infantry."

The enemy's tanks advanced cautiously, firing on the move. The lead tank stopped. It was a convenient moment. A green rocket went up in the air. Our antitank guns and rifles opened rapid fire on the sides of enemy tanks. Several were destroyed and the others rapidly reversed. The infantry followed them having taken many casualties.

The Germans' first assault had failed, but they came back twice more before overpowering Elin's 2nd Battalion, forcing the survivors to withdraw across the square and take up positions on its eastern side. Such was the intensity of the fighting that Elin's men ran out of mortar and antitank rifle ammunition, resorting to grenades, knives, and entrenching tools to defend themselves. By the evening, the German 71st Division controlled key buildings to the north of 9th January Square and Rodimtsev's right flank had folded, now splitting his division from the rest of Chuikov's army. His forward units in Railway Station No. 1 and the Univermag Department Store were surrounded and barely holding out. Rodimtsev ordered Elin to amalgamate what was left of the 2nd Battalion into other units, and the 39th Guards Rifle Regiment would shore up the left flank. Elin's remaining units would occupy the center, to defend the buildings overlooking 9th January Square—including Gerhardt's Mill—looking across to the new enemy positions. Separating the front lines stood two four-storey buildings—almost identical in design—that would now dominate proceedings for the next months. One of them would become legendary—"Pavlov's House."

The Germans had come within a whisker of eliminating Rodimtsev's headquarters, situated in the Dolgiy Ravine and housed in an enormous sewer pipe that ran into the Volga. The thick piping offered excellent shelter from the constant barrages and air strikes. Red Army engineers had built a wooden floor allowing the water to flow underneath and then established living accommodations for a small retinue of staff. The Germans had discovered its location, with the Luftwaffe originally attempting to bomb Rodimtsev out. Now, for this surprise assault, the German combat engineers decided to dam the pipe upstream and on the day of the offensive blow it up to suddenly flood Rodimtsev's position, now occupied by his 34th Rifle Regiment, and then assault it. The plan was as ingenious as it was deadly.

It came close to succeeding, the situation saved for the Russians only by Rodimtsev's clear-mindedness while under attack, organizing a defense by guards from his own headquarters and counterattacking with a reserve unit to drive back the attackers. The scene afterward was one of devastation, with bodies of his men strewn alongside the enemy around the destroyed position and farther back toward the German lines, only three hundred meters away. Some elements of the 295th had managed to circumnavigate past the fighting and established themselves in force on the Volga, between the 42nd and 34th Regiments, splitting Rodimtsev's positions.

By September 25, von Hartmann's 71st Infantry Division had thwarted all attempts by the Guards' 42nd Regiment to rescue their 1st Battalion marooned in the Univermag Department Store. German armored infantry was now finally arriving from the southern end of the city to link up with Lieutenant Colonel Roske's I.R. 194, thus closing the gap in the German lines and sealing the fate of the isolated Russian guardsmen. Fedoseyev, deputy battalion commander, radioed the regimental CP of his situation in the department store: two of his three company commanders were now dead, his 45mm antitank guns were now knocked out, and his garrison had been reduced to twenty-seven fighting men with limited ammunition and supplies. They were being attacked on all sides by enemy infantry and bombed relentlessly by Stukas. He had lost contact with Dragan's 1st Company, by the Nail Factory. This would be his last radio message, he said, for his battalion radio set was running out of power. He read out the oath his men had taken: "We will die, but we will defend the [position] to the last drop of our blood!"

From that moment on, 1st Battalion lost contact with the 42nd Regiment, and Dragan's garrison now acted independently. The three surviving platoons defending the headquarters of 1st Battalion in the Univermag and the guardsmen dug in by the Nail Factory were hopelessly encircled.[3] As Dragan recounted:

> It was clear that we needed to hold out as long as possible and not let the fascists go to the Volga at any price. I gathered all the remaining people and took command of the battalion. The guardsmen, gritting their teeth, fought off the enemy. The guards had vowed to die![4]

The surviving men of the garrison were gathered together; ammunition was collected from the dead and wounded, and the heavy Maxim machine gun was made ready for transportation. Together with what other survivors they were able to pick up as they fled, Dragan's battle group conducted a fighting retreat toward the Volga—all the while harassed on three sides by the enemy. Eventually, this small band of survivors, reduced to forty guardsmen, occupied one last three-storey stone-built house on Krasnopiterskaya Street, a stone's throw from the Volga. It would become their last line of defense:

> We barricaded the lower floor of the house. The windows were adapted for firing from the weapons we still had. In the basement, the heavy machine gun was installed with the last cartridge belt. We beat off the Germans with bricks, throwing them on their heads. They could not break into our house.[5]

More fighting over the coming days reduced the garrison to just nineteen fit to fight. Dragan decided to transport the wounded across the Volga on makeshift rafts, ordering Political Commissar Sterlev, Junior Lieutenant Dilenko, and one guardsman to go under cover of darkness to the river to gather material for their construction. They never returned. In reality they had deserted their comrades to make it to the safety of the opposite shore, though Dilenko had been killed when their raft was fired up by a German machine gun team. Commissar Sterlev had been wounded but then covered his desertion to the officers at 62nd Army HQ by stating that Dragan and his command were dead and that he had personally buried his commander. By this time, Dragan's position was untenable—they were now surrounded by armored infantry.

The seriously wounded were taken to the basement, the medics improvising bandages from torn strips of linen they found in a bedroom. Dragan's command repulsed several further assaults, losing men killed or wounded each time, until only twelve remained to fight on. In the afternoon of September 28, German troops approached under a flag of truce. Accompanying them were captured guardsmen, taken as their regiment retreated days earlier. The Germans stopped in front of the house, and a Russian voice shouted from a megaphone:

"Rus, surrender, you will die anyway!"

"You're mistaken," came an anonymous voice from within the house, "we will live for a long time!"—followed up with a burst of machine gun fire. The Germans attacked within a few minutes, the defenders again using bricks and the odd grenade for effect to keep them at bay. The garrison's limited firepower enticed the Germans to try one more time to attack. Soon the street was filled with infantry. Dragan seized his chance: "I put the last belt in the Maxim and fired point-blank along the street."[6]

He had chosen the right moment, as dead and wounded now littered the ground around the house, and the survivors quickly regrouped to pour on automatic and artillery fire. Beaten back by the intensity of the Russians response, the Germans ran for cover back along the main street, ducking into doorways and behind vehicles. Dragan, who had been wounded in his arm, abruptly ordered his men to cease fire and save their ammunition. Silence reigned for a while.

A few hours later, the familiar sound of heavy armor could be heard coming from the Germans rumbling toward the Russians' position. A lookout on the third floor of the house rushed downstairs to warn his commander that enemy armored assault guns were approaching their position from three directions. Dragan's heart stopped. *They would rather demolish the building and kill us that way*, he thought.

> We realized that our fate was decided. My soldiers began to say good-bye to one another. In my field bag, I put a certificate, my party card, Red Army book, Komsomol card [identification membership for the youth wing of the Communist Party] and some letters. All this was buried in the left corner of the house.

Several notes were scrawled on the wall. Dragan's orderly, Guardsman Kozhushko, took out his bayonet and etched into the nearby wall, "Rodimtsev's Guardsmen fought and died for their Motherland here."

The assault guns opened fire in a crescendo of violence. The defenders' world imploded in noise, brick, and dust, the aftershock sucking the air out of the room. The side wall of the house collapsed instantaneously, bringing the whole edifice down onto the sidewalk in a great cloud of dust. Fortunately for the survivors, the masonry and debris covered the basement window, plunging their world into darkness. It also smothered any noise that might give their position away. Satisfied with the result, the Germans continued their advance toward the river, to establish defensive positions along the shoreline, where they laid land mines and fresh barbed wire.

Incredibly, despite the destruction of the building, six of the defenders survived, including Lieutenant Dragan. Digging themselves out, they would remain in the basement for two days, until confident enough to try their luck and escape back across the Volga. Supporting one another, Dragan's men crawled to the river, lingering in the shallows to drink deep gulps. Amid the sound of distant gunfire and the glow of destroyed barges set alight on the river of burning oil, the survivors constructed a makeshift raft, pushed it into the river, and climbed on. The current would carry them to wash up on nearby Peschany Island, where a Red Army battery of antiaircraft guns were stationed. They were fed, patched up, and transported by boat to medical facilities on the east bank.

These were the sole survivors to return from the original six hundred guardsmen of the 1st Battalion that Rodimtsev had sent across the Volga in the first wave a little more than two weeks previously. Though it had been only fourteen days before, it must have felt like an eternity to these six men. The losses for the 13th Division were no different than those of other Red Army units, some of which were completely destroyed, but the position they held in the city at such a critical juncture earned them near immortality after the war. Such renown did not, however, hide the cost to the men who served within the division's ranks, as one soldier remembered:

> Before I went off to fight my mother gave me a written prayer, to act as a talisman. I put it in my breast pocket but never looked at it— I was, after all, a communist. . . . I was an atheist but being an atheist at Stalingrad was no longer enough. I could not explain how I was still alive or how our army was continuing to fight. The Germans should have destroyed us all that day. Reluctantly, I took out the prayer, opened it and gave thanks to God.[7]

The battle lines had been redrawn, but the fight for Stalingrad was far from decided. Paulus now focused his attention on subduing the industrial sectors of the city to divide and destroy Chuikov's command along the whole front. It was going to be a fight to the death.

CHAPTER TEN

Change at the Top

Let me thank you, my dear Paulus, for your loyalty and friendship and wish you further success as the leader you have proved yourself to be.

—Colonel General Franz Halder, Chief
of the General Staff, Army High
Command, September 14, 1942

Going into the third week of September with his rifle battalions suffering increasing losses, Paulus's repeated requests for fresh reinforcements were granted by Army Group B, who moved a rested division into the maelstrom to improve Sixth Army's options for the next offensive and the means to drive Chuikov into the Volga. Along the whole shoreline, the Russian 62nd Army commander had himself taken on significant resupply the same day. That evening a new rifle division had begun to come across the river to reinforce Rodimtsev. The 13th Guards by the time had been pushed farther back by General von Hartmann's 71st Division, supported by continuous airstrikes, the Germans retaking lost ground which now split Rodimtsev's division into isolated pockets. The 71st combat diary celebrated: "At 1200 hours, the German national flag was hoisted over the Theatre and the Party building complex by the commanders of I.R. 211 and 191."[1]

For outside commentators and those Nazi propagandists desperate for good news in Berlin, it seemed now the city was taken. Though he was pleased with the result, for Paulus the cost in men was concerning, while the expenditure in materiel was becoming a potential crisis. The Sixth Army would expend a colossal amount of supplies and munitions in the September battles: 25,000,000 rounds of small arms, 500,000 antitank rounds, 752,000 artillery shells, and 178,000 hand grenades. Each day the German forces expended 300 to 500 tons of artillery ammunition—one-third of the acceptable level for a formation of their size. One three-minute divisional barrage, vital to open up Soviet fortifications before any urban assault, used up 42 tons of ammunition. The exhausted troops' daily food rations amounted to 20 tons, their horse train 50 tons of fodder, while the Sixth Army's fleet of vehicles and armor drained 10 to 40 tons of fuel. Water was by now a major issue, with each line division's daily requirement coming to 150 tons, and those in combat 300 to 400 tons. The nearest supply railhead was eighty kilometers (50 miles) away, and the logistics supply line by truck stretched for more than a hundred kilometers (more than 60 miles) to the city itself. The mathematics were staggering for this daily route: four thousand tons per day meant two thousand truckloads reaching the Sixth Army's depot—not taking into account broken-down vehicles failing to deliver, creating a logjam of supplies and thus front-line units badly supplied with meager rations. As we shall see, such bottlenecks would have catastrophic consequences within a matter of weeks.

While Paulus and his commanders studied Chuikov's positions and agreed to switch their axis of attack toward the north, within the German High Command ruptures were appearing as to the overall strategy and the conduct of the whole summer offensive. On September 24, while reinforcements marched into Stalingrad on both sides, Colonel General Halder finally resigned his position as chief of the general staff at Army High Command. Worn down by incessant debate with the Fuhrer over Army Group A's inertia in the Caucasus and Paulus's bloody stalemate at Stalingrad, he could provide little consolation for Hitler at the conference table in Vinnitsa. Talk of the stagnation along Army Group Center's front and the ongoing failure to capture Leningrad by

Army Group North only intensified the struggle to maintain cordial, coherent discussions. Stating the facts of the situation had not been a policy worth pursuing, or risking one's career over up until this point. Until the beginning of 1942, Halder had continually enjoyed the benefit of having the protective arm of his predecessor Walther von Brauchitsch to handle Hitler's capriciousness.[2] Halder may have overseen the detail of Army High Command's plans, but it was von Brauchitsch who had walked through it with the Fuhrer. Halder had now been in his shoes for nine months, fighting his corner every day at the conference table as the summer offensive's objectives slowly began to unravel and Hitler tinkered to rescue it.

By now, the pair's relationship was in terminal decline, with Hitler barely able to listen to Halder's concerns for the coming operations, or heed his warnings as to the strength of the Red Army. At times such debates spilled over, with Halder enduring verbal tirades, explosions of temper, and public ridicule. Hitler ominously envied Stalin's own purges of the Red Army leadership and chided Halder for his lack of front-line experience in the Great War as opposed to the combat wounds he himself had won. Halder's strategic-minded, calm professionalism continually cut through Hitler's increasing levels of bombast. The Fuhrer's apparent determination not to accept the facts of where the battle and indeed the strategic goals as a whole were heading only served to crank up the tension between the two men. One could argue the plan going so rapidly off the rails was the one Halder had obligingly agreed to, yet now he seemed to Hitler to be the bearer of continual bad news.

Halder's final report sealed his fate as he presented the facts to his commander in chief, a report many colleagues at Army High Command now knew to be true but dared not publicly agree with:

> The Russians have assembled a million troops in the Saratov area and a further half million east of the Caucasus. The Soviet High Command will go over to the offensive, when the German forces reach the Volga. Stalin will launch an attack in this area, exactly similar to the one he launched against Denikin during the Russian revolution.[3]

Though the Luftwaffe's reconnaissance reports offered no credence to any increased buildup of Soviet forces on the flanks of Army Group B, the reality of the Red Army's continued ability to bring fresh divisions into the fighting at Stalingrad could not be denied. German military intelligence operatives could not detect the strength of what might be out in the steppe east of the Volga, but they did furnish Halder with the raw data for his reports on the Soviet's increasing overall armored strength, stating: "The Russians are producing 1,500 tanks per month, against a German figure of 600."[4]

Halder pointed to the front line, where the relentless casualty rates in the center of the city and to the north were gradually sapping the strength of Paulus's forces. The constant demands on the depleted German divisions to be reinforced from outside of the city, increasingly drawing away the very troops Paulus needed to guarantee his flanks, now manned by his Romanian and Hungarian allies. These Axis troops were badly lacking in antitank and mechanized support. He once again highlighted the serious concern of the army's line of supply in the east and to the south, with the lack of sufficient locomotive rolling stock. All these problems were, Halder stated, exacerbating the many issues along the Germans' line of logistics. In conclusion, the Wehrmacht's ability to supply major operations in Southern Russia was currently in danger of stalling just when it was needed the most. Sixth Army's daily supplies alone amounted to more than 750 tons. Such an epic undertaking at times took precedence over troop reinforcements reaching the front. Like a schoolmaster, Halder pinpointed each area of ongoing concern on the Stalingrad and Caucasus fronts, ominously concluding to Hitler: "I am warning you that a crisis is coming, and for sure."

As he had done on several occasions that summer, Hitler chose to cast aside Halder's opinions, German military intelligence reports, and the corroborative discussions he had held with Army Group B's frontline commanders von Weichs and Paulus twelve days earlier. Halder had clearly served his time as well as his usefulness to the Fuhrer. The supreme commander now dismissed him from his service:

You and I have been suffering from nerves. Half of my nervous exhaustion is due to you. We need Nationalist Socialist ardour now, rather than professional ability, to settle matters in the East. I cannot expect this of you.[5]

Since his gloomy meeting at Hitler's headquarters at what now seemed a lifetime ago on September 12, Paulus had been acutely aware he would not receive the reinforcements required to pacify the city and defend it from recapture. By September 24 he knew his army would be staying on the Volga for the winter. The news of Halder's dismissal hit him very hard; he had served under him before and during the early years of the war, coordinating the planning of Barbarossa. His connection to Halder was deeper than the chain of command; Halder had become a mentor and a friend, one who frequently offered him advice and support, especially once he had risen to replace von Reichenau as commander of the Sixth Army. In a letter sent earlier that summer to bolster his protégé's confidence amid the unexpected fierce fighting to break through the Don Bend toward the city, Halder had encouraged Paulus by reminding him of "that inner friendship which has for so long bound us old soldiers together."[6]

Now, his strongest supporter at Army High Command had gone, replaced by a man he only knew by reputation. Colonel General Kurt Zeitzler held a distinguished record. He was a highly competent staff officer, having served in the campaigns for France, Poland, and the Balkans, and then with Army Group South in 1941.[7] Still an ardent believer by September 1942 in the infallibility of Hitler's military judgment, he had impressed the Fuhrer with his energy and skill in maintaining the German divisions guarding the Channel Coast in western France and the Low Countries. Paulus had been warned, however, by colleagues at Army High Command that he was not to expect any new strategy to extricate Army Group B from their current predicament. Indeed, rumor was now rife within the corridors of the armed forces in Berlin that Hitler was now willing to elevate Zeitzler above more experienced, older candidates simply because he was an officer "who doesn't go off and brood on my orders, but energetically sees to carry them out."[8]

On September 25, the former chief of staff of Army Group West reported to the Fuhrer. Like Hitler, Zeitzler had combat experience from the Great War and was, the Fuhrer hoped, a kindred spirit in achieving the impossible. The old Prussian-led school of thought needed pruning back, and a younger wave of officers, such as Zeitzler, who understood mechanized warfare would be given their head. Another pivotal appointment Hitler made that autumn to control the backbone of the German Army was placing his own adjutant general Rudolf Schmundt as head of the Army Personnel Office. Now it would be a performance-based criteria that led to capable combat officers being raised to prominent and important positions of power within the Wehrmacht. The Fuhrer ran through with Zeitzler the positions of all four army groups on the Eastern Front, reviewed the mistakes his predecessor had made, offered more generalizations concerning the rapid capture of Stalingrad being now vital to provide the Sixth Army's base for winter quarters and thus protect Army Group A's rear. Discussions concerning the ongoing battles for the city, the diluting of German units from the flanks to support Paulus's next assault to capture it, and the concerns of the quality of Axis troops left to defend hundreds of miles of new front were brushed aside as Hitler ended the meeting: "For these reasons I have decided to dismiss Colonel General Halder and appoint you Chief of the Army General Staff."[9]

On the ground in Stalingrad, the next phase of Sixth Army's operations was underway. Rodimtsev's division now only held a narrow strip of land that stretched along the Volga for approximately fifteen hundred meters (almost five thousand feet) and to a depth in places of one to three hundred meters (three hunded to one thousand feet). To the German planners, they seemed bottled up in the ruins. Their own 71st Division,

Adolf Hitler at Army Group South's headquarters in Vinnitsa in the southern Ukraine with staff of Army High Command mapping out the summer offensive into the Caucasus.

Major General Alexander Rodimtsev, commander of the recently formed 13th Guards Rifle Division, receives the division's new Guards banner, March 1942. The division would see fierce action all throughout that year—from the disaster at Kharkov that spring to the stunning victory at Stalingrad the following winter.

3

Commander of the Sixth Army, General Friedrich Paulus, studies the city with his corps commander Walther von Seydlitz-Kurzbach, whose infantry divisions would suffer the heaviest casualties during the first months of the fighting to take the city.

4

The view of Stalingrad from the eastern shore on September 14 as the 13th Guards prepared to assault the embankment.

Damaged hull of a Soviet BK-13 armored naval boat from the Volga Flotilla, which ferried across countless reinforcements.

Stukas of the VIII Air Fleet give ground support to the advancing Sixth Army units as they attempt to capture the central district and reach the Volga. An armored Soviet motorboat can be seen in the distance.

7

Major General
Alexander Rodimtsev
with his divisional staff
during the fighting.

8  9  10

LEFT TO RIGHT: Colonel Ivan Pavlovich Elin, commanding officer, 42nd Guards Rifle
Regiment. Senior Lieutenant Fedor Fedoseyev. Lieutenant Anton Dragan.

11

Stalingrad's Main Railway Station No. 1 in present-day Volgograd.

LEFT TO RIGHT: Dropped into the fighting in early September 1942, Lieutenant Colonel Friedrich Roske would lead his regiment (I.R. 194 of the 71st Division) to dramatically seize sections of the Volga embankment. He was superbly served by his adjutant, First Lieutenant Gerhard Hindenlang, who would bring news of his success back to divisional headquarters.

The shattered railway tracks, damaged locomotives, and wagons resulted from incessant German artillery bombardments and aerial strikes before the 71st Infantry Division advanced to attempt to capture Railway Station No. 1 on September 13, 1942.

ABOVE: With support from mobile assault guns (Stug IIIs), troops from Lieutenant Colonel Friedrich Roske's Infantry Regiment 194 advance into the heart of the city toward the Volga on September 13, 1942.
RIGHT: Unteroffizier Albert Wittenberg would survive the intense fighting in the Factory District with the 50th Infantry Division and make it home.

The 62nd Army's evolution of "storm group" tactics proved to be a pivotal decision in the battle for the city. "Hugging the enemy" enabled the Soviet defenders to maximize German casualties through an "active defense" as well as nullify the superiority of Luftwaffe ground support.

Senior Lieutenant Alexei Efimovich Zhukov would distinguish himself in hard fighting for many weeks in the central district of the city and would oversee the defense of "Pavlov's House."

The newspaper reports would hail Guards Junior Sergeant Yakov Fedotovich Pavlov (*left*) as the hero of the siege but veteran testimonies point to Guards Lieutenant Ivan Filippovich Afanasiev (*right*) as the officer who took control of the defense of the building.

"Pavlov's House" after the battle, viewing the west gable of the building. Gerhardt's Mill is in the background to the left. Only one front section of the building was destroyed despite the fight that had taken place all around it.

22

23

LEFT: Lieutenant Juliy Petrovich Chepurin was a war correspondent for the 62nd Army's newspaper *Stalin's Banner*. RIGHT: He would write the first story of the defense of the house on 61 Penzenskaya Street and give it the name "The House of Pavlov," on October 31, 1942, which would soon pick up a wider, national audience.

24

The flag of the Third Reich is flown from the Univermag Department Store overlooking 9th January Square on October 1, 1942, by a regiment from the 71st Infantry Division. Hitler's boasts that the city would soon be completely occupied by the Sixth Army, and thus control of the Volga in German hands, was to prove hubristically false within weeks.

LEFT: General Paulus (*second from right*) confers with Major General von Hartmann (*far left*) at 71st Infantry Division's headquarters within the city at the Univermag Department Store. RIGHT: A few months later, surrounded by the Soviets and days from surrendering, von Hartmann was decorated by Paulus with the Knight's Cross.

Promoted to major general, Friedrich Roske seen here at his surrender on January 31, 1943. Roske's final letter to his wife, which was flown out of the German encirclement on January 22, 1943, read: "I trust in God, in our strength, and determined fighting community here—we will survive the fight well. Don't let yourself be too influenced by the reports from the Wehrmacht!"

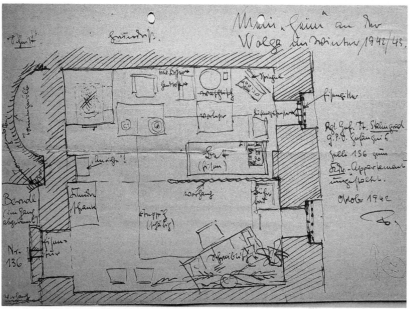

Roske, a trained architect, sketched the floor plan of his room (a cell) within I.R. 194's quarters within the GPU prison complex. His bed center right (with a "shabby carpet" around it on the floor) and clockwise: a bookcase, a desk at the bottom of the drawing (separated from the bed by a curtain), his orderly Berndl sleeping in the corridor separated by an iron door. There was a barrel vault near the space where Berndl lived outside the room. Back inside the room there was a wardrobe, a dresser, and an unexplained area (which could perhaps be the oven), a space for a small suitcase ("Handkoffer"), and a larger "military" suitcase, a sink, a mirror in the top right corner, and iron bars on the window.

If you know where to look—in this case the old worker's accommodation behind the Barrikady Gun Factory—you can still find original damage from the house-to-house fighting. A Soviet 120mm mortar tailfin, discovered on a walking tour of the Mamayev Kurgan.

The solemnity of Gerhardt's Mill is very powerful, even in the winter of 2020, a stone's throw away from "Pavlov's House" and the freezing Volga River.

33

LEFT: Alexandra Cherkasova, would lead the civic movement to rebuild the city. BELOW: The inscription on the front wall of "Pavlov's House" made by J. F. Pavlov: "The house received from Comrade Cherkasova, suitable for habitation. July 16, 1946."

34

35

Veterans of the 13th Guards greeting one another at a reunion in the 1970s at the site of their landing on the city's embankment, now called Rodimtsev's Wall.

ABOVE: The body of Marshal Chuikov lies in state prior to his burial in March 1982. RIGHT: No mistaking who this is! As one walks through the various platforms that comprise the Mamayev Kurgan complex, one encounters a bare-chested figure of Marshal Chuikov.

The resting place of Marshal Chuikov atop the Mamayev Kurgan today, looking out across the Volga River to the east.

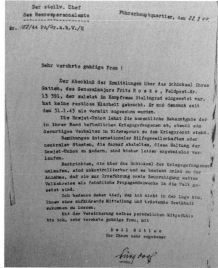

LEFT: The letter sent by Lieutenant General Wilhelm Burgdorf, the deputy chief of army personnel—Führer's HQ to Roske's wife, informing her that her husband is officially counted as "missing," as of January 31, 1943. ABOVE: Major General Roske would return to West Germany in one of the last batches of prisoners from Russia in 1955, yet the toll of imprisonment had clearly affected him. He would commit suicide on Christmas Day 1956.

ABOVE: Major General Roske's prison records between January 1943 and October 1955; includes imprisonment in Iwanowo (northeast of Moscow) in March 1946–47, a prison in Stalingrad (September 1948, where he was sentenced to twenty-five years imprisonment); in March 1949, he was sent to Workuta, north of the Arctic Circle, to a brick factory camp; 1951, a camp in Asbest in the Urals; 1954, a camp in Sochi; and then by October 1955, his arrival in Friedland by train.
RIGHT: Headstone of Friedrich Roske, in Dusseldorf.

43

What remains of the original "Pavlov's House" today is still a popular site for both tourists and historians of the battle.

however, was nearing exhaustion and in need of replacements, too, with all three of von Hartmann's regiments badly mauled from the incessant fighting of the past month, when tactics had evolved from one of combined arms and speed to one that was medieval in its nature and ferocity, as was recorded in the divisional combat diary on September 19, 1942:

> The Division Commander has decided to continue the battle in a form where every regiment tried to achieve headway in its sector with locally centralised assault troops supported by flamethrowers, because it has been demonstrated that each house has to be fought for individually and needs to be knocked out—a costly battle![10]

When studying the division's combat diary further one detects a pattern of the stress this type of combat was having on the division, with various notes of officers falling out of the line due to dysentery, pneumonia, jaundice, and pleurisy. This medical crisis was amplified by the losses sustained in the bitter fighting, the divisional log stating that now "many companies no longer have officers as their commanders and are still only 8–12 men strong."[11]

Paulus was well aware of the casualties, which mirrored the state of the bulk of the divisions he had sent into the city, contrasting sharply with Hitler's belief that the Red Army was in a similar if not worse condition.

For Rodimtsev's regiments facing them, despite the continued German fire on the Volga, reinforcements continued to arrive during the hours of night; either by boat or on the makeshift causeway constructed of floating barrels. His division had been fought to a standstill but remained in solid defensive positions on the embankment it had fought so hard to capture. Though the bulk of the men who had crossed in the first few days were now dead, wounded, or missing, their replacements enabled him to continue to harass the enemy. As we shall see in the next chapter, the fighting for the heart of the city would take on a new dimension as Chuikov switched tactics to maintain his toehold on the west bank of the Volga. The storm groups were coming.

CHAPTER ELEVEN

The Storm Group and
the Art of Active Defense

It was impossible, in Stalingrad, to conduct any strategic or tactical manoeuvre. All we could do was just sit there. There was no opportunity for any kind of Napoleonic brilliance.

—Lieutenant General Vasily Chuikov,
Commander, Russian 62nd Army[1]

By September 28, the past twenty-fours of fighting had Chuikov facing disaster. His own counteroffensive launched at 0500 hours the previous day, to relieve the pressure on Rodimtsev's narrow strip of land, had literally been blown to pieces by the artillery of LI Corps. Badly beaten and driven back within a few hours to their starting positions, the survivors now faced a renewed onslaught from LI Corps. It came on with a preparatory bombardment that consumed more than 450 tons of ammunition before German armor and supporting infantry attacked along the whole line, from Rodimtsev's positions in the center through to the Red October Steel Plant in the north. By the day's end, LI Corps units had recaptured the Mamayev Kurgan and pushed Chuikov's army into separate pockets as they occupied a long stretch of the Volga embankment. Yet again, the Luftwaffe had been the primary weapon for Paulus; unmolested by any Soviet fighter planes, it had inflicted enormous damage on Chuikov's forces: more than eight thousand killed, wounded, or captured. In a matter of hours, the 62nd Army had lost a sixth of its combat strength.

Fortunately for Chuikov, the German advance itself began to run out of steam as the 62nd Army commander ordered whatever forces he could gather to launch almost suicidal counterattacks to blunt the enemy's advances. Despite transferring extra units into the city, Paulus's continued push to capture the Red October Steel Plant was thwarted over the coming week. Chuikov survived by the skin of his teeth as yet more reinforcements crossed the Volga for him to initiate sniping counterattacks and artillery barrages to distract Paulus. Paulus had pulled out XXXXVIII Panzerkorps in the south to prepare for action in the north, leaving 71st Division to occupy an extended line now stretching from its positions opposite the 13th Guards right down to Kuporossnoye in the south. A lull came over the center of the city.

Amid the battering his army was taking, Chuikov had been studying the German's fighting strategy. He realized that he needed a solution for the disparity in firepower, which was nullifying any attack he planned. The German Sixth Army continued to implement combined arms to conquer the city, even after a month of intense fighting. As far as Chuikov and his commanders could ascertain, these assaults were carried out by large units, almost battalion strength, with the aim of capturing an entire block at a time with aerial and armored support—as von Hartmann's 71st Division had succeeded in doing at the start of the fighting. The German strategic goal of taking Stalingrad and controlling the Volga was entirely at odds with Chuikov's more localized ambition to simply deny him that objective through counterattacks and tenacious defense. September had been one of survival and keeping the German offensive off balance in order for the Russians to hold on to their scrap of the city's west bank. Both sides were now punch drunk from the fighting, the Germans having suffered more than forty thousand casualties, and the Red Army almost double that figure.

Within the total of Russian casualties, Rodimtsev's division had lost more than four thousand men within the first week of fighting alone and was badly in need of reinforcements if it was to maintain its tenuous position. Chuikov did his best to send what he could muster, but still the replacements came in a trickle, as the fight was now to the north, where both sides poured in whatever troops they had for the Germans' planned third offensive to take the Factory District. Amid the bigger picture, units of the 71st pushed the Russian 13th Guards out of their initial successes around Railway Station No. 1 and Red Square. In one such action, Lieutenant Colonel Roske himself was badly injured while leading I.R. 194, with shrapnel from a mortar round hitting him in the back. Though wounded, he refused to be taken from his position and instead directed events from divisional headquarters for the next few days, until he could move freely again. Chuikov bitterly accepted that the southern sector of Stalingrad was for now in the enemy's control, but the fight for the central district would continue. He needed to bleed the enemy of its strength, distract it, and provide proof his army was taking the fight to the enemy. But how?

The evolution of urban, house-to-house fighting and defending these buildings and built-up areas was seemingly born in Stalingrad in the winter of 1942. Up until the start of Barbarossa, Soviet military field manuals of 1929, and later in 1936 as the Red Army became more mechanized, had focused primarily on offensive tactics, with the emphasis for commanders on how to take towns and cities rather than on how to defend them, as the Red Army expected to be fighting a war of maneuver on foreign soil—be it Finland, Germany, or Japan.[2] The previous years fighting against the German army groups in western Russia had resulted in urban battles for occupancy of the key strategic cities of Smolensk and Kiev—but in both cases, the Soviet defenders were in the main fighting around the cities and not defending them street by street and house by house, as they now were in Stalingrad.[3] Equally, the fighting in the Crimea and the capture of Sevastopol by von Manstein's 11th Army had primarily been achieved through air and artillery supremacy, bombing the city's defenders into submission. Manstein's infantry had suffered losses in assaulting the defensive belts but not in actually taking the city port itself. Fighting for dominance along the Volga that winter, the tactics for conducting warfare amid the landscape of the ruined city offered potential benefits for one side and a death trap for the other. Chuikov realized this early on, as he recalled in an interview:

> The peculiarities of the fighting in Stalingrad, in terms of city defense and attacking whole cities, can all be applied to all combat situations. Any populated area can be turned into a fortress and can grind down the enemy ten times better than a garrison.[4]

Chuikov had learned something new. The Germans were up to that point predictable in how they conducted assaults. The 62nd Army, if it were to survive, would need to bring its troops as close as possible to the German units it faced in the streets and factories; if need be as close as a few meters, or a floor or room in a building. "Hugging the enemy" was to be the new mantra, which would test the nerve of all Red Army personnel over the coming months. Furthermore, Chuikov instructed his commanders to implement a new tactic for fighting in the city—one which Rodimtsev's men had accidentally begun in their defense of the city center as isolated small units of the 13th Guards had fought independently against neighboring German units of the 71st Division for the key buildings and transport hubs. Colonel Elin's 42nd Guards Regiment had attempted to storm the State Bank with small teams of assault troops armed with submachine guns, grenades, and satchel charges. Though initially successful in driving the enemy out, ultimately they had been forced to retreat by heavy counterattacks. But the lesson had been learned. Now, Major General Rodimtsev's regiments would go on the offensive to battle lost ground and attempt to establish a unified front line to maintain the 62nd Army's toehold. It was to be a savage and bloody back-and-forth campaign for the next three months.

Chuikov instructed his commanders that Soviet assaults were now to be undertaken by small parties or what would later be termed "storm groups" (*shturmovye ottriady, schturmoye gruppy*), who would utilize the advantages of combined arms to conduct patrols, seek out the enemy front lines, and use the terrain to mask their assaults.[5] His Order 166 on September 26 detailed:

I again warn the commanders of all units and formations not to carry
out operations in battle by whole units like companies and battalions.
The offensive should be organized chiefly on the basis of small groups,
with tommy guns, hand grenades, bottles of incendiary mixture and
anti-tank rifles.[6]

All front-line units of the 62nd Army now formed special raiding
parties—veterans from each company and battalion being selected for
these special operations due to their combat experience and performance
under fire—newcomers, unless absolutely necessary due to casualties, were
not encouraged for such roles. Scouting groups could be as small as four
to six men, whereas significant incursions into German territory might
entail fifty to one hundred soldiers. The groups would be led by junior
officers who for the first time in the war (perhaps the first time under
Stalin's rule) were allowed a modicum of initiative in the field to make
their own decisions based on what was presented to them by the enemy.

The men would trade in their standard Mosin-Nagant M.1891/1930
rifles[7] to be replaced with the lighter PPSh-41 submachine gun, an
excellent, robust weapon with its famous seventy-one-round circular
magazine.[8] That gun's firepower outmatched the thirty-one rounds
contained in the German's MP-40, which was critical for fire superiority
in urban fighting. The PPSh-41 was not designed to affix a bayonet, an
essential tool for close combat, but Chuikov's men fashioned the soldier's
"loyal friend"—the shortened spade—as a killing device.[9] Reminiscent
of the trench warfare of World War I, all Soviet raiders now carried
these sharpened spades into battle as they were particularly favored in
intimate, hand-to-hand fighting. Such was its success that Soviet propaganda declared: "Every blow with a shovel on the battlefield is equal
to a well-aimed shot. The spade makes a soldier invulnerable, and thus
terrifying to the enemy."[10]

Next to the submachine gun, the "pocket artillery" of the hand grenade was highly prized by front-line storm squads; it proved essential
for clearing the enemy out of bunkers, rooms, and foxholes, the men
carrying at least half a dozen each for their dirty work. Supporting the
small arms would be light and heavy machine guns (the Model 1910

belt-fed Maxim, and the lighter handheld DP-28 automatic rifle with its famous forty-seven-round disc). Once a building had been taken, the unit would be immediately supported by reinforcements bringing the necessary arms and equipment to fortify and defend it: laying minefields and barbed wire, digging supply and communication trenches.

If required or the situation demanded, the storm units could be reinforced with light artillery, or could call in an artillery barrage from the eastern shore. Many German operations over the coming months would be broken up prior to their jump off as Red Army spotters within the city would communicate the enemy buildup back to 62nd Army headquarters. As we shall see in the next chapter, such action resulted in the capture and defense of Pavlov's House. The storm groups were an innovative decision by a commander desperate to hold on to what positions his men still occupied.

On October 14, Hitler issued Operational Order No. 1 suspending all other operations along the entire Eastern Front, other than Stalingrad. The success of Case Blue now rested on the fight for the city. The next phase of German offensives to capture the Factory District commenced on October 14, with Chuikov's defenders coming under the heaviest artillery bombardment of the whole battle—some 859 tons—as well as a powerful aerial assault by the Luftwaffe. The Tractor Factory eventually fell to the Germans after heavy fighting, giving them a further portion of the Volga riverbank. Like the ruins of the central district, the northern industrial complexes were now a wasteland of twisted, tangled metal, burned bricks, wrecked tanks, and corpses, thousands of them. As one Soviet reporter described:

> The factory yards are empty now. Wind whistles through broken windows. When a shell explodes nearby, shards of glass shower down on the asphalt. But the factory, like the rest of the city, still fights. If it's possible to get used to the bombs, the mortars, the bullets and the danger, then they've certainly got used to them here. They've got used to them like nowhere else.[11]

As autumn progressed to winter, and with it shorter daylight hours for German operations on the ground and in the air, Paulus's soldiers knew too well that the Russians were on the move in the city (even through its sewers)—just the thought process and irrational fear that Chuikov wished to encourage in his enemy. To add to the stress of house fighting, the debris of battle confused identification of friend and foe alike, often playing into the hands of the storm groups as they ventured across no-man's-land, usually crawling silently at first[12] toward designated enemy fortifications. Each man was careful to stay apart from the others in case bunching up should give away their position, and to then take the fight to the Germans, as Chuikov summarized:

> People think that urban warfare is a matter of walking down a street and shooting. That's nonsense. The streets are empty, and the fighting is going on in the buildings, in structures and courtyards where you've got to pluck the enemy out with bayonets and grenades. . . . In urban combat you use hand grenades, submachine guns, bayonets, knifes, entrenching tools. You come face to face with the enemy and slash at them.[13]

As with many special units and scouting operations, the men would only carry what they needed, dress appropriately, no noisy accoutrements, steel helmets sometimes being replaced by forage caps (*pilotki*) or the quintessential headgear we know as the fur-lined *ushanka* (many soldiers had favorite headgear which they believed acted as a lucky charm). Gunmetal was blackened, and as the cold weather began many men dispensed with their normal single-breasted overcoats (*shineli*) and chose to wear just the padded bodywarmer (*vatnik*) together with the ubiquitous *plashch-palatka*, a light rain cape that could also protect the wearer from other weather. To maintain coordination and for each man to fully understand his own role in each mini operation, the 62nd Army now issued "fire cards," which illustrated the basic outline of the terrain they would be traversing and pinpointed the building to be taken, each enemy fire point outlined. As Brandon M. Schecter summarized in *The Stuff of Soldiers*:

Through fire cards soldiers and commanders reduced an unmanageably complex landscape into a set of clear, rationalized vectors for killing.

With offensive strategy primarily in the hands of the few men they sent out in the dead of night, the remnants of both Shumilov's 64th and Chuikov's 62nd divisions in the city had to now prepare for the expected offensive by the enemy to drive them from the west bank completely. Though the Sixth Army had suffered appalling losses in men and armored vehicles already in the city fighting by the end of September, Paulus still held the upper hand in terms of firepower, armor, and the Luftwaffe's domination of the Stalingrad skyline for the foreseeable future. Hitler drove Army Group B ever harder to capture what remained of the city, to focus the coming battle for the industrial district, and link up with Hube's Panzer and motorized divisions pressing Chuikov from the north. The Stalingrad Front had by now been ordered by Stalin "to turn every building and every street of Stalingrad into a fortress."[14]

Once again, the Soviet field manual from 1936 seemed unsuited to the fighting in the city. Though defensive strongpoints had been a mainstay of Soviet defensive strategy for many years, Chuikov required this to be refined to suit his purposes to hold a thin and precarious position against a determined attacker who wished to drive him into the Volga. His units needed a more coherent, interconnected, and unified system with which to beat off combined arms assaults by an enemy who was quickly coming to grips with how to take a building. The previous year's setbacks had seen formidable Red Army strongpoints swiftly outflanked, bypassed, cut off, and destroyed.[15] This could not happen again with so much at stake. The 62nd Army would quickly move to establish a fully integrated defensive system: separate strongpoints would now be tied together by interlocking fields of fire, and trench systems would offer protected supply and communication lines. Stavka expanded the brief that these fortifications would be:

Covered by antitank and anti-personnel obstacles, located under the effective fire of machine guns, mortars, and artillery . . . All buildings and entries into the yard and on the street should be taken under the field of fire by a system of flank fire. All stone buildings should be joined as centres of resistance and adapted for defence by means of holes in adjacent walls and the installation of communications trenches.[16]

This new strategy, driven by expediency, would have dramatic effect over the coming weeks of conflict. Though German commanders in the east had by now, after eighteen months of war, come to respect the tenaciousness of the Red Army's defensive capabilities, the prewar prejudices fueled by Hitler's racism, and Stalin's initial mistakes had reinforced the belief that the Red Army was incapable of successfully going on the offensive. As the following chapters will show, the Soviets would in the next few months prove how effective they could be strategically and succeed in launching coordinated offensives that would catch the Sixth Army, Army Group B, and the German General Staff by complete surprise. On a more local level the Germans would find that there was no imminent victory at hand, and the Wehrmacht would face a level of bloodletting not seen since Verdun in 1917. For the Soviets, who were frequently staring into the jaws of defeat to defend Stalingrad, the use of propaganda to celebrate small victories would crank up to a whole new level with the successful capture of one building.

PART IV

KEEP YOUR ENEMY CLOSE

For every house, workshop, water-tower, railway embankment, wall, cellar and every pile of ruins, a bitter battle was waged. . . . The distance between the enemy's army and ours was as small as it could possibly be. Despite the concentrated activity of aircraft and artillery, it was impossible to break out of the area of close fighting.

—Lieutenant General Vasily Ivanovich
Chuikov[1]

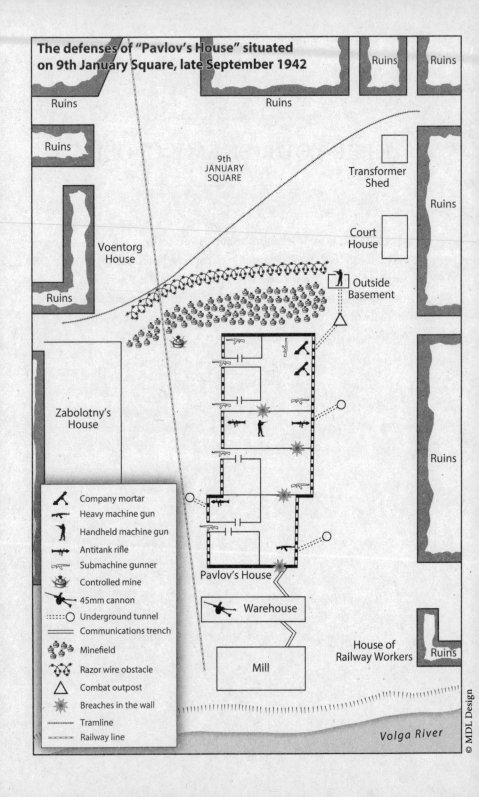

The defenses of "Pavlov's House" situated on 9th January Square, late September 1942

Ruins
Ruins
Ruins
Ruins
Ruins
9th JANUARY SQUARE
Transformer Shed
Court House
Voentorg House
Outside Basement
Ruins
Zabolotny's House
Ruins
Pavlov's House
Warehouse
House of Railway Workers
Ruins
Mill
Volga River

Company mortar
Heavy machine gun
Handheld machine gun
Antitank rifle
Submachine gunner
Controlled mine
45mm cannon
Underground tunnel
Communications trench
Minefield
Razor wire obstacle
Combat outpost
Breaches in the wall
Tramline
Railway line

© MDL Design

CHAPTER TWELVE

The Legend Begins:
The Capture of the "Lighthouse"

In war, do what the enemy regards as impossible.
—A. V. Suvorov[1]

In the center of Rodimtsev's defenses occupied by the 42nd Regiment of Colonel Elin lay the huge NKVD complex of departmental and residential buildings which by this point in time had been reduced to a labyrinth of ruins, propped up by strong walls best suited for urban combat. The bulk of these ruined buildings still offered some protection as their cellars, in the main, remained intact and were constructed from reinforced concrete, which could take continuous shelling. Facing the Soviet left flank held by the 39th Regiment, separated by a wide rubble-strewn street, stood two German strongholds: the four-storey School Number 6 and another five-storey building. They had changed hands several times in fierce hand-to-hand fighting, but on September 22, they were again stormed by the Germans and taken back from the defending Russian forces. Both had now been turned into mini fortresses.

To the north of the NKVD buildings Gerhardt's Mill, an imposing four-storey red-brick structure with reinforced basements, tied down the right flank of the 34th Guards Regiment. The weakness of this flank, however, was two deep ravines cutting through it and running into the Volga, breaking the 34th's lines and making a sustained, coordinated defense difficult. Opposite the regiment's lines sat two formidable buildings: the House of Railway Workers and the "L-Shaped House," still manned by the 295th Infantry Division. By now, like other German units in the center of the city, the "Lucky Division" of von Hartmann was severely depleted in manpower, having by now lost approximately 60 percent of its combat-worthy troops. Their main advantage was still the Luftwaffe's superior aerial presence above the city. These two key sites dominated the surrounding area, giving the artillery spotters a good view of Rodimtsev's overall positions and the Central Landing crossing behind them, where the Russians continued to bring in vital supplies and fresh troops.

The Germans had converted these buildings on both flanks into fortresses that potentially could close like a trapdoor to encircle Rodimtsev's whole command, as he later recalled in his memoirs:

> The entire enemy defence system was organized in such a way that the approaches to the strongholds were exposed to 2- to 3-layer frontal and oblique rifle and machine gun fire, as well as artillery and mortar bombardment; they were also defended with such field works as wire entanglements, *cheval de frise*[2] and minefields. In their observation points the Nazis had a view of 3–4 kilometres including the eastern bank of the Volga. They were able to control and keep under fire all the approaches to our crossings and the crossings themselves.[3]

The fate of the division and of Chuikov's 62nd Army's ability to remain on the western side of the Volga hung in the balance as each side now sought to locate the other's strengths and weaknesses. Chuikov realized that the weight of German firepower needed to be neutralized. The Luftwaffe was the protective shield, allowing Paulus to progress throughout the city's districts in the center and in the north without a significant increase in infantry. But though the air and artillery strikes were proving the Germans' advantage, the enemy was being punished for every meter of ground taken.

The German attacks were increasing in intensity again as the 13th Guards combat diary states:

In the early morning of September 22nd . . . the Germans went on the offensive along the entire sector of the Division's front . . . Enemy strength for this attack was approximately one infantry division accompanied by 100 tanks and with the support of airpower of at least 100 aircraft. The enemy tried to break through to the western bank of the Volga . . . [The] ultimate enemy aim was to split up our forces and destroy them in parts.

. . . Despite this, the 13th Guards Rifle Division stood their ground and repelled enemy attacks all day . . . Throughout the course of the day the 34th Guards Rifle Regiment repelled twelve enemy infantry attacks with tank support.["]4

The newspaper *Krasnaya Zvezda* later published a somewhat embellished account of the fighting for their captivated audience across the country: "The Guardsmen defending to the last man; repelling the enemy's attacks; the ground strewn with the corpses of German soldiers. The guards know that it is impossible to retreat, there is nowhere to retreat to. Stalingrad must be defended at all costs!"

The bulk of Colonel Elin's 42nd Rifle Regiment was now dug in directly across from 9th January Square, having suffered heavy casualties from enemy airstrikes as well as repelling numerous probes from German armor-supported infantry. The fighting for every room of each house and cellar was chaotic and murderous. Elin was aware the enemy was looking for a new weak spot with which to push him into the river and break the whole line. He needed to ascertain for Rodimtsev what the division now faced: Were the Germans reinforced and preparing for a new strike?

On the night of 23 September, I summoned to the command post of the regiment: the commander of the 2nd Rifle Battalion, Major Andriyanov, acting commander of the 3rd Rifle Battalion, Senior Lieutenant Zhukov (Captain Dronov was wounded), my Chief of Staff, Major Tsvigun, and the chief of reconnaissance of the regiment, Senior Lieutenant Roselman. It was necessary to clarify the positions of my

battalions and to immediately set the task of conducting reconnaissance, to clarify the position of the enemy.

Major Andriyanov would conduct a reconnaissance in the direction
of the House of Railway Workers. Senior Lieutenant Zhukov would
depart from the Mill Warehouse and head in the direction of the house
located on the 9th January Square, with the task of ascertaining if it
was occupied by the enemy or not. If so, how many?

Senior Lieutenant Roselman's men would conduct several recon-
naissances along Solnechnaya Street, in the direction of the Milk
House. Establish the front line of the enemy, his system of fire in the
area and take a prisoner if possible.[5]

Colonel Elin was keen that the house stationed alone on the square
should be investigated and if possible captured, as he outlined on his
map to Senior Lieutenant Zhukov. The large, elongated house stood
somewhat apart from other buildings in no-man's-land. It stood parallel to a similar four-storey building. The previous evening this target
had been searched by a squad led by Guards Junior Lieutenant N. E.
Zabolotny, who now occupied it. In the ongoing months of fighting, it
would be named on operational maps as "Zabolotny's House." Now the
neighboring building had to be taken. If this house could be captured,
then Elin's regiment could organize multiple firing points to suppress
the enemy's movements. The wide expanse in front of the house now
offered room for German forces to gather prior to any major new offensive, the building sheltering them from the 42nd Regiment's spotters. By
taking the house, Senior Lieutenant Zhukov could prevent the Germans
bringing up heavy artillery to blast the regiment's existing positions in
Gerhardt's Mill. Possibly the Germans weren't yet established in the
house in force, but Elin needed to know. He left Zhukov to make plans
and choose which men from his battalion's 7th Rifle Company to send,
as they were positioned directly in front of it.

Like all other units within the 13th Division, the 7th Company had
been badly depleted since it had crossed the Volga two weeks previously.
Zhukov was conscious that he required an experienced combat patrol
leader:

Returning to the battalion, I created an assault group headed by Sergeant Yakov Pavlov. The group was armed only with machine guns. In addition, each had a bayonet-knife, and three grenades. Why did I choose Pavlov? Because he was an energetic, courageous, executive and at the same time resourceful sergeant.[6]

Junior Sergeant Pavlov was indeed resourceful. Hailing from Novgorod, he had enlisted in the regular Red Army in 1938 and fought against the German Army Group South since the start of Barbarossa in the summer of 1941. He had come across the Volga with the 13th Division and managed so far to survive, despite being foremost in the house-to-house fighting. Zhukov briefed him accordingly and confirmed there would be a diversionary artillery barrage to mask their movements. Pavlov then went to choose the four men to accompany him as Zhukov waited for zero hour.

At 2200 hours, on my order, we gave the agreed signal, launching red and then green flares towards the Volga. Seconds later, the battalion's artillery opened fire over the house. The entire battalion also opened fire on the German positions. By this time, a tradition had already developed in Stalingrad, [which was that] as soon as an assault began in the sector of a battalion, regiment or division, our troops opened fire along the entire front in order to hide the true direction of the strike. And this time there was no exception. As soon as the first shots of the artillery battalion were fired, our entire front line in the city immediately rumbled.

The fire of our battalion artillery stopped, and I gave the command to Pavlov's group: "Forward!" They rushed to the house in dark shadows and disappeared into the gap in the wall.[7]

The official story was that Pavlov and his men stormed the building, encountered civilians in the cellars who told them the whereabouts of up to seventeen German troops occupying the upper floor and that he then surprised the Germans as they played cards, and finished them off with a submachine gun and grenades before sending a runner back to the 7th Company CP behind the position, at Gerhardt's Mill, with this message:

> To the battalion commander of the guard, Senior Lieutenant Zhukov. The house has been taken. I am waiting for further instructions. 28.9.42. Pavlov.

Colonel Elin waited at least twenty-four hours before then heavily reinforcing the building with a larger supporting group.

Lieutenant Ivan F. Afanasiev of the 7th Rifle Company, from Zhukov's battalion, studied the moonscape of 9th January Square, the remnants of the fires caused by the fallen incendiaries that illuminated the skeletons of already burned-out buildings. He winced as the thud of mortar and high-explosive artillery shells landed to the east of the square in front of him, indicating yet again how close the Germans were to his position. He gripped his PPSh-41 submachine gun tightly to his chest. In the failing light, up ahead, he watched as Rifle Company Sergeant Mukhin stepped warily forward, tensing up whenever a shell landed, and only looking back to give silent hand signals as to the best route to safely gain access to the house.

Behind Afanasiev came the reinforcements, including his PM-10 Maxim machine gun crew, who instead of pulling the heavy weapon along on its wheels had instead removed the heavy armor plate shielding and picked the gun up to carry, in order to lessen the noise. He appreciated their efforts. Next came two mortar crews, and bringing up the rear of the relief column, a half dozen antitank gunners toiled to carry their heavy armor-piercing rifles on their shoulders. He was relieved he had ordered the men to stow away their combat steel helmets and instead wear their distinctive *pilotka* side caps, making it easier to distinguish friend from foe in the dying light, and avoiding a sudden reflective glint from the fires. Any movement in this vicious street fight could earn them deadly counterfire from the German MG-34 machine gun strongpoint his scouts had detected two hundred yards away across the square.

Afanasiev surveyed the seventy yards of open ground from their positions to the side entrance leading into 7th Company's new outpost. His gut instinct told him it would be zeroed by enemy fire. He had the men dart across, moving in short, silent bounds, one by one. Suddenly, a green flare shot up. Afanasiev silently cursed as one of his men stumbled on masonry debris, his ammunition box clattering to the ground and inducing a sporadic and deafening salvo of enemy gunfire. Each guardsman now hugged the ground he had dived upon, refusing to move as the German bullets kicked up the earth around him. This was no place to seek shelter.

With tracer bullets cracking over his head, Afanasiev inched toward Sergeant Mukhin and shouted in his ear for the men to get moving and crawl to the house. Mukhin immediately pushed himself forward, dragging his bag of grenades with him, his submachine gun slung across and over his back, rapidly gesticulating for the group to follow. Frustrated at not hitting anything tangible, the German fire seemed to increase in its intensity. The men lying prone behind Afanasiev became desperate, and seeing their sergeant reaching safety, one soon broke cover, leaping over his startled officer and rushing to dive into the bowels of the building. Afanasiev recognized him as one of his antitank gunners, Private Nurmatov. Angry at his ill-discipline, he watched as Nurmatov looked to have made it, only to collapse in agony as a German bullet took him down at the knee. His screams penetrated the enemy fire, as he was hauled into the house by two fellow guardsmen who had been stationed near the entrance awaiting the company's arrival. The garrison laid down a base of covering fire as the relief group made their dash across the final yards, Sergeant Mukhin frantically dragging each man's arm as the man drew nearer, to speed up the process. They were in!

Leaving his men panting on the stairwell, Afanasiev made his way down the stairs and then along a dark, narrow hallway, reaching a man-sized hole in the wall from which a faint light emanated from an adjoining basement, into which he entered. In the dim light he adjusted his eyes to take in the scene. In the middle of this low-ceiling room was a large, roughly constructed wooden table. In one corner of the room he noticed an iron bunk and feather mattress, with a collection of blankets, pillows, and dirty sheets scattered on top. On the table lay a dozen hand grenades and a full ammunition box for a light machine gun. As he studied the room, his feet kicked against spent cartridge cases, old cutlery, broken pottery, and wastepaper. The bare cement walls were speckled with paint, and the basement stank of acrid smoke and stale sweat.

As the legend goes, a short, skinny junior sergeant in what looked like a Kuban brown fur hat approached out of the gloom, gave Afanasiev a salute, dust falling from his faded tunic as his arm snapped back to his side. He was dark-haired, with brown eyes, his face puffy with fatigue and what looked like three days of stubble growth. He stared at the officer. It was Sergeant Pavlov of the 7th Company. Afanasiev returned the salute and greeted Pavlov. Controversy still continues as to whether Pavlov's assault group actually encountered and killed the German garrison, or whether the house had in fact been unoccupied when they arrived. Afanasiev updated the squad and announced they would be staying and fortifying the building. He was now the de facto leader until his company commander Senior Lieutenant I. I. Naumov arrived.

Afanasiev introduced Pavlov to his men, ordered Company Sergeant Mukhin to feed them all and return back to their company entrenchments together with the wounded Nurmatov. Turning to Pavlov, he asked the young sergeant to show him the layout of the basement and upper floors. Bowing their heads to exit the basement, they walked toward the ruins of the end part of the building, where a young soldier stood guard with a submachine gun.

"Private Alexandrov," the guardsman reported clearly, then said briefly that he had heard some Nazis talking loudly across the square.

"If you see anything, let us know at once before opening fire," warned Pavlov.

Afanasiev inspected the upper floors and picked out the best spots for placing his heavy machine gun and antitank rifles. The basement consisted of four insulated compartments divided by load-bearing walls. The basement windows would serve as gun openings, with wide fields of fire. The first and fourth compartments had wooden partitions, too. The families of the specialist workers and Party functionaries who had originally lived in this apartment block, before the war came to Stalingrad, had stored their possessions there. Even now, there were civilian belongings scattered around, such as metal and glass dishware and wooden crates.

Between the second and third stairwells, there was a special basement entrance from Solnechnaya Street. A heating boiler stood there, with rusty pipes going from it in different directions. All basement sections on the south side of the building had isolated little rooms, where for now—according to the legend and to Afanasiev's surprise—the elderly, women, and children were sheltering from the firestorm.

The four house entrances faced Solnechnaya Street, whereas the western end wall and the northern wall were overlooking the square itself. Outside, and inside, too, the house was already badly damaged by mortar and artillery shells, especially the western part, which had fallen in. But the floor structures on all the four stories remained intact, which ensured the strength of the building and gave Afanasiev confidence that he could hold it, even if the Germans brought up armored support. The fourth floor provided a view of not only the square but also the ruins behind it. When he climbed up to the top, Afanasiev realized finally why headquarters had attached such importance to the house. Its strategic position on the front line meant it was now a physical wedge into the German positions and as such an important tactical stronghold not only within the regimental but also the divisional defense system.

The elevated view it provided of the Volga, with the eastern shore beyond and the entire city surrounding the square, for a good five kilometers in any direction was a priceless asset. They could easily spot German movements and direct Katyusha and artillery fire with great accuracy. Afanasiev immediately set to work establishing a spotter team, one of whom was rifleman Terenty Illarionovich Gridin of the 7th Rifle Company in Zhukov's command:

From the roof of this house it was easy to observe enemy actions in the city and on the Mamayev Kurgan. Therefore, the command set up an observation post [with the call sign of] "Lighthouse" on the attic floor. This [would be] connected by communication with the Mill No. 4 [Gerhardt's Mill] and the command post of the Trans-Volga artillery units.[8]

Content with his ability to defend his position, Afanasiev returned to the relative safety of the basement to brief his men, allocate their positions, and order them to fill in the windows with bricks and sand-filled crates, establish fire points, lay communication cables, and prepare their weapons and ammunition. By midnight the work was completed to his satisfaction, and the soldiers released from duty collapsed to find rest.

Senior Lieutenant Zhukov had achieved the acquisition of a prized asset in the regiment's new defensive system and now needed to consolidate it:

> I ordered to mine all approaches to the house from the enemy's side with anti-personnel mines, and where tanks could pass—with anti-tank mines. When I reported the measures taken to the regiment commander, Colonel Elin, he fully approved them, but in conclusion he added the position required a more senior leader if the garrison was to be expanded and heavily armed: "Look, Zhukov, you are responsible for this house with your experience!"[9]

Zhukov agreed but consented to remain back at 7th Company headquarters in Gerhardt's Mill to oversee the battalion and ensure the new garrison sticking out of the existing defensive system was supported. He now placed Senior Lieutenant Naumov in charge of that new garrison.

The accepted story of Pavlov's House—which I have read from Pavlov's and Afanasiev's own memoirs—describes the intense fight for the building: As the weather turned colder, German infantry, often supported by Panzers, assaulted the house daily, sometimes several times, trying to dislodge the stubborn defenders. They would rush the lower windows incessantly and pushed the barricades aside, only to be met by everything from withering machine gun fire to chunks of hand-thrown masonry, or they were fought off with a sharpened spade. Stukas dive-bombed from above, destroying the facade and killing many of the garrison. At one point they called in pinpoint artillery fire from across the Volga to drive off an attack in the nick of time. Pavlov himself is said to have used an antitank rifle and fired upon advancing armor from the rooftop, to which the Panzers could not elevate their gun, and thus he destroyed up to a dozen during the siege. This is all "boy's own adventure" and is well written in Afanasiev's postwar memoir, as well as recounted in testimonies and letters I read in the city's archives. Is it true? Who knows for certain, but from scanning actual records and combat diaries of both sides in the fighting, I cannot find any mention of the siege. Neither Paulus nor Chuikov mentioned it in any orders coming from their respective headquarters, and Paulus certainly did not have the house pinpointed on any operational map.

What the defenders did do, along with the defenders of other houses along the embankment, was to tie down the attention of a well-entrenched and still very active German force positioned around the city center. There were continuous firefights, and the garrison was kept busy, and I am sure Pavlov found himself at the center of this, being the combat veteran he was. The garrison's occupation of a tall building stuck out into the German lines was valuable, forcing the German command to maintain a stronger presence in an area they had believed to be almost subdued. Communication and supply tunnels were secretly dug linking the house back to Gerhardt's Mill, where the 7th Company's headquarters were situated, so that the house offered the divisional command an excellent vantage point to monitor the enemy and keep Chuikov informed of movements against the Mamayev Kurgan. Rodimtsev and his regimental commander Colonel Elin were said to have both visited Pavlov's House during the battle. Strategically, occupying the position was important to the division's operational strategy, but as we shall see later, the building would assume a new identity and storyline that for Soviet forces fighting for survival across the whole city was far more significant than merely the actual fight for the house itself.

CHAPTER THIRTEEN

Trouble in the North

We are hunters—come and see how we work.
> —Motto of Red Army marksmen
> in Stalingrad

One of the most famous legends of the Stalingrad fighting was the fear and healthy respect Sixth Army forces within the city held for the skill of the Soviet marksman. Throughout the war both armies, as per regulations, contained excellent snipers who were assigned to all infantry commands, but at Stalingrad the bombed-out ruins created a perfect landscape of camouflage for German and Soviet riflemen to ply their trade. What the Soviets were able to do, much like the creation of a mythology of the storm groups, was to have their top-class marksmen mythologized by the regime's propaganda apparatus. In some cases, their skill at shooting from great distances or their kill totals were reinvented to make a stronger story. The effect this had on German morale was palpable and gave the Russians the psychological edge as the battle continued into the winter months. With the Sixth Army still in the ascendancy after three weeks of heavy fighting, Paulus was now looking to subdue the final northern sector in the city. The coming weeks of the German's final attempts to crush the 62nd Army would see born the cult of the sniper that would be celebrated across the country. As the writer Ilya Ehrenburg demanded from his readership: "Unless you've killed at least one German in a given day, your day has been wasted."[1]

The government wasted little time in promoting this notion, alongside the burgeoning numbers of Red Army soldiers who took up the challenge to accumulate German kills. Though the likes of the more famous Vasily Zaitsev and his early mentor the Siberian marksman Alexander Kalentyev established their credentials, more often than not ordinary men on the front line decided to test their skills in the hope of not only killing the enemy but also becoming recognized for it. This would have a debilitating effect on the Sixth Army, already wary of night attacks from Russian storm groups starting to operate in the ruins. Combat leaders were now being killed or wounded at a higher ratio than other ranks, affecting German morale as well as fighting performance, as the following personal testimony shows.

By late September, after surviving a malarial infection picked up in the Crimea, *Unteroffizier* Albert Wittenberg fighting with the 50th Infantry Division had been ordered along with three companies of Pioneer Battalion 71 to Stalingrad. The unit would bulk up the fighting ability of the 295th Division, which had suffered heavily in the fighting for Mamayev Kurgan. These fresh troops would be welcomed to assist Paulus's thrust into the Factory District and to capture the worker's villages by the Red October Steel Plant.

The urgency for more combat units meant the battalion's journey would not be via vehicle or train; this time it would be courtesy of the Luftwaffe. Although a luxury compared to the relentless marching along dusty unlaid roads of the summer advance, the men of Wittenberg's unit were now filled with a sense of unease as to what was to come. They knew the fighting for the city was proving hard and bloody. Clearly, they were needed urgently at the front. Wittenberg stared out the window of his Ju-52 transport:

> Flying has always been my dream. The circumstances weren't so nice, but I would fly, *what the heck*, I thought to myself. We even had escorts, six Messerschmitt BF 109s flying alongside us. The flight was great, the world from above. The great forests gradually gave way to endless expanses, the Russian steppe. [*Compared to*] *our "Little Germany" how insignificant we are*, I thought to myself.[2]

The battalion arrived at a dirt airstrip at Peskovatka, approximately 40 kilometers (25 miles) northeast of Kalach. The unit disembarked to waiting trucks and was driven to the outskirts in the southwest, where the Fourth Panzer Army was situated. The sounds of sporadic fighting were continuous, though shelling could only have been faintly heard toward the north of the city. They were then housed in a former Communist Party administration building, one of the few still left standing. They would not go straight into action but acclimatize to their surroundings and await final orders. The next few days were filled with talks from Stalingrad combat veterans, from the 295th as well as other infantry units, giving the pioneers advice on the fighting they would now experience, the seriousness of which magnified the importance of the nighttime drinking sessions that took the men's minds off what was coming. Wittenberg in particular struck up a friendship with a young lieutenant who played the piano, accompanying the NCOs, who sang a famous song of the time, "You should be able to play the piano, then you have luck with the women."[3] This officer was to play a role in saving Wittenberg's life weeks later.

By now, with the south of the city a mopping up operation, Rodimtsev's 13th Guards tied up in the center, Paulus now looked north to catch Chuikov off balance and split the 62nd Army in two on the western bank, then isolate and destroy each pocket. He would use battle groups from LI Corps for this purpose, in a twin strike on the Mamayev area and one aiming for the Red October Steel Plant. The new arrivals from the Crimea would be joining the 295th Division for a planned night attack in the city on October 1. After three weeks of intense fighting, German commanders and their men were learning from their experience of fighting the Red Army in urban combat to avoid becoming easy targets for their artillery positioned across the Volga, or snipers. A new method was required, as the newcomers from the Crimea soon learned, as Wittenberg remembered:

> We got something like a crash course in house-to-house fighting, we had already learned the essentials in our basic training. We were mainly trained in the use of explosives. This included all types of hand grenades, mines, concentrated charges of different sizes, tube charges, stretched charges, cutting charges and the explosive cartridge. It was

done by a sergeant who gave us the tricks of how best to survive. It really frightened me, I couldn't imagine that at all.

The sergeant said: "In house-to-house warfare, it is not the mass of soldiers that counts to take a house, I need the mass so that it provides fire protection. To get in the door I only need two or three men who are brave enough to open the door. Then they jump in. And don't think you can use your carabine there. You can only shoot once then you can use the thing as a club, if you are not already dead by then. The first to jump in there have submachine guns or hand grenades, only that is effective. If you don't have both, take your folding spade and try to hit the artery below the edge of the helmet. A little tip sharpens the edges."[4]

The battalion quickly set to work preparing for the assault by training in the south of Stalingrad, with the men going out in squads and splitting the houses into teams of two or three men.

Toward the end of September, they were moved north, taking up quarters in an abandoned warehouse. After forty-eight hours they were informed of their objective and to make ready equipment. They then marched off to their jumping off point, close to the front line, with the Mamayev Kurgan in the distance.

Our staging area was a ravine that led down to the Volga. So we had reached our destination and stopped. There were a lot of soldiers in the ravine. We got the order to eat and then we could rest.[5]

Wittenberg was astounded to see Russian civilians, obviously escaping the battle in the city, now sheltering in the gorge itself. Dozens of pieces of cloth flapping and billowing in the breeze revealed man-made holes dug into the red clay, the odd one or two revealing a face staring at the mass of soldiers. The Luftwaffe flew overhead on bomb runs, with the explosions breaking the low murmur of noise the assault teams created as they made ready to go into the attack.

As always, we walked behind the team leader, Emil, as always, next to me. We marched cautiously through the ravine and after a while turned left and reached railroad tracks. It was pitch dark so that you could hardly see your hand in front of your eyes. To the right of us was a railway embankment that protected us, to the left the area was overgrown with bushes and small trees. From time-to-time flares rose up behind the embankment, then the shadowy outlines of buildings that looked like apartment buildings could be seen.

We continued along the embankment and slowly we got used to the darkness. Flares continued to rise. The troop leader, a sergeant major, said: "The Russians are doing this to disrupt communication between the troops. Do not look otherwise you will be blinded afterwards and see nothing at all."

We then crept right across the embankment and infiltrated the city. There were houses that were still completely intact, some were completely destroyed, many halfway. There was rubble everywhere and it was very dark. A flare went up and in the light I saw a flap opening in front of me, less than ten meters away. A Russian soldier threw something in my direction. I instinctively shot. The soldier slammed back into his hole, at the same time something hit my helmet and landed somewhere behind me.

"Grenade!", someone shouted behind me, and then it exploded. A sergeant jumped to the hole and threw a stick grenade into it. Our team leader came back and said: "Is anyone injured? Take cover up here and examine each other."[6]

Wittenberg, along with three other members of the assault group, had been hit by splinters from the Russian grenade, not seriously, but enough to prevent them continuing with the advance, as the team leader explained.

The team leader said: "Listen, we can't stay here long, the medics will leave you bandages and then you will treat each other. Then you stay in position here. We'll move on and on the way back we will pick you up again. See you later."[7]

The five wounded soldiers searched nearby for shelter, Wittenberg and his comrade discovering the empty cellar of a ruined house where they could assess their flesh wounds and stay hidden waiting for their team to return. Two men took up position in the cellar while the other three found refuge in a nearby bomb crater. In front of their position was a small square, and some distance beyond was a multi-storey building. Their defense reasonably secure, they passed the time keeping watch and listening to the distant sound of fighting. It was intensifying. As the nighttime hours passed by and with no sign of their assault team returning, they debated whether they should try to head back to their starting positions or remain in their holes. If they were to leave, they needed to do so under the cover of darkness.

Was that our unit? Hours passed, we took turns with the watch, so that everyone could doze a little. Emil said: "Where are they, hopefully they won't forget us here. Before it gets light we have to get out of here. It would be better if we would run away right away."

The comrade from the side hole said: "We can't do that, you heard what the platoon leader said."

After a while it started to get dark. Nobody came, it was quiet, the noise of the battle could no longer be heard.

Emil: "Hey comrade, how long do we want to wait, let's go. Just get out of here."

The soldier from the next foxhole poked his head out, but before he could answer, a shot rang out. There was a sound like hitting a saucepan. He dropped backwards, lifeless. A bullet had grazed the edge of his helmet and then struck his head. The other two soldiers ducked down but were panicking.

"Don't move," I said.[8]

Panicked by the sudden death of their comrade, the two remaining men tried to get his body out of the hole and into the shelter of the cellar. Two clear shots rang out in quick succession, taking both men down, too quickly for one shooter. Wittenberg feared they were now under fire from two separate positions. Now there was only the two of them left. What should be their next move?

Wittenberg's comrade now attempted to assess the perimeter and where they could move to try to escape the area. Another shot rang out and he fell back into the cellar, shot through the chest, but still breathing. Wittenberg recounted:

I pressed a bandage pack over his wound and crawled to the cellar stairs. I took a few deep breaths and then ran up them, once I was at the top I ran back towards the embankment. When I was almost over it, I felt a tremendous blow in my right thigh. I felt like I was flying several meters through the air and landed on the other side of the embankment. *That's it*, I thought.[9]

It was then that Wittenberg was joined by an officer who knelt by his side. He had been on patrol and had advanced toward the gunfire. Though in agony, Wittenberg recounted what had happened over the past hours, the Russian snipers, and his injured comrade still wounded back in the cellar. Wittenberg was bleeding badly from his wound, and despite his objection the young officer instructed one of his patrol to tie off the sergeant's thigh with wire to stem the bleeding while they gathered him up in a canvas blanket. They would not sacrifice another man going back to find Wittenberg's wounded comrade; they needed to get Wittenberg to an aid station. As he recounted:

I didn't reply, despite everything I was glad to be safe. After they tied my leg with the wire, they put me in a tent sheet and carried me to an aid station. That was backbreaking work and I supported my rescuers by lying on my stomach and supporting myself with my arms.[10]

When he arrived at the aid post, he received basic care to prevent bleeding out and a shot of painkiller. He was transferred to the rear lines and placed on an ambulance for the nearest airfield. Wittenberg was then flown in a Ju-52 to the Stalino field hospital, 120 kilometers away from the fighting. Once there, he waited in line to be examined by a doctor and, depending on the urgency, selected to be taken to the operating room.

> It was my turn pretty quickly and I was pushed into an anteroom. There was blood everywhere and severed limbs lay in one corner. A soldier's lower leg was still stuck in a boot. I felt sick and panicked. A doctor came to my stretcher.
>
> "What is wrong with him?" he asked.
>
> "Shot through the thigh," replied the paramedic, "he has lost a lot of blood, we should operate right away."
>
> "They'll prepare everything," the paramedic said to me.
>
> "Please don't cut my leg," I said in panic.
>
> "We'll do our best boy, don't worry," the doctor replied.
>
> That with all this horror someone could still be so calm and friendly impresses me to this day. From then on everything went very quickly, I was anesthetized with ether, then it went black. When I opened my eyes, the first thing to do was vomit because of the ether. I didn't know where I was. What actually happened? The sniper? My leg? These thoughts shot through my head. My hand slowly slid towards the thigh. It was still there, what luck![11]

A few days later more men from his battalion arrived in the hospital. Wittenberg approached them for news of his comrade and the officer who had saved him. The news was terrible. His assault team advancing had suffered casualties, with several men killed and their bodies recovered a few days later. There was no news of his shot comrade in the cellar and the officer Wittenberg described who had rescued him had been killed in the continued fighting.[12]

As with the destruction of Wittenberg's unit over the next few days, the fighting for the northern district would degenerate into vicious localized firefights, attack, counterattack, and intimate brawls that consumed whole units. Red Army officers being very aware that there was nowhere else to go if they did not halt the German assault. Chuiko signed off on his final words to his commanders:

> The enemy must be destroyed at whatever cost! Shoot soldiers and commanders who willfully abandon their foxholes and positions on the spot as enemies of the Fatherland.[13]

Yet still, despite the losses and the Germans' remorseless grinding their way into the Factory District, the 62nd Army managed to hold on to some semblance of the western bank, even though by now it was merely a few hundred yards in depth and Chuikov's own headquarters was under constant bombardment. At a higher level, the Stavka had finally reorganized the running of the campaign to a more manageable structure, splitting the Stalingrad Front into two commands: the Don Front and the Stalingrad Front. Both fronts would be reinforced from the reserve forces husbanded farther to the east, with Chuikov supplied just enough to keep going. This was in stark contrast to Paulus's urgent pleas for fresh troops for a final push, which were rebuffed by Army High Command. He was hamstrung to effect a positive result as his artillery tried to thwart the steady flow of fresh troops coming across the Volga to block his every move forward. A lull now set in across the center of the city, as both sides contemplated the next and perhaps final move.

CHAPTER FOURTEEN

The Last Assault of the Sixth Army: Operation Hubertus

The Bolshevists attack until total exhaustion and defend
themselves until the physical extermination of the last man
and weapon. . . . Sometimes the individual will fight beyond
the point considered humanly possible.

—Das Schwarze Korps,
October 29, 1942[1]

In his November 8 speech to old comrades of the Party faithful who
had been with him since the Beer Hall Putsch in Munich, Hitler
infamously boasted that Stalingrad's fall was now imminent. He basked
in the applause and laughter as he celebrated nine years since taking
power. The handpicked audience lapped up the Fuhrer's apparent belief
that his Sixth Army was about to deliver the killer blow to the enemy
at Stalingrad. What is striking is a later line from that speech where he
discussed the doubts many in the country and possibly in the Party felt
at the losses that were mounting up. The regime could manipulate the
news, but it couldn't hide the vast numbers of wounded being shipped
back from the east, or the telegrams arriving at the doors of German
families with news of their son's or husband's death. For Hitler, with
the summer campaign a clear failure, now was the time the country
needed to make itself ready for the prolonged war he knew too well
awaited them:

We have opponents. There can be no mercy allowed them. On the contrary, there is only one possibility: either we fall, or our opponent falls. We are aware of that, and we are men enough to look this knowledge straight in the eye, cool as ice. And that differentiates me from those gentlemen in London and America; if I demand much of the German soldier, I am demanding no more than I myself have always been ready to do also.[2]

In reality Paulus's army was by now exhausted from the continued fighting to take the Factory District. The Soviets were in no better shape, as Chuikov fed into the maelstrom whatever reinforcements Yeremenko could give him without upsetting the buildup of General Zhukov's forces for the big offensive being secretly assembled. From the beginning of November right up to the point of Hitler's speech a lull had settled over the ruined city as the Soviets tried to predict the next move and the Germans prepared their newly won territory in the Factory District for what they hoped would be the final offensive to claim victory. Paulus now occupied the vast portion of the city's southern and central districts and had almost free movement in the Tractor Factory, the Barrikady Gun Factory, and at least half of the Red October Steel Plant. Hence Hitler's boasts. The Russians still clung on to the worker's settlements along the river and the Chemical Plant. They were so close to the river now that Chuikov joked he could actually dangle his legs into the freezing Volga. His ace in the hole was now the massed artillery assembled on the eastern bank, which could send across deadly accurate barrages onto any German formation 62nd Army spotters in the city could detect. The survivors awaiting the final offensive were anxious of the coming fighting, but Chuikov and his staff clung to their belief in Stalin's Order No. 227: "Not One Step Back!"

During Stalingrad the desire to kill seems to have reached an obsession, as Ivan Vasil'ev, head of the Political Dept of the 62nd Army at Stalingrad, revealed, "I should say that I didn't see or hear or get any intelligence about Red Army men under any battle conditions showing any sort of pity for the Germans. What is more, even if there wasn't anyone to stick with a bayonet, they would stab the dead."[3]

Sixth Army's repeated pleas for fresh troops and armor were appeased to a degree when Hitler agreed to send five battalions of assault pioneers, experts in urban combat, armed with submachine guns, satchel charges, and flamethrowers into the city for the task ahead. Supporting them would be combat engineers and several amalgamated new storm companies consisting of combat-worthy troops from tired-out divisions. With a shortage of combat commanders Sixth Army administrative staffers had been concerned at the low turnout of non-commissioned ranks to be candidates for officer training, with many of the men questioned stating that they preferred not to go into the front line as an officer. Fresh armor was also provided—a dozen new, very powerful self-propelled guns, perfect for house assault, as well as powerful 210mm howitzers. These would be complimented by twenty-two newly arrived StuG IIIs to replace the losses from the previous assault. All told it was a dynamic, heavily armed, combat-ready force thought powerful enough to finally kill off the 62nd Army.

November 11 saw the temperature drop yet further, bringing a stinging cold wind from the east as the waters of the Volga within a few weeks turned from slush to become floating, drifting ice. Such was the power of the flowing current that the river rarely froze over solid. But the arrival of wintry conditions, by its very nature, worried any Sixth Army veteran from 1941. Paulus had delayed the coming attack hoping the ice would be his ally in preventing Chuikov from being resupplied as the crossing became dangerously unstable. But the Volga continued to offer a viable pathway, despite the Luftwaffe operations, which were now being contested by a resurgent Soviet air force. Aware of German forces massing for a fresh assault, Chuikov's forces had been busy over the past days rebuilding their lines during the hours of darkness:

A powerful fortified defence net had taken shape on our main line. In a month and a half [from the beginning of October to mid-November] over 150 blockhouses and pill boxes and more than fifty dug outs had been built and equipped. Sappers had laid more than ten thousand anti-tank and anti-personnel mines.[4]

Chuikov had also instructed his commissars to go into the front-line positions to maintain discipline—he was aware his troops were exhausted and fearing the worst. He now brought in penal battalions—units comprised of soldiers found guilty by NKVD tribunals of coward-ice or political misconduct[5]—who were given the necessary weapons for tank hunting. The defenders were badly in need of food and supplies, with little ammunition to spare. They would meet the assault by seven German divisions across a five-kilometer front with ferocious defense.

As both sides made their preparations, civilians still trapped in Sta-lingrad tried to survive. Five-year-old Valentina Savelyeva's family had survived the bombing that August, and the multiple aerial assaults and artillery barrages, until their home had been destroyed in the fighting in late October. Now, as winter set in, she and her mother had fled to a nearby ravine leading down to the Volga. She remembered:

When I close my eyes, I can see the Volga on fire because of spilt oil. We dug holes in the clay to live in—not trenches, but holes, like real animal holes. Soon there was heavy fighting inside the ravine. German tanks moved up and down, while female Soviet pilots dropped bombs on them, and therefore on us. Everything was on fire and we heard thunder and planes roaring. The most horrible moment was around November when the Germans broke through down the ravine towards the Red October plant. It was very scary.

At first we just sat there in our dugouts, then our parents went out to help the wounded with their disjointed limbs. They would bandage the hands and legs, then medical staff would appear and take them away. Down by the Volga there was a hospital.

There was no food, only the local mud, which happened to be slightly sweet. We ate clay and nothing but clay, and we drank water from the Volga. My mother would throw away the bits of clay that were soaked in blood, and then take the rest and filter it through a piece of cloth.[6] [The sugar in the clay kept her alive, but not her little brother who died of hunger and cold].

On November 11, Valentina, along with the rest of the city, was suddenly shaken by a series of tremendous explosions before dawn, at 3 a.m., as a sudden preparatory barrage paved the way for the new German offensive—Operation Hubertus—to roll out. Paulus's gamble to destroy the 62nd Army's final forces became yet another back-and-forth bloody struggle as German armor and infantry were ground down against fanatical Soviet resistance, inflicting significant casualties. In the fighting of what became famous as "Lyudnikov's Island" (named after the Soviet commander Colonel Ivan Lyudnikov), the survivors of Lyudnikov's 138th Rifle Division matched the performance of any Red Army unit in Stalingrad. The unit rushed across the Volga to blunt Paulus taking the Barrikady Gun Factory worker's village—defending a strip of land 700 meters by 400 meters (approximately 2,300 feet by 1,300 feet) that was surrounded on three sides, with only the frozen Volga to their backs. All efforts to relieve the trapped Soviet division failed, but they maintained a presence as Chuikov bamboozled German radio monitors with fabricated calls to Lyudnikov telling him reinforcements were on the way. He had none to spare. At one point of the attack a German unit was forced to bring in a 20mm flak gun to suppress Soviet snipers as they made multiple assaults to take a fortification. German pioneer squads drove Soviet defenders into cellars, ripped up the flooring, and poured gasoline down on them before setting it alight. Again, operational goals became bogged down in brutal house-to-house and room-by-room shoot-outs and knife fights. By November 17, what remained of Paulus's shattered divisions were forced to a standstill yet again, mirroring the failure in the Caucasus of Army Group A, which had halted less than a hundred kilometers from their target of the oil installations at Grozny.

Russia's 62nd and 64th Armies had performed their duty and bled Army Group B to exhaustion, as they conducted a fighting retreat from

July through to the fighting subsiding in Stalingrad on November 18. In terms of casualties in men and tanks the Red Army had suffered a disparity of 5 to 1 compared to Axis casualties.[7] Yet the Russians had the ability to endure such losses, in readiness for the sledgehammer that was about to hit their weakened enemy's flanks.

PART V

THE GREATEST VICTORY

Everything is indeed changing. And the Germans who had broken through to one street in September, had ensconced themselves in city apartment blocks, and danced to the noisy music of mouth organs, those Germans who had gone about at night with torches and had by day brought up trucks of ammunition have now had to hide in the earth and stone ruins.

—Vasily Grossman, *Red Star,*
January 1, 1943

CHAPTER FIFTEEN

"Twentieth Century Cannae": Operation Uranus

The Russians no longer have any reserves worth mentioning
and are not capable of launching a large-scale offensive.
—Chief of the General Staff, Colonel
General Kurt Zeitzler[1]

On November 18, Chuikov received a call from Yeremenko's headquarters to expect a special order at midnight. He and his staff knew
nothing of the new offensive, code-named Operation Uranus. Stalin,
Vasilevsky, and Zhukov had deliberately kept it from the Stalingrad Front
commanders to maintain security and to ensure that the men would
continue to fight with intensity. Chuikov later offered the opinion that
he and his senior officers had a "feeling" a fresh offensive was coming:

We had sensed that our high command was preparing a major attack,
but we didn't know where exactly. We had sensed this from the very
beginning of November. We were being given less and less help. We'd
been used to talking to people from front HQ every day, but now
they'd all vanished. Khrushchev wasn't here, and Yeremenko came
only once.[2]

The Stavka still needed the remnants of their respective armies to
be the bait in General Zhukov's trap to tie down the bulk of German

forces in the city and give the counteroffensive the best possible chance of success. Chuikov ordered all 62nd Army units to undertake probing attacks along his line of defense. Rodimtsev's 13th Guards Division made nightly advances from their fortifications in the central district to find out what the Germans were now planning and whether it was possible to recapture strategic points lost in the fighting the previous weeks.

For Paulus and German Army Group B staff officers the buildup of Soviet forces had been sporadically noted for many weeks. As far back as October 15 an increase in new units had been monitored against Army Group B's northern flank but was considered smaller in threat to a noticeable convergence of Soviet armies elsewhere. German military intelligence indicated that an offensive against Army Group Center's Ninth Army was more probable once the autumn rains had passed. Hitler, although focused on Stalingrad, and wary of the reliability of the threat, nevertheless ordered Colonel General Zeitzler to move reinforcements guarding the English Channel and reallocate them to shore up Army Group B. By the time of Paulus launching Operation Hubertus in his final push to take the city, daily reports were arriving at Army High Command telling of the arrival of new Russian tank armies opposite the Romanian Third Army's positions, and of a new front headquarters suddenly appearing (the Don Front), indicating a whole level of activity, but still there was no hint of panic. German intelligence now concluded that the picture was not clear enough to make a definitive assessment of an imminent attack.

Since their first discussion with Stalin during the crisis of mid-September, Zhukov and Vasilevsky had expanded and refined their operation. While Paulus battered his way through Chuikov's defenses, the Russian pair had overseen a massive escalation of armored and infantry forces around Stalingrad. From the Soviet railheads miles behind the front line, hundreds of horse-drawn columns supported twenty-seven thousand mainly American-built trucks to create the fuel, ammunition, and supply dumps necessary to sustain the new military buildup: 4 tank armies, 3 mechanized corps, 14 independent tank brigades, and 3 tank regiments, backed up by 115 Katyusha battalions containing more than 1,000,000 men and a rebuilt Soviet air force of 1,100 aircraft.[3]

This would be an overwhelming force. The Russians had learned their mistakes the hard way over the previous eighteen months. The level of secrecy in husbanding their forces and coordinating a two-pronged offensive with armored infantry deep in Army Group B's territory was stunning in its conception. On the night Chuikov was informed of the following day's offensive, an exasperated Paulus was confiding to a war correspondent at 389th Division's headquarters: "I do not know what I have got left to fight with." Paulus's cry for help almost sums up how the German high command's relationship with their supreme commander had disintegrated into paranoia and mistrust, compared to how Stalin's ability to learn from his mistakes (and they had been highly costly ones) had freed up his most talented strategists to provide genuine solutions to achieve strategic victory.

Meanwhile, in Moscow on November 13, Stalin finally instructed Zhukov and Vasilevsky to present their plans for Operation Uranus to the stunned (but impressed) members of the Politburo and the Stavka, and lecture all attendees on their intended plan for an all-arms coordinated offensive and the makeup of every unit that would achieve it.

Operation Uranus began at 0720 hours the following morning with the issuing of the code word "siren." The weather had taken a turn for the worse, with heavy snow landing on the rock-solid ground, perfect conditions for the hundreds of T-34 tanks about to be unleashed on the German Sixth Army's northern flank. Ten minutes later, to the north of Stalingrad, Chuikov's units, buried in the ruins of the city and fighting atop the Mamayev Kurgan, heard the distant rumble of an offensive beginning. It was the combined might of the 3,500 guns and mortars of the 21st Army and the 5th Tank Army of General Nikolai F. Vatutin's Southwestern Front and the forces of Lieutenant General Konstantin K. Rokossovsky's Don Front launching a ferocious eighty-minute artillery barrage upon the beleaguered Romanian Army. As soon as the shelling finished wreaking its havoc on the barely sufficient Axis defenses—in many cases simple trench works dug in the frozen steppe—Russian infantry and tanks went in along a two-hundred-mile front in the first wave, to exploit openings. The following day, to the south of Stalingrad, the Soviet 51st and 57th Armies of Colonel General Yeremenko's Stalingrad Front launched their own offensive against the Romanian IV Army, which had only recently taken command of the VI and VII Romanian Corps. Yeremenko's assault covered a 125-mile front. Though not as powerful as the northern offensive, it had the same effect on the Axis forces it faced—sheer terror, some sporadic defense, and then rapid withdrawal in the face of Soviet armor.

The Red Army outnumbered the Romanians in infantry by a factor of three to one, the latter having little in the way of adequate antitank capability to match the T-34s advancing through the fog and snow toward their weakened positions. As with the previous winter offensive, outside the gates of Moscow, the Russians used their Cossack horse cavalry to venture deep into Axis lines and capture strategic points and supply dumps, and to confuse and bewilder the enemy. As the flank attacks would progress, Shumilov's 64th Army would make local attacks around the city itself to tie down the German IV Corps. Chuikov's 62nd Army would continue to fight tenaciously for every scrap of land in the central and northern districts, against the bulk of Paulus's shattered forces.

As Halder, Zeitzler, Army Group B's commander von Weichs, and now Paulus himself had feared, there was very little in the way of infantry or amored reserves to prevent the Russian assaults developing into something more serious. The weight of Soviet forces broke like a wave against the Axis armies—though isolated Axis units managed to hold the enemy at bay for a few hours, the Germans' lack of solid defenses guaranteed eventual breakthroughs by Zhukov's armor. The rout began as the Romanians in the north broke first—thousands fleeing westward and south toward the city. Amid the freezing conditions, the roads became clogged with lines of beleaguered stragglers, hundreds of abandoned vehicles, the carcasses of shot horses too exhausted to continue, and human corpses everywhere. All the while the retreating forces suffered the constant panic of whether more enemy attacks would appear out of the low-lying mist that enveloped the fields all around. In scenes reminiscent of the disintegration of Tsar Nicolas's own imperial army in the Great War, the Axis forces' discipline was now disintegrating under pressure, and Paulus's own reserves were not enough to stem the tide. The Red Army swept along, continually encountering fierce resistance from isolated units, which they either fought and enveloped if they were armored, or simply bypassed for the second wave to deal with. Frozen bodies were littered in their wake, as one Red Army officer based in the city noted:

> Their clothes were simply wrong for the weather. . . . The winter of 1942 in Stalingrad was unprecedentedly cold. Locals said it was the coldest one in many years. Windy, too: when those winds from the Kazakh steppes would start . . . this is what we wore: regular underwear, thermal underwear (made of cotton, but thick), then a shirt-tunic, then regular pants and on top—quilted ones, a cotton wool-padded jacket (officers had them from goat or sheep wool), then a sheep-skin half-coat, felt boots over two or three layers of foot cloths.[4]

Both sides were now in a race westward, the Russian forces to join as intended at the confluence of the Dona and Chir Rivers, miles behind the original German front line, at the pivotal transport hub of Kalach, while the Germans attempted to mobilize what armored formations they could to attempt a counterattack at local levels—all micromanaged by Hitler, who had excused himself weeks earlier back to the Berghof, the home in the Bavarian Alps where, other than the Wolf's Lair, he spent the most time. On November 19 Paulus was ordered to cease operations in the city against Chuikov and assemble what armored and infantry divisions he could spare to move out of Stalingrad to save his left flank from collapsing as the Russian armies closed around it. While this was underway, the rest of the German Sixth Army would adopt a defensive posture. It would be a wasted opportunity due to the German Panzers running out of fuel before they closed with their enemy. The fresh offensive in the south now caught them off guard as the Romanian VI and VII Corps supposedly supporting Fourth Panzer Army's flank turned tail and ran from the onrushing T-34s. The Fourth Army was split in two as a result, the majority of it marooned in the encirclement. This was no local offensive, but a strategic earthquake across southern Russia.

The scale and ambition of the Red Army's plans had been shielded by their use of *mashirovka*, the art of concealment through camouflage, disguise, and deception. During the buildup, troops had been under strict orders to only be transported at night and remain bivouacked undercover during the day to avoid the attentions of von Richthofen's Luftwaffe reconnaissance planes. The technique had been perfected over the past three months and was now making the Germans pay the price of their mistaken belief that the Soviets were still unable to coordinate and implement multiple offensives. The German leaders faced a "three-front" offensive: to not only encircle and destroy Paulus at Stalingrad and envelop all Axis forces stretched thin along his flanks, but to then close the door to the north of Army Group A by pushing on to recapture Rostov and control the whole of the Caucasus. Fresh offensives would then launch against Army Group Center farther to the north. Adolf Hitler's dreams of early summer lay in ruins as his whole southern army now seemed bound to become trapped and destroyed.

The Germans could only react with what was at their disposal. At the local level the Sixth Army, caught out in the freezing steppe countryside, fought a bitter fighting retreat eastward back toward the city, supported by whatever armored units Paulus could muster. Hitler left his Bavarian retreat to reach his headquarters in East Prussia and conduct discussions with Field Marshal Erich von Manstein, the conqueror of the Crimea with his 11th Army, as to how to stabilize the whole front and relieve Sixth Army from its predicted encirclement. Army Group A would need to pull back from their southerly positions to form a secure new defensive line and be redesignated Army Group Don. The main question was whether Paulus's Sixth Army could stand

and fight while an effective relief across more than one hundred miles of enemy territory was organized and implemented.

Within two days of Uranus being launched, with Hitler now ensconced in East Prussia, Russian armored formations rolled toward their target of Kalach, to seal Sixth Army's fate. At Paulus's headquarters his staff hurriedly destroyed documents amid the sound of distant Russian artillery fire getting closer. They departed in time from their base at Golubinsky as T-34s appeared on the horizon, Paulus flying twenty miles southwest to set up at Nizhne-Chirskaia, which he had already intended to make his winter quarters. Awaiting his arrival was a communiqué from Hitler with clear instructions as to next steps: "The Commander-in-Chief will proceed with his staff to Stalingrad. The Sixth Army will form an all-round defensive position and await further orders." A second order followed soon after: "Those units of the Sixth Army that remain between the Don and Volga will henceforth be designated 'Fortress Stalingrad.'"[5]

Paulus received a visitor before dawn the next morning: Hoth of the Fourth Panzer Army. Both men discussed the continuous flow of signals coming in from Axis units spread across the steppe, all fighting desperately in a confused state to escape Russian armor appearing out of nowhere. It was similar to the near catastrophe of Moscow the previous December. Reports came in that the vital crossing outside of Kalach had been taken by Soviet tanks unopposed, and the Germans now faced the inevitable conclusion—they were surrounded. The new line of defense the five German corps and their allies fell back to from the onslaught now measured approximately fifty-six by thirty-two kilometres (thirty-five miles wide by twenty miles in depth). Seven Soviet armies with ninety-four divisions between them now surrounded twenty German divisions (fourteen infantry, three Panzer, and three motorized), what remained of three Romanian divisions, and a single Croatian infantry regiment. General Zhukov and Colonel General Vasilevsky believed the success of Uranus had yielded 85,000 to 90,000 Axis troops trapped in the encirclement, but in reality it was close to 320,000 men, with approximately 100 tanks, 1,800 artillery pieces, 10,000 vehicles, and 23,000 horses. Though it would take the Soviets days to realize the size of the German pocket they now had to crush, to Paulus and Hoth and their respective commanders the scale of their predicament was all too evident.

Paulus was a fervent believer in the chain of command. Unlike his predecessor, von Reichenau, this Sixth Army commander was not one to take the initiative, as some of his most senior officers reminded him when they argued the best course of action. Unaware of similar arguments erupting from within Hitler's Wolf's Lair, Paulus's head of LI Corps, General Walter von Seydlitz-Kurzbach, now attempted to force the issue, encouraging his own divisional commanders to take the necessary steps to make the men ready for a breakout west. The 94th Infantry Division would take the lead in the northeast of the new perimeter, with the hope that it might well instigate a knock-on effect to other formations and a full-scale march to the southwest. As night came, the division's units began to burn all supplies and equipment and blow up ammunition dumps, and then they vacated their well-built positions opposite a division of the Soviet 66th Army, whose soldiers were astonished at the burning glare coming from across the frozen steppe. Caught out in the open, the 94th Division was mercilessly attacked by Chuikov's forces and almost destroyed. On hearing the news, Hitler believed Paulus responsible, when in fact he'd had no idea of the insubordination of his corps commander. The Fuhrer now took the first step in sealing the fate of the Sixth Army by issuing a direct command that "Sixth Army will adopt hedgehog defense. . . . Present Volga front and northern front to be held at all costs. . . . Supplies coming by air."[6]

While Paulus digested and then complied with the order, all that day back at Hitler's headquarters the debate raged as to what would be the final decision: fight or flight? Hitler had initially been convinced by his senior commanders such as Zeitzler that a breakout was the only option to save Sixth Army, which had now as little as six days' worth of supplies left to defend itself. Zeitzler had been convinced his argument had swayed the Fuhrer, only to then witness Hermann Göring declaring that the Luftwaffe would achieve the impossible and supply the trapped

Paulus with the estimated five hundred tons of supplies he needed per day to survive. Had this not worked the previous winter with the Ninth Army trapped at Demyansk?[7] The lack of suitable aircraft, the weather conditions, and the growing threat of the Soviet Air Force apparently did not factor into Göring's thinking. An incandescent Zeitzler raged at this foolhardy promise, arguing statistics and figures that undermined Göring's claims, only for Hitler to come down on his longtime ally's side. They would scour the operational theaters for enough aircraft and pilots to do the job, Hitler explaining a few weeks later to his crestfallen general as von Manstein's rescue offensive began:

> I have, on the whole, considered one thing. . . . We must not give [Stalingrad] up now under any circumstances. We won't win it back again. We know what that means . . . to imagine that one can do it a second time, if one goes back and the materiel is left lying, that's ridiculous. They can't take everything with them. . . . What isn't brought out by motor will be left behind. . . . We can't possibly replace that stuff we have inside. If we give that up, we surrender the whole meaning of this campaign. To imagine that I shall come here another time is madness. Now, in winter, we can construct a blocking position with those forces. . . . We are not coming back here a second time. That is why we must not leave here. Besides, too much blood has been shed for that.[8]

Despite now agreeing with his Fuhrer's directive to form a hedgehog defense, Paulus still faced internal disputes from his own officers as to what they should or shouldn't be allowed to do to rescue the situation. The commander of LI Corps, von Seydlitz-Kurzbach, cabled Paulus:

> The [Sixth] Army is faced with a clear alternative: breakthrough to the south-west . . . or face annihilation within a few days. . . . Unless the Army Command immediately rescinds its order to hold out in a hedgehog position it becomes our inescapable duty to the army and to the German people to seize that freedom of action that we are being denied by the present order, and to take the opportunity

which still exists at this moment to avert catastrophe by making the attack ourselves. The complete annihilation of 250,000 fighting men and their entire equipment is at stake. There is no choice.[9]

Within the confines of their well-entrenched positions in the city, the 71st Division had begun to follow what their corps commander had initially ordered the 94th Division to do—prepare for breakout. In the relative protection of the GPO Prison complex where his regiment was now ensconced, Lieutenant Colonel Roske managed to write his thoughts to his wife about the ongoing crisis:

> *My dear good Bärbel,*
> *We, the whole Sixth Army, are enclosed by the Russians, and re-inforcements are cut off. In the North and in the South, the Russian broke through to the Romanians with masses of tanks, and they [the Romanians] apparently partly went over to the enemy, partly came back in floods, completely broken. After we had previously heard about these assaults, the General called us to a meeting, saying, "The situation is serious—very serious." He explained the naked truth: The Führer wished to have a period of consultation until 7 a.m. the following morning (24 November), for him to decide as to whether Stalingrad should be evacuated and for our troops to break out OR whether to stay and hold out. In the meantime, all preparations had to be made in order for our forces could be made mobile. Because we had some of our horses far back (where the Russians are now positioned) in so-called "Recovery Areas" because of difficulties with feeding them in the city; we have lots of winter clothes, ammunition, food provisions, equipment for the winter fighting—but putting all that weight onto trucks was going to be difficult, let alone being pulled by horses.*
> *The reported news and increased rumours made everything more difficult. Soon I had composed myself again and told General [von Hartmann] how long we [71st Infantry Division] still had provisions. We had already baked our own first bread. We had set*

up the mill again and brought wheat from the old [grain] silo. I
had experience of this from the previous winter's fighting in Russia.
We also still had enough horses to slaughter. So, whether we had
to remain and defend our position and wait for a break-through
was possible. The thought of breaking out and planning for it was
discussed, too.

The divisional admin staff, officers, and radio operators, etc.
burnt all written correspondence, orders, and files. Horses that
are still healthy were brought into our positions, vehicles, carts,
equipment, and personal items would have to remain if we broke
out. Orders were [then] issued in case of having to leave our current
positions—and routes back through were scouted out. The prob-
ability of breaking out back to the rear, "was a ninety per cent
certainty" we were told.

The thought of dismantling everything and destroying supplies
is awful for everybody. You need to have a strong disposition to
become used to this thought. You need a bit of gallows humour and
cynicism to help you through that. I cannot write any more now, I
am going to have to catch up with it at some other time.

Your husband,
Fritz.[10]

With the circulation of Hitler's latest directive, the officers and men,
like the rest of their Sixth Army comrades, now knew they were staying
until Manstein would rescue them, his cable to Paulus at Sixth Army
headquarters the same day stating:

Will assume command on 26 November. Shall do everything in my
power to relieve you. . . . In the mean time it is imperative that Sixth
Army, while holding the Volga and north front in compliance with
Fuhrer orders, forms up forces in order, if necessary, to clear a supply
channel toward the southwest. Manstein.[11]

News soon spread that "Manstein *kommt!*" ("Mannstein is coming!")
Roske again wrote to his wife the news:

Then—at noon—"breakout is not likely." At the meeting of com-
manders in the cellar of the warehouse we received the liberating
radio message: "The Army will remain and defend!" The joy in our
hearts at this revealed to us how this undercurrent of pressure had
been weighing down on us all. Back in the prison at lunch we had a
bottle of champagne—in small glasses, so that there was enough to
go round. I was able, with a shaky voice, to thank the Führer, and
to express our vow that we would indeed defend and hold out.[12]

As the Sixth Army finally settled upon organizing an effective pocket
defense, inside the central district of the city both the German 71st
Infantry and the Russian 13th Guards Rifle Divisions remained locked
in sporadic combat. It would again entail heavy fighting for control of,
among other strategic areas, the 9th January Square and a tragic set of
events that would decimate the garrison of Pavlov's House.

CHAPTER SIXTEEN

The Relentless Fight

Every house [in Stalingrad] has become an impregnable fortress. . . . Stalingrad's defenders are fighting for every house, every barn, and every garden. Every house has become a firing position. Stalingrad's defenders are performing miracles of bravery, dedication and loyalty to and for the motherland.[1]

Once Operation Uranus had borne fruit with the successful encirclement of Paulus's army, Chuikov needed to maintain the pressure on his trapped foe, the Germans now hastily reassessing their positions within their pocket or *"Kessel"* ("cauldron"), as it would be known, some miles outside the city. Within Stalingrad, the fighting died down to a degree as the remnants of Chuikov's 62nd Army dug in after the final assault on the northern district. More reinforcements were making their way across the Volga to be fed to the final redoubts around the strip of land where the Soviets had fought the Germans to a standstill. Rodimtsev's units, still facing a strong and motivated enemy in the central part of Stalingrad, were ordered to dig in where they were, to hold the line along the streets the men had taken, and ensure that their position was fortified to hold back any enemy incursions. Though badly understrength, Rodimtsev was instructed to keep the German center bottled up and to secure the main crossing point by the central pier. Across from his lines, the 71st and 295th Infantry Divisions of the German LI Corps were doing the same as they awaited news as to what the Sixth Army would do: fight or flight? In the meantime, strategic decisions had to be made on the Russian side concerning the imposing buildings—now fortifications—the Germans controlled almost overlooking the central embankment. These needed to be eliminated. Afanasiev's small garrison within Pavlov's House would soon be called into action, too.

Using what units he could from the 42nd, 39th, and 34th Regiments, whichever was closest to the designated target, Rodimtsev would continue the task of attempting to push the Germans out of strongholds they had held for more than two months. By now, very much like the Russians' own defenses, the enemy had heavily fortified their positions with minefields, barbed wire entanglements, and well-constructed firing points offering clear fields of fire that interlocked the whole front. It was an incredibly tough nut to crack. Rodimtsev's guardsmen had been forced to perfect their techniques of assault the hard way—through trial and error, costing many men.

They had tried and failed numerous times to take and hold various buildings, but were continually beaten back by German counterattacks and artillery. The Soviet assault groups had also suffered from a lack of morale to maintain an attack if the designated leader was killed. Each time this happened, the survivors lost focus and retreated, and thus caught out in the open, or with their flank exposed, they suffered further casualties. There was also an issue of failing to quickly reinforce what gains were made in the initial assault, allowing the Germans to respond, too. All these areas needed to be resolved. They would be eventually, but not before one more disastrous assault, this time involving Pavlov's House.

On the evening of November 24, Lieutenant Afanasiev picked up the receiver in Pavlov's House and heard Battalion Commander Zhukov's voice: "We are paying you a visit! Alert the men—they'll have work to do." Half an hour later Zhukov arrived with his deputy Senior Lieutenant Naumov; the commander of the company's machine gun section, Senior Lieutenant Aleksey A. Dorokhov; Commissar Avagimov; and Junior Lieutenant Alexei Anikin, who was commanding the small garrison in "Zabolotny's House" a few hundred yards away. Behind them, heavily armed, followed about two dozen soldiers. The party made their way down to the cellar, where the new assault troops sat to rest in an adjoining room while Zhukov discussed the upcoming attack with his officers.

The engineers would provide pathways through the minefield and then cut gaps in the razor wire entanglements that had been originally put in place by Afanasiev weeks earlier to protect Pavlov's House. Zhukov gathered his officers around the map table and placed a diagram of 9th January Square in front of them. He pointed his finger at a familiar building they all had come to hate—the "Milk House," garrisoned by the German 295th Division and directly opposite the Russian positions across the square. The officers and men were electrified by the news—the whole garrison of Pavlov's House would be going on the offensive. For the first time in almost two months of continuous fighting they would be leaving the place that they had rendered habitable.

The Milk House had been a formidable and deadly objective since Rodimtsev himself had ordered its capture. Much like Pavlov's House it served as an excellent spotter's vantage point for German artillery to rain down accurate fire on the Volga and on the Mamayev Kurgan. Lieutenant Afanasiev recounted in his memoir that from his position atop Pavlov's House he had a bird's-eye view of the proximity of the Russians' own 42nd Regiment fortifications behind him, and to his left and right the various buildings that stood like sentinels overlooking his division's lines. All the buildings had been heavily reinforced by German forces, including the 71st Infantry Division, and with the encirclement they were being strengthened further:

> We had code names for all the nearby buildings: "the Milk House" (named after the colour of its outer walls), the L-shaped house, the House of Railway Workers, the Voentorg House, the Brewery, etc. Some buildings bore the names of commanders: on the left, not far away from us, there was the Zabolotny's House, too.[2]

* * *

On the morning of November 25, the assault party went in, quickly scrambling across the square, jumping from crater to crater as Soviet artillery laid a barrage in front of them, pinning the German defenders in their shelters as Naumov's team advanced. They were soon upon them, driving the Germans out with grenades and machine gun fire. Then disaster struck. The building was by now coming under more fire from a German counterattack, mortars landing all around the Russians' newly won position. Naumov's men looked for any cover they could find amid the intense barrage but discovered to their horror that the Milk House, unlike the vast majority of buildings occupied during the battle, did not possess a cellar. They were now trapped in the house, unable to safely retreat and coming under attack by German infantry who lobbed stick grenades through blackened, windowless holes. Several attacks were repulsed by Naumov's garrison throughout the day and into the night. By the next morning the Germans had brought up an artillery piece which blasted the walls, driving the survivors to seek protection under the intact stairs within the house. By now it was desperate. Naumov rushed across the square to inform headquarters of their predicament but was cut down and killed. Colonel Elin ordered a retreat. More of the assault team were killed as they ran for cover—both Lieutenant Afanasiev and Junior Sergeant Pavlov were wounded as they reached the safety of the regimental line. The square was littered with corpses as both sides continued to pour on suppressing fire. By the evening hostilities had died down. Most of the men from Pavlov's House who had ventured out were now dead. Sergeant Pavlov himself was carried away with a serious leg wound, Lieutenant Afanasiev scrambled back with multiple flesh wounds and suspected shell shock. Senior Lieutenant Anton Dragan, recovered from his dramatic escape from the first week's fighting, was now ordered by Colonel Elin to take command of 7th Company.

As the fighting intensified for the other buildings in the 13th Guards Division's operational area, on the German side, Lieutenant Colonel Roske of I.R. 194 was in the thick of it. As his letters home to his wife display, the combat was intense:

Stalingrad, 24 November

Since the day before yesterday, the Russian has been trying to break into my left flank. [They] penetrated two of the larger houses [fortresses], the "Alex" and the "School," during the night. In the "Alex" they came over collapsed parts of the sixth floor; my men remained on the ground floor and in the cellar. In the "School" he [the Russian] was on the top floor, and part of the ground floor; we remained on the ground floor and in the cellar.

Despite this chaos: "I ventured bravely with my senses . . ."[3]

I ordered more men and a PAK[4] be brought to me and had those parts of the building in Russian hands be shot to pieces. The places where the Russians were above us, I ordered to be blown up. We used hand grenades continuously. The Russians held out for a further twelve hours after having repulsed several of our attacks. We had to throw 5-kg loads of explosive through the windows. When this still didn't work as we hoped for, I called for help from the other building, who joined with my men to blow holes through the adjoining walls and attack that way. It was almost impossible to protect the artilleryman, whom we had quickly tried to train in our assault tactics. They couldn't keep up, didn't fully understand the situation, and it was difficult to instill strength and maintain their morale with all the blood and death around us.

Stalingrad, 25 November

That afternoon the "Alex" house collapsed into rubble. The Russians were trying to burn down the remaining parts—which [they didn't realise] was also in our interest; I didn't disturb them during this time. They weren't successful though. Where the School ruins were—which was still partly offering us protection the previous day; we then tried to clean it out [of Russians] with three separate assaults—all of which were partly successful. We were entrenched opposite the enemy when he attacked my left flank with 80 subma-chine gunners—which was repulsed. The men carry on in their duty day and night without protection in this hell, food is poor, no time

or possibility of rest. Last night I brought chocolates and cigarettes
for everyone with me to the "School," which I had saved for when the
situation might become more desperate. Still all night the Russians
would attempt to work around our positions and capture the School.
He definitely had to take it—and we had to hold on to what we had.

My battalion commander now had to appear again from [his
CP]—two of his company commanders had fallen, the only ones he
had had in the front. I promoted two junior officers to replace them.
Both great lads. I ordered the battalion commander to personally
assimilate the reinforcements we were expecting to join us. In
the meantime, I circulated the news to the men about the bigger
picture: Most of the base camps are still in our possession! And the
supply depots, too.

The School and our First Aid base were attacked by Russian
tanks. We let them get close, and then put mines over their caterpil-
lar tracks. We had to fight hard to repel them. My whole regiment
fighting now towards the west. Yesterday I received a company
artilleryman for that, who now, without any artillery, horses
or vehicles, belongs to the I.R. 194. Onwards: the fronts looking
towards the South, West, North, stands still. Reinforcements from
the Luftwaffe has been rolling in. The Sixth Army received a radio
announcement from Manstein: "Hold out! I'll bash you out!"
Everywhere I tell this story, there is a great atmosphere.

Stalingrad, 26 November

It was soon going to be morning. I was sleeping when my Adjutant,
Hindenlang, reported to me: "The Russians were still occupying
the School." I make plans to recapture it. My main concern: are
they in the cellars, too? I give an order for a raiding patrol—our
regimental reserve force, including our regimental musicians too,
who have been trained recently to shoot properly. I called Captain
Münch (Commander of the 3rd Battalion) to lead it. I later report
[to Major General von Hartmann] that Combat Post E and the
ruins of the School are [back] in our hands. The Russians have
left behind many dead—no prisoners at all. In the past thirty-six

hours—four Officers lost. And 3rd Battalion's adjutant (Lieutenant Koch) is seriously wounded. (He was leading the assault on Fighting Station E.) My commander of the vehicle pool (Lieutenant Willig, an extremely young person), will now remain as commander of the School garrison.

Now my main concern: Caring for my people and how to keep them warm. The School is now in ruins. I have the cellars inspected, whether one can still go in there, whether they can still be heated. The dead Russians had to be thrown out! It was 9 a.m. In five hours it will be dark again. The pioneers begin to construct new defenses in order to prepare for a counterattack, so that at dusk our positions can be protected. Prisoners are quickly put to work building of barbed wire defenses because in the last few days we have been able to work in here. The ruins of fortress "Alex" need to be staffed, for the protection of the construction workers. Earthworks [built] to our front etc. in order to establish a stronger defensive position, as well as provide some protection from the cold weather. Are there any working fireplaces? Ammunition? Save and ration, distribute, ration. The Russian is bound to come back at night.

Later, I go to inspect the Fighting Station E where my new artillery infantrymen are based and then review the men at the School. Their relief [upon my arrival] is obvious. The Russian artillery forces us to seek shelter, but the men must be able to see their commanders, so that they don't feel like they have been deserted. All the officers have to give advice and build trust for us to succeed. Much has to be done to help, to find out issues, and to solve them.

Well, Bärbel, that's what fighting means. It's a manly job. Hard, but good. We will succeed.

Your old soldier and husband,
Your Fritz

By the first week of December, as Field Marshal von Manstein prepared to launch his rescue offensive for the Sixth Army (Operation Winterstorm), Rodimtsev continued to push his commanders to capture

German positions. After the failure of the Milk House raid, they were adapting to what was required of them and how best to achieve results. Units from Colonel Elin's 42nd Regiment would be chosen for the next task of clearing out enemy positions overlooking and adjacent to 9th January Square: the L-Shaped House and the House of Railway Workers, both formidable fortresses that dominated the central embankment. The capture of the L-Shaped House in particular was coveted by Rodimtsev as it served as the main operational hub for the German sector and as such was heavily fortified.

The two houses were now designated a priority for capture. Elin and his intelligence officers had spent days analyzing the mistakes their assault groups had made and how best they could be reconfigured to ensure success. Intelligence and reconnaissance were improved by scouting intended targets beforehand, working out the enemy's fire plan, and coming up with solutions to neutralize them: digging trenches close to targets, cutting off communication links, seeking blind spots to attack, and using suppressing fire. Attacking in daylight now seemed the preferred option to guarantee good coordination between assault groups and supporting fire from behind, but they had to get across and engage the enemy quickly as well as then rush in reinforcements to hold what they had captured.

Colonel Elin's men had attempted two assaults by tunneling, which had failed as they miscalculated where the German-held building was and came up short. Now they would leave nothing to chance, as he recounted:

The best forty people were allocated to the assault group. They were armed with three grenades and one knife each and eight crampons with ropes, one for each window on the second floor of the building. In addition, the group was reinforced with eight flamethrowers—one flamethrower for each enemy firing point. Six sappers joined them with explosives. They would go in the second wave with a support group of seventy-five men with four heavy machine guns. The 32nd Artillery Regiment would support with concentrated fire. To suppress and destroy the German firing points in the house, 76mm guns and antitank rifles were allocated to be zeroed in on a specific position. When the assault went in the guardsmen took the House of Railway Workers quickly and held them successfully . . .

Elin concludes:

> The assault was, one might say, classic. The assault group during the assault itself did not lose a single person, the losses were insignificant during the battle in the building, the support group suffered small losses—several people were wounded. The German garrison was captured.[5]

The assault and fight for the L-Shaped House would be more intense, with the Soviets making successful entry and driving the enemy out of the various rooms and corridors of its six floors. The Germans fell back but would not be dislodged from their final redoubt at the northern end of the building, as well as putting up a defiant defense of the cellar. The resourcefulness that had now been instilled in the Russian assault group had them lay 250kg of explosives on the main wall protecting the German defenders and blow it up, collapsing one end of the house. Stunned German infantry staggered back to their lines or surrendered to the guardsmen storming in. It was a remarkable victory amid the many costly failures the Russians had endured.

As Rodimtsev's commanders now mapped out further operations most of which would end in stalemate—all German eyes in the city and in the outlying defensive positions of the *Kessel* turned optimistically toward the southwest. Operation Winterstorm was about to be unleashed.

CHAPTER SEVENTEEN

Hope Extinguished:
Christmas in the *Kessel*

He [Field Marshal von Manstein] is the best tactician and commander we have.

—Field Marshal Wolfram Freiherr
von Richthofen

Perhaps Adolf Hitler missed the one opportunity that might have saved Paulus's trapped army in the first week of the encirclement: pull Army Group A back from the Caucasus and drive toward the Volga to open a credible link to rescue him. But at the time, the desire to succeed in the Caucasus and belief that the Luftwaffe could indeed supply the Sixth Army had led him to the needless, almost futile decision to green-light von Manstein's efforts to rescue Paulus and his men with his newly designated Army Group Don. The force von Manstein assembled was never up to the task of breaking the stranglehold the reinforced Russian fronts now had many miles to the south and west of Stalingrad. Operation Winterstorm in theory looked possible, if the forces at von Manstein's disposal had all been fully up to strength and the Luftwaffe could guarantee aerial supremacy. As it was, only the the 6th Panzer Division relocated from France was fresh in men and materiel (Hitler had promised von Manstein four) while the other was depleted of men and machinery. The weather they would be fighting in was atrocious, the terrain was hard going, and the enemy was implacable and well reinforced despite Hitler's assessment that this was only on paper and these units must, in fact, have been denuded of their strength since the encirclement.

Commencing with a short artillery bombardment to break Soviet front-line defenses in a localized area on December 12, von Manstein's relief force at first took the enemy by surprise in the angle of their attack. German armor moved from the farthest point away from Paulus's besieged army and into the Soviets' southwestern front. The Russians had been expecting a frontal assault where the German front line was closer to Stalingrad. By taking this longer approach, von Manstein's forces made good ground in the first day. The Stavka were outmaneuvered and also surprised by the speed with which the Germans had organized a relief operation. Yet, within twenty-four hours, German forces were running into stiffer Russian resistance. Field Marshal von Manstein appealed to his chief of the general staff, Zeitzler, for more support, but Hitler refused once it became apparent the Soviets were about to assault his weakened left flank, manned by the remnants of the Italian Eighth Army. Standing next to Zeitzler at the situation table, Hitler pointed to the city by the Volga: "We cannot, under any circumstances, give that up. We will not retake it. And we know what that means. If we give that up, we sacrifice the whole sense of this campaign. To imagine that I will get there again next time is insanity."[1]

Insane it was. Operation Winterstorm continued for a further four days, making progress but not enough for the cost in men and materiel, though by now Hitler had agreed to support von Manstein with a further motorized division. The Germans managed to get to within thirty-five miles of their Sixth Army a week into the offensive, but such was the weakness of Paulus's forces in terms of lack of fuel to maneuver that von Manstein knew it would be impossible to open and maintain a corridor for their relief; they would have to break out themselves. He sent a message to Paulus of his new plan, Operation Thunderclap, for the Sixth Army to shed their equipment, take only what they could carry, and break out and meet their rescuers, who were bringing resupply. Unbeknownst to the commanders in the pocket, Hitler had forbidden the plan, as Lieutenant Colonel Roske of I.R. 194 recounted:

In bright sunshine and crystal-clear sky, I visited an artillery observation post in the roof of a multi-storey building high above the Volga. I looked through the binoculars towards the enemy across the area beyond the Volga River. I stopped short several times, as I believed I could hear the thunder of guns in the distance. I said to the artilleryman that there must be an artillery battle going on far behind us. I ordered a hole to be made through the roof and asked for the telescope to be placed there. As well as the sound of the thunder we could now also make out the unmistakable clouds of explosions! That had to be the Fourth Panzer Army, led by Hoth, who were attacking from the south-west and were going to relieve us.

An air of excitement went through us, as we were now hoping to be rescued. I was baffled though why we, the 194 Regiment, or indeed all the Sixth Army, wasn't involved in this fight, and falling into the backs of the Russians who were now standing against Hoth. We weren't particularly mobile anymore, but what wouldn't we have enabled, in order to get us out of this "kessel"!

Feverishly, Roske called divisional headquarters to ascertain where the relief column was and what plans were now in place for their breakout:

My telephoned enquiries with the division resulted in knowing that our assumptions had been correct, but that nothing was known about any participation from our side. We clutched our heads in disbelief and didn't know whether it was us or the highest command which was not in their right minds. The most obvious tactical decision was to break out when there is a relief attack, and it was simply being ignored. The fuel was only going to last the troops about thirty kilometres. But the Fourth Panzer Army was fifty kilometres distant. Did nobody even have the idea to just be brave, or to transfer the fuel from some tanks to others, leaving the empty ones behind? The Fourth Panzer Army eventually had to give way, after it had been surrounded from all sides. And with this, our last remaining hope of rescue was gone, although we probably didn't realise this with such clarity at the time. For us the priority now was to bind the enemy down for as long and as much as possible, until we died of hunger, cold, or were shot dead.[2]

Over a newly installed high-frequency telecommunications system, Paulus and von Manstein conferred about the potential of Thunderclap to succeed and what plans needed to be put in place should the Fuhrer allow it. Both Paulus and his chief of staff, Lieutenant General Arthur Schmidt, confessed their chances were slim if the Soviets offered stiff resistance, forcing the beleaguered troops to fight out on the frozen steppe through lack of fuel for their vehicles and still miles from the safety of German armored forces. Both men recognized this was the death knell of the Sixth Army if Thunderclap did not go ahead. Once the Soviets launched their assault on von Manstein's left northern flank, threatening to encircle his troops, he was forced to retreat on December 23 back to defensive positions close to the Don River.

Over the next few days, the Red Army of the Don Front, under the command of Lieutenant General Rokossovsky, planned to break up the Sixth Army piecemeal with each mini pocket created then bottled up and systematically destroyed. As the effects of the freezing temperature and diminishing food supplies took effect, multiple artillery bombardments and armored and infantry assaults began to squeeze the life out of Paulus's forces. The 71st Division in particular would find itself supplying ad hoc units to plug gaps in the line to stabilize the defenses in protecting the southern wing of the *Kessel*, house Paulus himself once he and his staff finally decided to relocate to what was left of central Stalingrad, and to negotiate some kind of surrender. At the heart of these events would be Lieutenant Colonel Roske.

As Christmas 1942 approached, with all hope now vanquished for a rescue, like many German field commanders trapped in the *Kessel*, Roske and his staff of I.R. 194 sought to keep the unit busy to maintain morale. For all German soldiers on the Eastern Front, especially those trying to survive in Southern Russia, thoughts of home pervaded everything at this time of year. Roske's staff attempted to distract the men, as he recounts in his unpublished memoir:

> I fell back on something familiar and worthwhile by my men: the German Winter Relief. I tasked the regiment for a particularly high donation. What a Result! In just two days 43,000 Reichs Marks was collected. Never before had I campaigned for the *Winterhilfswerk*,[3] but here I employed it as another raft to which my soldier's minds could cling to, which can be witnessed by the enormous amount they donated. Also, the men's spirit had to be raised by highlighting our future plans for the battles ahead, and by organising special food and decorations for Christmas.

The remnants of von Hartmann's division were firmly ensconced in strong positions south of the Railway Station No. 1, with the Tsaritsa Gorge acting as a natural barrier for their flank. Preparing for the Russian winter, each unit had constructed deep, well-maintained dugouts along the shelter of the gully, with underground communication systems and good lines of supply. Roske's men had also spent time shipping tons of wheat from the grain silos in the south of the city to be ground for baking bread by the Russian auxiliaries pressed-ganged into working in the German regiment's impromptu bakery they had constructed. The division also benefited from a soap-making plant to aid the soldier's continual battle against lice, and a slaughterhouse provided whatever meat could be found and prepared. The local troops knew it as "Hartmannstadt."

What remained of the formation's strength now held a pivotal position in the center of the pocket, with Roske's men turning several buildings on the corners of their perimeter, such as the Univermag Department Store, the local NKVD Prison, and the Bath House, into mini fortresses connected by trenches and communication tunnels. Roske's units weren't attacked directly but were continually skirmishing with Red Army storm groups on the left flank of their front line, where another division was under assault. The Russians' pattern of urban fighting hadn't changed since late September, always looking to take advantage of the enemy's reluctance to engage during the hours of darkness, as one sergeant recalled:

They continuously conducted assault sorties at night, which we fought back with heavy losses for the enemy. During the day, the Russians launched attacks either at dawn or at dusk. Before the attack, his infantry opened fire from heavy weapons, artillery, mortars and salvo launchers. With such raids, we suffered heavy losses. Then the Russians attacked with flamethrowers, destroyed our machine-gun nests and tried to break through. If they found a gap in the defense (usually where everyone was out of action), then they immediately rushed there and had to be beaten back out with a counterattack. Usually no one slept at night, during the day they slept in turns—one hour to sleep, one hour to watch.[4]

Christmas was approaching as the men of von Hartmann's division sought to make do as best they could. Private Willi Jettkowski of I.R. 191 recalled the surreal encounter he had when bringing back supplies from Gumrak airfield:

I drove with our [improvised] sleigh to the airfield. The Ju 52 arrived at the airfield, which was shot and ruffled. It was Christmas Eve. It had snowed once again. And then we saw them: The Christmas trees. They were unloaded from the airplane and thrown onto a truck. Having arrived at the Ju 52, I grabbed one. "Hey you, there!" someone called. "What are you supposed to be doing?"

"Order from Major General von Hartmann! Getting a Christmas tree for the Command post" I replied just as snappy. That trick always worked. We threw the post bags with our field post number onto the sleigh. Some provisions were added to that. Then we made a move again in direction of Minina-Tsaritsa Gorge, where our battalion was located by the bank of the Volga.

What had been a typical soldier's adventure to scavenge some supplies at the airfield suddenly took on a bigger problem, or so Jettkowski thought:

The railway embankment south of the Tsaritsa Gorge emerged in front of us. We turned to the side and stopped in front of the command post. General von Hartmann, with the knight's cross at the neckline, came out! He waved his hand [for us] to stop. We unloaded both post bags for the unit. Then the General sat next to us on the sleigh, and we continued to the battalion. Close behind the rail embankment, which here formed a curve, was the low hut of the command post.

Though enjoying a welcome respite amid the constant shelling, Willi Jettkowski would be wounded within hours by Soviet artillery and flown out the next day.[5]

Major General von Hartmann's mood had darkened as discussions at LI Corps and with other commanders fixated on what the Soviets would do next to reduce the pocket. Drinking schnapps outside his own billet on Christmas Eve, he mused with IV Corps commander General Max Pfeffer as both men looked up into the clear night sky: "Looking from the viewpoint of [the star] Sirius, Goethe's works will be just dust in a thousand years, and the Sixth Army will be just a name that nobody knows anymore." In front of Roske's I.R. 194 positions, the Soviets parked a truck with a large loudspeaker attached to its roof. Within minutes, the defenders in the regiment's forward positions could clearly hear German Christmas songs. In between the songs, a German voice called: "Come over. You want to get home safe? That's why you've got to come over!"

On Christmas Day, snow fell in thick, heavy flakes and the city was blanketed in a suffocating gray cloud. German and Red Army sentries monitoring each other from their respective ruins tried as best they could to cover up from the biting wind as temperatures dropped below minus twenty-five degrees. The German dead were not able to be buried anymore as the ground was frozen too deeply and hunger had weakened the living. The snow took that task from them, however, as bodies piled up alongside cellars and dugouts like stacks of cordwood. The

Christmas music had now been replaced as the Soviet's loudspeakers broadcast a clear but brutal message: "Every seven seconds a German soldier is dying in Russia. Stalingrad is a mass grave." The message was then enhanced by the sound of a clock ticking for seven seconds.

Up until the New Year, Roske was ordered five times to move a company-strength battalion here or there in order to stabilize a crumbling situation on his left or right flank as slowly the *Kessel* pulled back. Individuals and whole units, or what was left of them, began to simply disappear in the maelstrom of the fighting, as he recounted:

We never saw these battalions again. In one such case I had to hand a battalion over to Captain Hindenlang,[6] since I had no more officers who could have responsibly led a troop. With a heavy heart we had to separate. After many days, believing we had lost Hindenlang and the battalion, he suddenly reported into me. In white camouflage smock with machine gun and munitions belt he appeared haggard and emaciated. The greeting: a cognac. Followed by another one. Hindenlang had been deployed at the southwest front with his troops. In icy coldness they had fought and stabilised the enemy incursions. Eventually one Russian assault succeeded when his battalion's ammunition ran out, despite the Red Army units attacking without any tactical formation, more in a jumbled mass, running in the direction of a red flag. Here and there a German with ammunition was still shooting at them. Hindenlang stormed a Russian machine-gun nest, took the gun away from the Russian attacker, turned it around and shot him. A German Luftwaffe officer next to him kept replenishing cartridges into the machine-gun belt so that Hindenlang could shoot again, until it was finished. Senseless, pointless, without any ammunition, without any food and with frozen limbs. He still wanted to come back to the regiment though and came via an airport in which wounded men were being loaded onto planes who kept their engines running in order to take off immediately.[7]

As with some fighting men across the war, those who had left their mother unit for whatever reason felt a pull to return. Hildenlang was one such, as he confided to Roske back at regimental headquarters:

After the final firefight with the Soviets, Hindenlang sat down on a box of rations and watched them retreat. A pilot approached, sitting down and talked with him for a while. The Luftwaffe officer encouraged him to fly out with him so as not to perish here. Hindenlang refused, saying that he needed to report back to his regiment. He arrived here and was until the bitter end a role model of a courageous officer, always with an exemplary uprightness whether he was fighting or imprisoned. In January it was already impossible for the Army to stop the break-ins of the Red Army. The Kessel was shrinking more and more.

For all the attempts to alleviate the men's minds from the mental and physical stress of the fighting, their freezing conditions, and the dwindling supplies, the reality brought out desperate acts, as one of Roske's battalion commanders, Captain Münch, described after the war:

At New Year's Eve my own company commanders came to me and said that, since all of this did not make sense anymore . . . shouldn't we all shoot ourselves together? We discussed for a whole night with each other what we should do. And at the end of this discussion, it was clear that, as long as soldiers had to be led under our command, we did not have any moral right to commit suicide.[8]

The fighting in the steppe to the west of the city was more ferocious as German units lacking adequate protection and with many of their antitank guns destroyed grimly took on T-34s with improvised explosives and machine guns. It was a one-sided and bloody series of skirmishes as the Axis forces retreated back into the city. Paulus himself later confided to Lieutenant Colonel Roske his memory of inspecting their positions prior to pulling back into the southern pocket:

"The men of a battalion are lying waiting in the snow. The battalion commander points to the hill opposite, where a long row of 'Stalin-Organs' are driving into position, just as in other places, equally undisturbed, the Russian artillery had done the same. They are marginally further away than can be reached by the shot of an infantryman, and we don't have any artillery munition anymore. The battalion commander asks me what he should do. His people are about to get shot to pieces. What could I say? I said they should stay lying down." This is what the Supreme Commander of the Sixth Army told me! Is that murder? The battalion was indeed shot to pieces.[9]

As the new year progressed, the intensity of fighting took its toll, and more survivors of other fragmented divisions arrived to seek shelter, putting pressure on the division's already plummeting stocks of food and ammunition. Roske, witnessing this flood of frozen and disheveled humanity and listening to their horror stories of the fighting, now began to question where it might end:

But now, when we were running short of provisions, of clothing, munition and combat-ready troops. Could or should I now give orders to these men to undertake orders of whose success I myself wasn't convinced? Was it possible to go to battle relying purely on the spirit of the troops (which bordered on the miraculous) and on the limitless trust given to me by a simple soldier of my leadership? No, my men would not be deprived of their trust in my leadership, which was still strong, even if my own trust in leadership at the very top was diminishing more and more.[10]

The Soviets could sense the enemy was on his last legs, as Russian war correspondents conveyed while they monitored events on the front lines around the *Kessel*:

Everything is indeed changing. And the Germans who had broken through to one street in September, had ensconced themselves in city apartment blocks, and danced to the noisy music of mouth organs, those Germans who had gone about at night with torches and had by day brought up trucks of ammunition have now had to hide in the earth and stone ruins. I stood for a long time with binoculars in the fourth floor of a burnt out building looking at German-occupied parts of the city—not a whisp of smoke. Not a single figure moving. There is no sun for them. No daylight for them. Their ration is now 25–30 bullets per day. Their orders are to only fire at attacking forces. Their food rations are limited to a 100 grammes of bread and horsemeat. They sit there like shaggy beasts in stone caves. Of a night they crawl up to the surface and sensing fear before the steadily-closing pincers of Russian troops they yell out: "Hey, Russ, shoot my legs first, then my head!"[11]

On January 7, the first ultimatum of surrender from the Don Front commander Rokossovsky was delivered across the German front lines by a party of three junior Red Army officers. The message was then publicized to all and sundry by Soviet planes dropping leaflets and loudspeakers blaring the words across from Red Army positions. Stating his position untenable, the terms were generous should Paulus agree to accept within twenty-four hours. All German troops would be treated humanely, medical care administered to his sick and wounded, and the men permitted to keep their personal belongings and meager rations. Extraordinarily, Rokossovsky offered that upon an eventual Soviet victory over Hitler's Third Reich, Paulus's men would be repatriated to any country they chose. Paulus, alongside his chief of staff Schmidt and his aide-de-camp Colonel Wilhelm Adam, took the news to confer with his remaining generals. News was now cabled from Army High Command of a proposed new relief operation planned to commence in early February. "They all spoke against surrender. They assured him [Paulus] this was also the opinion of the divisional commanders."[12] As the conference ended, a fresh directive landed from Hitler which for the time being settled the matter: "Capitulation out of the question. Every day that the army holds out longer helps the whole front and draws away the Russian divisions from it."[13]

A chance to save countless lives and spare the misery Paulus's men were living under was missed. He now appealed to his officers and men to reject any call to surrender from Communist propagandists, for their relief would surely soon come from the west. The fight would continue. As would the desertions. The search for food was overriding the need to defend the pocket for many, as one infantryman from the 71st Division recalled:

> The Russians were attacking from all sides now and found very little resistance. Also, food had become worse. There was no salt for cooking, and only occasionally could a dead horse, having died many months before but being preserved in the ice, be found to eat. This was done by cutting pieces from the carcass, placing them into a steel helmet in slushy water to warm up a little, and then devoured by the men.

The remnants of the 71st Division, with the survivors from sister divisions from LI Corps, the 371st and 295th, on its flank, now faced south and east, looking across the frozen Volga. Lieutenant Colonel Roske spied the odd Russian scout moving around on the eastern shore and could hear the constant hum of Katyusha mobile trucks being placed in position, amid the familiar rumble of the T-34s. Crouched in one of the regiment's fortified bunkers, he took in the same vast forested countryside he had first encountered four months previously, now coated in a heavy blanket of snow. A lunar, icy landscape that was his home for the foreseeable future. The freezing wind blew across the water, blasting his face and any skin not protected by his leather overcoat and gloves. It made peering through his binoculars problematic if he did not wish to have his eyelids frozen on the lenses. He continually wiped his eyes and nose to thwart frostbite and wore a scarf to protect his clean-shaven face. He was not a fan of the beards his emaciated troops were now sporting to protect their own. His combat instincts drove him and his few officers to maintain a watchful eye for the expected Russian response to Paulus's refusal of surrender.

Fearing the enemy would attack, I wanted to make some reconnaissance right across the Volga into the area beyond in order to ascertain what was actually brewing in front of my very nose. Whether for instance the Russians were going to attack over the ice. I didn't have the necessary forces to undertake such an in-depth reconnaissance, crossing the 1,800-metre-wide Volga and into the area beyond that. I didn't have the appropriate men, but also there was a lack of boldness and physical strength for such a task. In the end I myself sometimes wandered, slightly wistfully, along the Volga, carefully avoiding mine fields and barbed wire to see what "Ivan" might be up to.

The answer soon arrived, the next day.

On Sunday, the forty-eighth day of the *Kessel*'s existence, at 0805 hours, Rokossovsky's Don Front unleashed the final act in the Stalingrad drama—Operation Ring. The Stavka had now reinforced his mauled rifle divisions with 20,000 replacements, giving him a force of more than 212,000 men supported by 6,860 artillery and mortars, backed up with 257 tanks.[14] A thunderous artillery and Katyusha barrage lasting several hours preceded an all-out assault on the Sixth Army's perimeter stretching thirty-five kilometers (more than twenty miles) in diameter.

From the north swept the 66th Army, and across from the west came the 65th Army, and surging from the south was the 64th Army with elements of the 21st and 24th Armies. Chuikov's 62nd Army pinned the defenders down within the city itself, around the Factory District and the Mamayev Kurgan. Though the survivors of the bombardment put up whatever defense they could muster under the circumstances, the Sixth's radio report to Army High Command over the next few days clinically plotted its demise:

```
11 January, 09:40 Hours: Enemy broke through on a wide
portion of the front line . . . isolated strongholds
still intact.
```

11 January, 19:00 Hours: Resistance of troops diminishing quickly because of insufficient ammunition,
extreme frost, and lack of coverage against heaviest
enemy fire.

12 January, 08:00 Hours: Army has ordered as a last
means of resistance that every soldier has to fight to
the last bullet at the place he is holding right now.

13 January, 09:30 Hours: Ammunition is almost
exhausted.

In the west, Paulus's lifeline of Pitomnik airfield was finally overrun
on the evening of January 16,[15] German troops and Luftwaffe personnel fleeing Soviet T-34s advancing down roads already littered with
broken-down vehicles and thousands of frozen corpses. Behind the
Soviet armor poured Red Army infantry advancing in line to mop up
the survivors not crushed under tank tracks or pulverized by their artillery. The fleeing German motorized columns heading back toward the
city spared little time to pick up their comrades on foot, in some cases
crushing them under wheel in the panic for safety. Only the airfield at
Gumrak, fifteen kilometers (about ten miles) west of the city center,
was for now able to take heavy aircraft, with the Stalingrad Air School
in the city operational for light planes.

German casualties stood at 60,000 troops killed, wounded, or captured. Now Soviet commanders realized they were dealing with a far
larger besieged force than previously thought. The losses for Rossokovsky's
Don Front reflected the fierce resistance such strength could muster—
Russian dead and wounded stood at 24,000 men and 143 T-34 tanks
destroyed.[16] It did not diminish the Don Front's momentum in penetrat-
ing each defensive line the Germans attempted to set up, after each mini
retreat in the face of overwhelming numbers. Resistance was proving
stubborn in the north of the city, though, the survivors of the XIV Panzer
Corps using the same terrain and defensive tactics Chuikov's 62nd Army
had so successfully implemented against them the previous autumn.

Rokossovsky ordered his Don Front units to dig in and await reinforcements and resupply for the final phase to begin on January 20. Soviet fighters dominated the sky above the city with daily air supplies, with the Germans dropping less than ten tons as a consequence. The Luftwaffe could only effectively deliver supplies under the cover of darkness. Amid the silence of the battlefield, and with Pitomnik gone, Paulus had made the decision to move his staff into the city, and to settle upon the divisional headquarters and become extra mouths to feed in "Hartmannstadt," the 71st Division,[17] which was now close to Stalingradsky airport. Taking only essentials, burning all else, the trek by Paulus and his men into their new accommodation was heartrending as they drove down the "Road of Death" past the detritus of the retreating army and into the center of the city:

> Innumerable dead lay alongside the roadway. Many were the corpses of wounded and sick who had only wanted to lie down for a short rest to try to regain some strength. They had fallen asleep from fatigue and frozen to death. The dead also lay on the street. Nobody made any effort to remove them.[18]

Paulus's command of approximately 120 staff were accommodated by von Hartmann, who housed them at first in the division's established winter quarters along the Tsaritsa Gully. For Roske and the divisional commanders still active, another set of visitors caused a bigger headache:

> Amongst the masses who, defeated, arrived back in my battle area in Stalingrad (at first only from the west), there were above all field hospitals with thousands of wounded, frozen men. Soon they couldn't be housed in the few habitable cellars we still had. An underground tunnel [an evacuated Soviet command post originally used by Yeremenko and then Chuikov] was turned into accommodation for the patients. The air ventilation wasn't working any more, which eventually would have the most gruesome consequences. No power in the world would have been able to change the outcome for these seriously wounded men.

The spirited attitude of Roske's remaining soldiers able to fight or offer logistical support provided a counterweight to the sense of pessimism such sights caused in their operational area. In his newly discovered memoir, Roske celebrated the camaraderie of his men and their officers in carrying out their duty and in the letters they sent in the final transport home.

Even as late as 21 January my Adjutant First Lieutenant Hoßfeld wrote to his relatives back home: "The spirit of our regiment is quite excellent," at a time when quite a few are already counting on our demise, ". . . as nobody knows what may happen next," he writes, and adds in his own words what I had once said to him: "Whether we live and when we die is totally irrelevant. The only eternal value for the future is purely how we live and how we die."

I never heard a single complaint from those hungry and dying fighters in Stalingrad. Whether I spoke to them in the holes where they had been posted, or in a shelter, they were able to sense my care for them and also sense that I was unable to truly help them. So it happened occasionally that they comforted me, me who was supposed to give them strength! "Sir, the hunger is not so bad, we'll pull through." I heard this and similar expressions from time to time.

Despite the privations, while the Don Front was preparing its coup de grace to launch on January 22, the men of the 71st Division, and those of I.R. 194 in particular, attempted some kind of normality amid the sporadic breakouts of calm along their front line, not least when it was their own commander's birthday on January 20. It was a birthday for Roske unlike any other he would ever experience:

I had forbidden any kind of celebration. But I couldn't prevent the items which had already been made by my men to be given to me. Wood carvings, metalwork, sketches, a model of a company dug out and even poems.

Roske's regimental staff and battalion commanders were then meeting with their CO that evening to drink to his health, when suddenly the eerie silence of dusk was broken by a tremendous crescendo of horned instruments, coming as if from beneath the ground. The officers watched on as from the narrow gangway of the prison cellar, with uniforms as clean as they could get them amid the misery, the regimental band emerged.

> How uplifting, how exhilarating, in the depths of the battle. They played a march! Everyone received a cognac. I recalled that on my arrival at the Volga last September, I had given the military band the opportunity to collect their instruments and to practise them. Soon they were asking me to check their musical progress. Eventually I found the time to go into their accommodation and was deeply moved to hear music, even just marching music, and I said a few words of praise. I told them that my plan was, when we liberated Stalingrad, to have military bands play from the rooftops of the tall department store—fanfares to announce the triumph; and encouraged them to think of a programme for the occasion. Partly I expressed this idea in order to boost morale and give confidence, and I myself was still feeling more confident at the time—although not as much as my words may have conveyed. I wasn't lying to myself so much as utilising an essential means of battle if one is at all determined to carry on.

By January 24, the existing pocket's perimeter had been reduced by a third, with the loss of Gumrak airfield and, in the northern sector, the Germans retreating back to the Factory District. Across the city's mangled front lines isolated German units, sheltering in ruins, cellars, and burned-out apartment blocks, waited for the end.

> The Russians took their time now, moving carefully in squads, in platoons, over the mounds of snow-covered wreckage. In countless minor engagements in the side streets of the city, the command "*Raus!*

Raus!" echoed when the shooting stopped, and Germans climbed out of their holes with hands held high. The Russians kicked a few, punched others, but led the prisoners away without further incident.[19]

Discipline was fragmenting and desertions continued among the *Kessel*'s divisions, from the lowly infantryman to the highest-ranking general. The commander of I.R. 191, Lieutenant Colonel Kurt Corduan, overseeing the cornerstone of the 71st Division's defense, the NKVD prison, had reached his own point of no return as Lieutenant Colonel Roske recounts:

That night [of the 25th] Lieutenant Colonel Corduan phoned me and asked me to come to him immediately. I declined and postponed the meeting to the following morning. When I then arrived, he was with some other officers, so I asked, "What's going on?" Corduan said he had decided yesterday to put an end to this battle (Regiment 191 had not even been attacked yet at that point), by talking to the Russians on behalf of the Army. That was why he had called on me the evening before, to ask my opinion and to know whether I would join him. And since I had not come over, he had then sent an officer to go over to the enemy to negotiate. But the officer in question turned around, plagued by a guilty conscience, and didn't fulfil his task. Now he (Corduan) had just found out that his officers were against such a step too.[21]

Needing to nip such actions in the bud, Lieutenant Colonel Roske acted, ignoring his divisional and corps commanders and driving directly to Sixth Army headquarters to speak with Paulus in his cellar room of the 71st Division. *Was everyone allowed to break out and start negotiations?* he pondered. *Or does the fighting continue resolutely?*

When I arrived at the hospital cellar (the office of the staff of Army), I put my questions to the Adjutant of the commander, Lieutenant Colonel Adam, who immediately went with me to see the Supreme Commander. He was in a small cellar room with destroyed windows, where they were both housed, and where they had just recently been slightly injured by splinters of bombs. I spoke to Paulus and said I required clarity.

"Of course we continue to fight," he said. "Everything else is a confusion, and only excusable, if that is indeed the case, because of these extraordinary circumstances."[22]

Colonel Adam now spoke up, informing the colonel that their front to the south had already collapsed, with the Russians expected to assault their positions soon. He and Paulus had lethal injections waiting in order to be able to take their lives if necessary. An incredulous Roske replied, "Ha, sir, it's not that bad yet! There is plenty of fight left where we are, and there will be some time yet."[23]

Paulus smiled at his bravado. "Yes, Adam told me about his visit to you yesterday and was impressed with the buoyant mood there."

"Well, sir," replied Roske, "you are welcome to come over to us, especially if things are finished here soon. Mind you, I only have space for a few officers."[24]

Paulus called his chief of staff, Lieutenant General Schmidt, and informed him about the suggestion. Schmidt declined, stating it wasn't necessary to move accommodation so soon after arriving in "Hartmann-stadt."

In the evening, though, Paulus, Schmidt, Adam, and the entire com-munications team appeared at my Regiment's base camp, together with their head of department, Colonel van Hooven.[20] Space was made for them, three rooms, in the cellar of the department store, and we others were then jammed in closer together. Seeing the Commander in Chief gave the officers and soldiers a tremendous uplift.[25]

On January 24, 1943, Paulus cabled Hitler's headquarters with the dire situation report. He still could not and would not bring himself to take unilateral action to save his men, despite the death, destruc-tion, and futility of continuing the defense. Perhaps pushed by his senior corps and divisional commanders into some form of protest, he did not hold back in detailing the hopelessness of the Sixth Army's position:

> The troops are without ammunition or provisions, parts of six divisions are still reachable. Sign of dissolution occurring in the South, North and West Fronts. Consistent leadership is no longer possible. The East Front has only minor changes. 18,000 wounded without the minimal help of bandages or medication. The 44th, 76th, 100th, 305th and 384th Infantry Divisions are destroyed. The front has been torn open from many sides as a result of massive break-ins. Further defence is pointless. Collapse is unavoidable. In order to save the lives of the men still here, the Army requests immediate permission to capitulate.[26]

His senior officers knew the truth, and his immediate staff, Chief of Staff Schmidt included, were aware of their untenable position, but Paulus nevertheless awaited the confirmation that the agony would soon be over for all of them. Surely any sane leader would see this? Later on the same day the response came to Paulus in his cellar of the department store: "The Army is to hold its position to the last man and to the last bullet.—Adolf Hitler."[27] As word passed around Paulus's senior leaders, the chief of staff of LI Corps, Colonel Hans Clausius, left the Univermag and called his officers together behind a ruined building for a private conference. As they stood in a huddle, stamping their feet to keep the icy wind at bay, Clausius calmly lit a cigarette and announced his decision: "Gentlemen, you may do and 'not do' whatever you wish. The battle is lost. I wish you all the best."[28]

CHAPTER EIGHTEEN

The Last Commander
of the "Lucky Division"

For me, the first duty of a soldier is to obey.
—Field Marshal Friedrich Paulus[1]

The end game for the *Kessel* was fast approaching by January 25. Everyone knew it. On all sides of their perimeter, the German troops who were still fit for fighting could see the strength of the Red Army forces now arrayed against them. Three separate Soviet motorized formations were now converging on the Univermag Department Store. In the side streets could be heard the familiar rumble of T-34 tanks. Artillery and mortar shells intermittently dropped all around the German bunkers, foxholes, and the ruins surrounding Red Square. Casualties were increasing, with nowhere left to house or treat them. Hundreds of the dying and corpses lay strewn among the rubble in the open streets. The lucky ones bled, froze, or starved to death in temporary field hospitals set up in bunkers or cellars. The order to defend Stalingrad to the last man, the last bullet, was more than carried out. Defeat was in sight.

The previous evening, over dim candlelight, Major General von Hartmann had decided what needed to be done. Taking one final drink with his divisional compatriot, General Richard Stempel of the 371st, and the commander of IV Corps, General Max Pfeffer, he had joined the other two veterans in mulling over the fate of the Sixth Army, the state of the Eastern Front, and what might possibly happen to Germany itself. Their fates indeed seemed sealed, but should they surrender? As more German stragglers and whole units drifted into captivity by simply walking over no-man's-land to the Russians, there soon wouldn't be an army left in the southern *Kessel*. Lieutenant Colonel Roske had already estimated the garrison to be seventeen thousand men of all ranks, with merely two to three thousand troops still able to fight. The units now intermingled simply to form a defensive ring. The will to carry on amid such privations had already taken its toll throughout January, as Lieutenant Wuster of the 71st Division recalled:

> The reason these new motley units disintegrated and suffered high losses was due to the fact that they were so intermingled that lines of command and supply routes became tangled. Neighbours to the left or right side were not known, and some soldiers simply disappeared into the darkness and returned to their original units. Even many experienced infantry-men gave up and vanished into the underworld of the destroyed city. Soldiers who had quit the front did not look out of place in the chaos.[2]

With the southern *Kessel*'s lines slowly disintegrating, staff of the IV Army Corps took it upon themselves to issue the following order to their commanders still actively fighting:

> Out of consideration for the wounded, there will be no fighting nearer to the centre of the city than the present frontline. This line will be held as long as possible, but when further resistance becomes pointless, it may be abandoned and this made visibly evident to the enemy.[3]

At the beginning of the summer campaign the previous July, von Hartmann, Stempel, and Pfeffer had commanded tens of thousands of men, motorized vehicles and artillery pieces. Now, in a dimly lit wooden bunker, they sat on upturned ration boxes, drinking schnapps from iron mugs as they stared into the light of a candle. Major General von Hartman's division had now been reduced to less than two hundred fighting men and a few artillery pieces. Together with what was left of 14th Panzer Division, they were still capable of offering some resistance, despite being heavily outnumbered, but his mind was now made up. His son had died the previous July on the Eastern Front, as he outlined to his comrades with his intentions:

> An officer has to die in battle. I shan't shoot myself, but I'll sell my skin for the highest possible price. . . . My wife is a competent woman, she'll surely get on as best she can without me: my son has been killed and my daughter is married. We shan't win this war and the man who is in Supreme Command is not the man we took him for.[4]

A few hours after the generals had bade farewell to one another, Stempel now back at his own quarters, believing his own son fighting in the city with the 14th Panzer Division had died attempting to escape the encirclement, ordered his staff to make their own decision as to their next steps, closed the door to his room, took out his revolver, and shot himself.

The following morning another dank and freezing day began for the exhausted remnants of I.R. 194, as the men lay entrenched along the railway embankment approximately six hundred yards away from the Tsaritsa. The five months of Lieutenant Colonel Roske's leadership had bonded cohesion into what remained of their number, and they acted and fought like a unit compared to the motley crew of troops defending the rest of the line nearby. They would not simply walk across to the Russians as other units had done over the previous days. Through the morning mist, the sunshine outlined the shapes of five figures coming toward them from the rear, their hands thrust deep into their pockets as they slowly walked upright toward the *Kessel*'s front line, seemingly oblivious to the thump of mortar rounds landing in the distance. The infantrymen looked on in astonishment. Russian snipers were still very much active in their sector should anyone stupid enough want to stand upright to offer them a target. The first lieutenant on duty, crouched with his men in their positions in the snow, was astonished to now realize it was von Hartmann, accompanied by General Pfeffer, artillery commander of IV Corps Major General Hans Wulz, and the regimental commanders of their own division, Lieutenant Colonels Corduan and Bayerlein. All five men had carbines slung over their shoulders as if it was just another day on their divisional shooting range back home in Osnabrück.

Hartmann greeted his junior officer, who continued to lie prone on the ground, squinting his eyes to focus on his commander. The young officer gave him the situational report and the current strength within their positions: 183 men, 7 non-commissioned officers, and 3 officers, the majority of whom were lying to the left and right of his position. The general thanked him and gestured that he remain lying on the ground. He then unslung his rifle. He stared across at the enemy positions. The Russians were becoming agitated at the movement in the German lines; activity could be seen in the Russian positions. The sound of more mortar rounds landing was heard behind the German forward positions as the morning peace was shattered. Shots suddenly zipped past von Hartmann's group, kicking up spurts of snow near his feet. The lieutenant ordered his men to offer covering fire, but their divisional commander ordered them to remain inactive. He took up a shooting stance with his front foot perched on the snow hillock the officer lay behind, and chambered a round. He shouldered the rifle, shouted, "Take cover! All take cover!"—the traditional order on a rifle range before a practice shoot—and took aim.[5] Pfeffer and Wulz soon joined in the engagement.

Informed of the incident, Paulus sent a verbal order via his staff officer Major von Below, with instructions "to persuade the Generals to stop behaving like lunatics and for the spectacle to cease immediately." He was curtly dismissed by the generals as the shoot-out continued. A suitably chastened von Below crawled slowly back to the Univermag to report the conversation to Paulus, only to be sent out again with a written order directed at the most senior officer involved, General Pfeffer:

```
The IV Corps is ordered to withdraw to the city bound-
ary. The Corps Commander will report to the Commander-
in-Chief. Paulus.⁶
```

By this time, however, von Hartmann, of the "Lucky Division," had finally run out of luck. Though eyewitnesses claim he did wound several of the enemy as they worked their way toward his position, a Russian sniper managed to get into position and kill him instantly with a shot to the right temple. His men dragged his body back from the front line and buried him in a foxhole dug into the frozen earth of the railway embankment. As the news spread, many of the men admired the fact that their commander had taken an "honest bullet." Lieutenant Colonel Roske himself was appalled at the group's actions:

> Major General von Hartmann had definitely taken his leave of the Division too soon . . . [and had] accelerated its disintegration. Now, as the Commander of the I.R. 194 I was the 71st Division's last living regimental commander and swore never to leave my men to their fates or to the Russians alone.

Paulus was quick to act to restore some semblance of order to the morning. Roske would now command the entire central *Kessel*:

> Sixth Army 10:45 Hours: "I have assigned Lieutenant Colonel Roske, commander of the Infantry Regiment 194 with the leadership of the 71.ID. This proven, exemplary brave, energetic commander has reorganised in the shortest of time the completely mixed-up units and transferred his absolute/unconditional will to persevere onto his men. I request his promotions to general major to decree/order via radio. Paulus, General Colonel."[7]

Though clearly suffering from dysentery and preferring the sanctuary of his camp bed, Paulus briefed his new commander of his responsibilities:

1. Only to leave the command post if given explicit permission to do so, so that he would always be available.
2. When he thought it necessary, to inform Paulus the end was coming, in order he might receive further instructions.

Moreover, everything within the *Kessel* was to be in his jurisdiction (which was the case already), and he would now be responsible for the distribution of any food provisions.

Roske recounted in his memoir the state of orderly panic that now settled upon his headquarters:

> In my command post there were now a lot of officers and orderlies, all crowded together. There was artillery equipment lying around throughout the department store, and in the yard outside there were grenade launchers. Our windows were soon destroyed by the enemy's artillery fire, the men constantly repairing and protecting the gaps in the walls with wooden planks and sandbags.[8]

The entire *Kessel* operation was now being conducted from his cellar room. He was the de facto commander of the *Kessel*, with authority over everyone other than Paulus:

> Soon it became impossible to think straight, because the arrival of officers and messengers was so frequent that work, or getting some rest, were out of the question. Having a lookout at my door was of no use, so I posted an [armed] officer with a steel helmet there, who was ordered not to let anyone in without permission. Even this measure proved futile as the wounded and those seeking shelter now turned to him. Also, I started to notice more officers arriving with bad news of a particular incursion by the enemy (often untrue) and asking for shelter. Many of these men had simply lost their nerve. I had to again increase the strength of the guard around the department store.[9]

Unbeknownst to Roske, Paulus and the remaining officers and soldiers of the Sixth Army, within their own defenses, "Fortress Stalingrad," had now been split in two. Rokossovsky's Don Front forces had once again driven deep into German lines, his forward detachments of 21st Army and 65th Army finally linking up with Chuikov's besieged 62nd Army north of the Mamayev Kurgan, behind the Red October Steel Plant area. Rodimtsev's 13th Guardsmen greeted the tankers and infantry after they all recognized one another's green signal flares. Chuikov's army had fought alone for over 140 days. Now the enemy was split in two, with the bulk of General Karl Strecker's XI Corps dug in to the north of the Factory District. Roske's men of the 71st Division were now part of the southern pocket containing what remained of LI, IV Army Corps and XIV Panzer Corps—the latter two units' commanders having been flown out of the pocket by now, leaving their men to their own fate. Within forty-eight hours, another Soviet assault would bisect the southern pocket, forcing Paulus to make a final stand in the very heart of the city that he had captured in the first weeks of September. Roske would now be his de facto combat leader.

The colonel struck up a cordial and somewhat personable relationship with his commanding officer in those last few days of the defense, the older officer discreetly informing him of his dealings with the upper echelons of Army High Command, with Hitler and of his own misgivings at the start of 1942 as to whether Case Blue was even feasible, confiding to Roske that he had overseen a war-gaming exercise before Barbarossa about invading Southern Russia to capture the oilfields and Stalingrad, with the conclusion it could not succeed:

> From Paulus's recounting . . . it became clearer and clearer to me that I would never receive an order from the High Command to end the battle because the order from Hitler was not to negotiate. It was obvious to me that, as commander of the defence of the ring in which the headquarters were situated, the initiative and the decision regarding the way the battle should end, had [now] fallen to me.
>
> I realised one final thing from all of this. Someone would have to end the agony; would have to try to prevent our men from being robbed and beaten by the Red Army if we surrendered. These soldiers who were mainly unfit for battle, apathetic, frozen, starving to death in cellars, in ruined buildings and on the streets. How I was to solve this problem? I didn't know yet.[10]

In the meantime, Roske was now promoted to major general of the 71st Division on January 27 and belatedly received the Knight's Cross for his actions in getting I.R. 194 to the banks of the Volga the previous September—a lifetime ago amid the fighting. The greatest news of all was that delivered by Paulus, who had made contact with Roske's pregnant wife back home in Germany:

> Towards the evening Paulus came to me in my dark cellar room lit only by candles and informed me, "And now I have something else for you: from your wife!" And he gave me a scrap of paper, a radiogram, on which was written: *A son, all is well.*

The stress and fatigue of the months of fighting, the loss of comrades, the pressure of commanding the *Kessel* now sweetened with the joyous news of the birth of his son was too much to bear: "I left the O.B. [*oberbefehlshaber*, or Commander in Chief] standing there, turned away from him and went into the pitch-black corridor, so that my tears would not be seen."[11]

His perimeter was now being inundated with the desperate and the wounded from other parts of the city. The word had spread that one division was strong enough to put up a defense, offer safety, and might have sufficient supplies. Hundreds now made their way there, to seek whatever shelter they could find in the cellars and dugouts along the Tsaritsa and to try to find food to eat. As for fighting, Roske could only depend on his own men now:

> I vividly remember the O.B. coming into our room one morning; we greeted each other. Only Captain Hindenlang was still in his bed, under his blanket. We all happened to look in his direction, so I jokingly said, "Well, Hindenlang, you old lazy bones, you might want to get up soon!" Hindenlang extracted himself from his blanket and laughed: "I wouldn't mind sleeping occasionally, Herr General sir; there was quite a lot happening last night!" And it turned out that he

had been called out three times that night because the Russians had broken in at the mouth of the Tsaritsa River; and three times he had hurried down, had gathered some people together and had thrown the Russians out with no ammunition, just with a "Hurrah!" and a bayonet!

Paulus just shook his head. Then the telephone rang. Hindenlang spoke joyfully with an officer who must have been well known to him. "Well, that's great. Of course we can do with you. Come on over, there's tons to do!"

Paulus shook his head again and said to me, "See, Roske? Strength begets strength."

It was important to me to determine the right moment for a ceasefire—which wouldn't be able to be delayed much longer; in other words, to keep the battle going even if only for a short (and undeterminable) time, as long as there was still hope left, or at least a purpose to it.

By January 28, Russian armor and infantry were only as far away as the width of Red Square (one hundred meters, or a little more than three hundred feet) to the south and only one street away from the Univermag Department Store to the west. Roske had prepared his final stand. The front of the store had been heavily mined, one heavy artillery piece was a few hundred yards away in the Bath House, guarding entry on one flank, and groups of soldiers made ready with what weapons they still had for the final assault. The nearby Gorki Theatre was a shell, its enormous vaulted roof having completely fallen in. Roske now required his last combat-worthy men to take positions in the ruins of the top floors of the department store to defend their position. But by then many were not standing at their posts anymore, most having apathetically drifted away the night before. He made his way down to the overcrowded, stinking cellars and corridors, crowded with the dead, dying, and the wounded, to rouse those still willing and able to fight:

No amount of barking orders could change that, and certainly no rebuking. I spoke with one of the men still resting in the basement—an otherwise splendid soldier. He said, "Herr General, sir, there's just no point anymore." I laid my hand on his shoulder and said that up until now he and his comrades had been able to rely on me and that they could do so again now. So, he went off again in order to set himself up in the top floor.

Occasionally that morning, a single aircraft flew by, looking for a dropping point. Once I was standing in thick fog, by night, in front of the department store. An aircraft was buzzing just above us, circling. Again and again the pilot circled above us, attempting to find the dropping point conveyed to him via the radio, and eventually pulled away again without having any success. A brave man![12]

On January 29, 1943, Roske reported to Paulus of their situation— the 29th and 36th Rifle and 38th Motorized Rifle Divisions had finally linked up in the center of the city—their position was now firmly surrounded:

On the 28 and 29 January the enemy had pushed forward from the south, the west, and the north to within threatening distance to my positions in the department store. The sounds of battle then decreased. The resistance of the troops as well as the attacking strength of the Russians, both of which had already been fairly low, sank even further. Both sides were exhausted. Around midday on 29 January, I walked out of the entrance of the department store in order to gain a better picture for myself. I ascertained:

1. Right across the other side of Red Square the Red Army soldiers had already mixed in the approach roads with our countless unfit-to-fight men. There was now no more talk of a battle of the howitzers which I had put into place in the side streets through the artillery leader Ludwig. Still at least the Russians were keeping their distance from the guns.

2. Towards the north there was only one street's width between the Russian tanks and my position. Everywhere Germans and Russian positions were now intermingled.

3. In the north-east, where the Romanians had been positioned to

defend the northern flank, those very same were already talking with the Russians about surrendering.

4. Where the Tsaritsa and Volga Rivers met, the Russians had advanced to somewhere close to one of my support camps.

5. My occupation of the department store was only partially holding out. Here and there some shots were still being fired towards enemy positions. But wasn't every shot also hitting our own comrades? I said this to the O.B., and added, "The battle is suffocating. I could perhaps organise some small centres of firing, but we would inevitably also hit our own. I can now no longer guarantee the defence of the department store.

The O.B., to whom I had only a few days previously spoken of my commanding the last unit of good fighters, responded, "You see, Roske, I told you so." And now the misgivings regarding the morrow, 30 January, were talked about, which I understood. I also understood that it was, from now on, my task to act without orders from the O.B., independently, and therefore to relieve him of all decisions in that respect.

On January 30, as Soviet tanks ground their way forward through the streets toward his position, and whichever units were still holding out in the outlying ruins and entrenchments were being driven out or killed, the ever-mindful Paulus sent a congratulatory note to Hitler on his tenth anniversary of taking power in Germany. By midday, with Russian units now parked in the side streets a few hundred yards from their positions, Roske reported to the chief of staff of the Sixth Army, Lieutenant General Schmidt, that through Colonel Ludwig of the 14th Panzer Division he had asked a Russian negotiator to come to his office.[13] Schmidt was still of a mind that the men should carry on fighting on the anniversary of Hitler taking power.

When I got back to my room, Schmidt caught up with me and said in the doorway, "But Roske, you have got to be the one to negotiate!"

"Naturally; that was my intention," I replied.

[Captain] Hindenlang heard this exchange and, as soon as Schmidt was outside, said, in his brazen, straightforward way to me, "That was mean of him, Herr General, sir," to which I replied by telling him that it was right it had to be this way.

January 31, 1943, was the day on which Roske himself would negotiate with the Russians and the southern *Kessel* would go into captivity. By this point it consisted of only the department store and a small area toward the north and east. This story of the surrender has never been published before.

Just after midnight, Roske requested from Hindenlang that he not be disturbed for at least an hour, just so he had time to collect his thoughts as to how he could protect his men as well as Paulus. He wanted to prepare himself to meet the Russian delegation. Headquarters staff informed him the Soviets had now cut their telephone lines. He asked his orderly to find him some clean water to shave and to brush up his one usable dress uniform. While he waited, Roske's mind went to a dark place. As he describes it in his unpublished memoir, he was clearly suffering from post-traumatic stress. He questioned how good a commander he had been to his men since his arrival the previous September, how he would avoid meeting the seriously wounded or make excuses not to. Despite the fact his men respected him greatly, upon taking command of the division's positions around the Univermag, he now preferred to stay alongside Paulus as ordered, and made excuses not to inspect those units on the front line of his perimeter. Ultimately, he was a gifted and brave officer who after five months of intense combat felt powerless to save his men but still resolutely fought to the end.

The race for the various Red Army divisions now surrounding Paulus's position to take the main prize resulted in various parties attempting to make contact and speak with Roske's command. At around 3 a.m. a party of Russian negotiators arrived at the locked main door, requesting to be let in.[14] They had come supported with a dozen armed soldiers—some of whom carried grenades in their pockets ready to use should the enemy open fire. One Red Army lieutenant was allowed access to the building with two aides, entering via a side entrance due to Roske's previous order to mine the front of the store. Whether this young tankman actually met with Paulus is refuted by Roske's memoir, he only states the lieutenant was informed to radio for a senior Red Army officer to attend, in order to agree to terms that could be guaranteed. In the morning a new delegation headed by a Russian colonel,[15] with supporting officers and guards in attendance, appeared wishing to speak to the German commanding officer. The Russians by now had brought up almost a battalion-strength unit to train arms on the building. They were made to wait until Roske and Schmidt spoke with Colonel Adam. Paulus was left to rest in his quarters next to Roske's room. Again, both Roske and Schmidt balked at handing over the field marshal to someone so junior in rank. While the Russian colonel's message was taken back to Soviet lines by one of his subalterns, Roske sought to ease the tension of his Soviet guest who sat opposite:

> I had a need for a cigar and offered one to him as well. Soon after he had lit it, he quickly put it to one side. He must have had second thoughts whether such a thing was permitted, or whether it was perhaps poisoned, or he just wasn't used to that sort of thing. I talked with him about a possible approach to the battle and also about my terms and conditions. He was of the opinion that these would surely be listened to. There would be a lull of a few hours before the Russians finally sent the right man.

The Red Army officer was impressed by his opposite number: "Roske looked very sharp and clean. He made the best impression of the group. . . . All of Roske's aides looked neat. All of them with dozens of medals."[16]

While they waited for the new senior delegation to arrive, Roske had taken the opportunity to say his farewell to Paulus. Hindenlang had already informed Roske of the cable from the Fuhrer listing the raft of promotions Hitler had bestowed on the officers he could not rescue, a final bauble to dangle in front of desperate men so they would go down fighting. Roske was now addressing the field marshal of the Sixth Army—or what remained of it.

> With an air of gloom, I congratulated him on his promotion. We stood opposite each other in his small room and could sense how close we had become, and how well we had come to know each other during these difficult days—as men, as soldiers, and as comrades. He said to me, "Roske, do you think the Führer has promoted me to the rank of Field Marshal because it's never happened before that a Field Marshal was taken into imprisonment, and never should be?"
>
> It shot through my head that once before I had advised him not to take his life. Everything inside me railed against this thought: *If the O.B. were to take his life, the fault of this defeat would fall on us all.* I asked, "Does Herr Field Marshal feel himself responsible [for the failure of the battle]?" And then I remembered a slightly lame comparison: "Anyway, Field Marshal Mackensen went into imprisonment."[17] Well, those two sentences together seemed to offer a final straw to him, onto which he clutched. We shook hands and he thanked me, visibly moved.[18]

Roske returned to his own cellar room to dictate one last order for his men of I.D. 71, but more important those left from his old I.R. 194, whom he had served with through the last five bitter months of fighting:

> *Hunger, extreme cold and lack of ammunition have made it impossible to continue this battle. We will all continue to stand together as good comrades, for then we will endure even the worst hardships.*

Within under an hour the Russian delegation, headed by Major General I. A. Laskin, chief of staff of the 64th Army, arrived together with Major General Ivan Burmakov, commander of the brigade surrounding the department store, all the party like the previous Russian officers, resplendent in good, clean winter coats, hats, and heavy felt boots. Their attire stood in sharp contrast to the disheveled and worn-out uniforms of the

German troops they noticed lying in the darkened rooms of the cellars. Laskin's party had sped across from 64th Army's headquarters at Beke-tovka, on behalf of their commander, Colonel General Mikhail Shumi-lov. With Lieutenant General Schmidt and Colonel Adam in attendance, Roske took a chair and dismissed the Russian interpreter,[19] preferring to use his own, who quickly brought the Red Army commander up to speed on his position in the southern *Kessel*. Paulus was still nowhere to be seen, nor did the Soviets realize his close proximity—yet. In the squalid corridors outside his room many of Roske's officers and their men stood in tears as defeat finally now stared them in the face.

Roske opened up proceedings:

"I have made the decision," he said, "that under certain conditions, because of the innumerable wounded and soldiers unfit for fighting, to cease fire should the Red Army meet my specific conditions."

"Which conditions are they?" Laskin asked.

"The safety and lives of my soldiers has to be guaranteed, and any looting or marauding particularly of my weaker soldiers is not to be permitted. I will only end the fighting if I get a guarantee right now that each of my soldiers is allowed to return home as soon as the war is over."

Laskin pondered a few minutes as the German commander's words were translated. He held up one hand to then stab a finger down on the table as he spoke: "All that is already mentioned in the original Capit-ulation Document, but there is one exception, seeing as this was not accepted. The officers are not permitted to keep any weapons!"

Roske turned to catch Schmidt's eye. Both men realized they must now come clean as to their trump card to play. He leaned forward to speak clearly and meet Laskin in the eye as his words were translated to him. "In my encampment I am housing the O.B. of the Sixth Army, General Field Marshal Paulus."

Much as the Russians all hoped this was the case, Roske had finally supplied the concrete evidence that Paulus indeed was still in the city and had not been flown out of the *Kessel*.

Laskin interrupted: "Do you mean Commander General Paulus?"

Roske shook his head and repeated (with emphasis): "No, I mean *General Field Marshal Paulus*, for whose safety I am responsible. I will only lay down our weapons when he has been driven away with dignity, without him being harassed in any way."

Laskin studied the German's face and looked around at his own delegation and at the rooms leading off from where they sat, trying to perhaps guess, before finally inquiring:

"Where is Field Marshal Paulus?"

Without blinking, Roske calmly replied, "Somewhere within my encampment."

Digesting the incredible news of the fish they were about to catch, Laskin remained silent for a few seconds before firmly stating: "Your weapons must be lain down immediately!"

Without waiting for any recognition or words from Schmidt, Roske shook his head. "Only once these conditions have been met. I will draw your attention to the fact that I still have a small but capable garrison of soldiers!"

Laskin and Major General Burmakov's faces remained immobile, both men saying nothing for a few seconds, a disconcertingly long time for the German delegation. Finally, and abruptly Laskin declared, "*Tak!*" ("So be it!"). The interpreter looked and nodded to Roske, intimating that the Russian had agreed to his commander's terms. The game seemed to be over, bar the final, dramatic denouement. Lieutenant Colonel Vinokur nodded in agreement, but his soldiers still kept a firm grip on the F-18 grenades stowed secretly in their pockets.

Obviously, and immediately, his eyes on the bigger prize, Laskin now wanted to know Paulus's whereabouts.[20] Sixth Army's Chief of Staff Schmidt had gone out in the meantime in order to inform Paulus, who this whole time had been lying on his camp bed, alone with his thoughts in the room next door. When Schmidt returned, Laskin asked again about Paulus. Roske replied that he would meet him shortly in an adjoining room. The Russian major standing near to the conference table asked Laskin whether he could personally take Roske to army headquarters at Beketovka himself. Laskin nodded to his request as Roske looked on and listened to his interpreter's translation. *Will he be rewarded nicely for an imprisoned general?* wondered Roske.

Before Laskin left the room, Roske's official secretary arrived to take down his last order to the troops:

> I asked Laskin to excuse me, as I had to now sign an order. I read and signed around twenty copies of it. Laskin asked whether he was allowed to know what the contents were of this order. I had it translated to him and permitted him on his request to keep a copy. Then all the Russians left my room in order to see the Field Marshal, who had meanwhile prepared himself and who was subsequently driven away in General Laskin's staff car.

However, Paulus's transfer would not be as smooth as promised. Konstantin Duvanov had fought with the 62nd Army in his home city of Stalingrad until the end of the battle. By chance he was standing in Red Square guarding a captured German communications vehicle when Paulus walked out of the basement of the Univermag Department Store and was led to a waiting Red Army car.

"Half an hour later," he recounted, "we saw a sergeant carrying three captured German machine guns over his shoulder. He went up to the car and saw Paulus inside. He said, 'Ah! The general who killed so many people just sitting there in the car as if nothing happened!'

"So, he loaded a machine gun and aimed it. Paulus opened his mouth and became white as paper. Because you know—in one millisecond there would be no Field Marshal. But suddenly a lieutenant emerged and pushed the machine gun away. He shut the car door and shouted to the driver: 'Move for God's sake, otherwise he'll be killed here.'"[21]

The Russian major remained with Roske, waiting for him to make ready to leave and follow Paulus and his staff to the 64th Army's headquarters. Roske ordered his orderly to pack his belongings as he sat motionless in his office.

> The next question came to me. What do we do now? The Russians, being very proper and correct, had granted all our requests. I asked my men: "Well, shall we give it a go?" These words came as a relief to

them, and they loudly cheered my suggestion. Since we were to lose our weapons anyway, we rendered them useless and threw parts of them into the fire, which was busy consuming my personal papers, photographs, identity documents and money. Our army doctor then provided me with a phial of cyanide which I could take with me "just in case." As he gave me the little bottle, he said, "If Herr General were to drink this, it would kill him three times over." I hid it away in my trouser pocket.

As well as leading the 71st Division, I had also retained command of my old I.R. 194. Apart from Major Dobberkau, Captain Hindenlang, First Lieutenant Hoßfeld, and the officers of the regimental staff were all housed in a small room adjoining the entrance hall to the cellar. I had only visited their living space there one single time. Now that things were coming to an end, I wanted to see them one last time and say goodbye. I went into the entrance hall, which was pitch black, without a lantern, and was unable to find the doorway to their quarters. Apathetically, but with an enormous sense of regret, I turned back and never did see them.

Roske returned to his cellar room, packed his clothes and bedding into an enormous washing bag, and added one piece of hand luggage. It was here he was surprised by the Russians' empathy, or generosity even. The Soviet officer ordered sufficient transportation to ensure that all the remaining men, officers, and their luggage could be transported safely:

Eventually I agreed to this, after having been persuaded by my gentlemen and not really minding either way myself. After some hours a truck and a car arrived. Dobberkau, Hindenlang, Hoßfeld, the severely wounded Adjutant of the I.R. 191 First Lieutenant Wegener, Berndl my orderly, and all the luggage, went into the truck. I then got into a separate car.

For the Russian troops now celebrating, some firing their weapons into the bright sky, others sitting quietly with their comrades sharing stories, while others danced, the final resting place of their enemy was to some a befitting end. Anatolii Soldatov, the deputy political officer of the 62nd Army, described "an unbelievable stench" near the German headquarters at Stalingrad, where German soldiers had used the corridor as a bathroom, leaving piles of feces "up to your chest."[22] As Roske had stated to Laskin, who also commented on the site, such was the ferocity of the Soviet artillery and mortar attacks on anything moving in the Germans' defenses it had proven impossible to organize and maintain an effective latrine system.

After a difficult off-road trip the motorized column transporting Roske's officers finally arrived in the evening at Beketovka, the staff quarters of 64th Army. He recalled,

> I was led into a farmhouse which was being used by the army staff. The truck with all my comrades drove on. When I protested at this, I was reassured that I would see them all again the following day and that I was just here to be introduced to the Commander of the 64th Army of the Southeastern Front, Major General Shumilov.[23]

Roske's war was now over. He took from his pocket the parchment of staff paper his orderly had handed him, perhaps for its historic significance. It was the final radiogram sent by the division to Army High Command before they destroyed the communication equipment and their Soviet captors arrived to take them away.

```
11.02 Hours: Radio station of the 71.ID signs off.
Greetings to all relatives.[24]
```

The Lower Saxony "Lucky" Division, the premier infantry formation that had served with Sixth Army to "storm the heavens," mustering a strength of 11,361 men at the start of Case Blue, had like many of Paulus's formations now ceased to exist. Roske crumpled up the radiogram, dropped it into the slushy snow, and walked in to meet his captors.

He would serve almost thirteen years in Soviet gulags based in

Siberia and the Urals, before returning home in 1955—one of the very last batch of German POWs to be returned by the Soviets to West Germany.[25] He would be one of approximately five thousand survivors from the ninety-one thousand men who had marched into captivity that freezing January day. Less than a year after his return, at Christmas 1956, "Fritz" Roske, who had survived five months of hell in Stalingrad over a decade before, leading his men with distinction in an offensive he knew would fail, would commit suicide. One of the last lines he wrote in a letter to his wife on the days before the surrender summed up his quality as an effective combat leader:

> The spirit within our regiment is quite marvellous. We are so very proud to be able to be in such a community of true men in Stalingrad. What will be, nobody knows. It's not really about "what." It's more about "how." And we will take good care of that.[26]

CHAPTER NINETEEN

The End

The army is moving out. It wasn't easy to see them go, these comrades I had shared so much with.

—Veniamin Yakovlevich Zhukov[1]

The thousands of Axis forces now surrendering were, like Roske and his men, leaving the city to an unknown, grim future. Lieutenant Wuster of the 71st Infantry Division recounted in his memoir *An Artilleryman in Stalingrad*:

Large and small groups of prisoners were guided through the rubble of the city. These trickles then merged into one huge column of prisoners, at first a few hundred, later thousands. We walked past German positions that had been overrun. Shot up and burnt-out vehicles, tanks and guns of all kinds bordered the route formed from hard-packed snow.

Dead bodies, frozen stiff, were lying everywhere; completely emaciated, unshaven, often curled up in agony. In some places the corpses lay entwined in large mounds, as if a crowd had been driven together and cut down by automatic weapons. Other bodies had been mutilated until they were no longer recognizable. These former comrades had been run over by Russian tanks, regardless of whether or not they had been dead or alive. Their body parts lay scattered about the area like pieces of shredded ice. . . . I had lost my comrades in the war years, had experienced death and suffering first-hand, but never had I seen so many dead soldiers in such a narrow area.[2]

*   *   *

For Red Army officers and soldiers alike, though the victory was cherished, their hatred of the enemy was engrained with little sympathy, given to the horrendous sites the central *Kessel* provided now that Roske had formally surrendered his position. For tank commander Lieutenant Joseph Mironovich Yampolsky, now recovered from his wounds fighting the previous October in the Factory District, there was little emotion left in him to warrant showing pity:

> All the basements were packed with wounded German soldiers and officers, dying of their wounds, hunger and cold. It was hard to look at their suffering, but after what we had experienced during the autumn battles, nobody felt any pity. . . . Our paramedics were physically unable to provide assistance to all the Germans. The order was enforced not to kill the prisoners. Anyway, some of us wandered among the rows of the wounded, looking for SS-men. Those identified by their SS uniforms were shot on the spot. One more thing struck us: almost one in ten of those wearing German uniforms were former Red Army soldiers. Summary execution was applied to them also. The bitterness of people was overwhelming. All the streets were littered with frozen corpses of Germans. The German prisoners themselves cleared the pass ways by pulling the corpses to both sides of the roads. . . . The Germans ripped off jackboots from the dead bodies of their countrymen. The technology was simple: they would hit with a crowbar on the ankle, it would crumble and then they could easily remove the jackboots.[3]

The human drama playing out on the ground was matched by the political machinations in Berlin. On February 1 Hitler raged in his headquarters against Paulus's betrayal in not taking the poisoned chalice of a glorious ending to the legend the Fuhrer's minister of propaganda, Joseph Goebbels, was constructing for the German people: "In peacetime in Germany about 18,000 to 20,000 people a year chose to commit suicide, even without being in such a position. Here is a man who sees

50,000 or 60,000 of his soldiers die defending themselves bravely to the end. How can he surrender himself to the Bolsheviks!"[4]

The Fuhrer knew the reality too well, as reports and firsthand eyewitnesses had spent the past few weeks being brought in front of him to report the situation as the Sixth Army disintegrated.

The scale of the fighting and number of dead were staggering, both to comprehend on an official report and for those still alive to witness firsthand in the city itself. Death and destruction was all around as Nikita Khrushchev would later recount:

> Thousands of German corpses were dug out of the frozen ground, stacked in layers alternating with railway ties and set afire. "I didn't go back a second time," Khrushchev recalled. "Napoleon or someone once said that burning enemy corpses smell good. Well, speaking for myself, I don't agree."[5]

More than 2.9 million bombs had landed on the city districts—whether artillery rounds, mortar shells, or dropped from the air by the thousands of sorties flown by the Luftwaffe. The Factory District—born of Stalin's Five-Year Plans—the jewel of the new city, were now a smoking, lunar landscape. Eight hundred and fifty thousand square meters had been destroyed, taking with them 126 of the city's industrial enterprises and the 8,630 major machine works housed within them. All three major industrial centers where the major fighting had occurred—the Red October Steel Plant, the Barrikady Gun Factory, and the Tractor Works—were now ruins. Of the 666 industrial buildings on these sites, 546 had been completely destroyed. The estimated cost for all three complexes was approximately 1,200,000,000 rubles.

The city itself was unrecognizable. Approximately 41,000 buildings were now in ruins, with only 12 percent of civic housing still standing. The battle had destroyed 110 schools, 15 hospitals, and 68 healthcare centers. The streets of the city were now simply pathways through a wasteland, with barely any distinguishing landmarks for casual observers to navigate to their destination. A division commander recalled when at Stalingrad, after 156 days of combat, he saw an intact house for the first time: "We were so used to ruins—that seemed normal to us—that an intact little house was a remarkable phenomenon and attracted our attention. We even stopped, looking at this surviving house."[6]

Of the city's 400,000 or so residents (which had swollen pre-battle to 850,000 due to the mass influx of refugees fleeing the German's initial advance eastwards), only 9,796 remained upon its liberation.[7] Soviet figures stated that 64,224 civilians had died in the fighting at Stalingrad, including 1,744 who were shot and 108 who had been hanged.[8] The city had no local police force or active militia to monitor and protect what buildings were left standing that might attract looters and those German troops that had not surrendered but instead chosen to fight on and survive come what may in the ruins.[9] Stalingrad's Defense Committee requested support from the NKVD to secure the city's boundaries, set up checkpoints, and recruit and train a new police force.

The magnitude of the destruction in Stalingrad was so great that regional and national government-level discussions took place to seriously argue the case that perhaps leaving the ruins of Stalingrad as a monument to the war was the best option, and then rebuild the city at a new point along the Volga. As the BBC correspondent on the ground, Paul Winterton, testified:

> Every yard of it, literally every yard has been fought over and frozen corpses still lie amongst the wreckage of trenches and dugouts and under blasted walls. . . . The streets of Stalingrad, if you can give a name to open spaces between ruins, still bear all the marks of battle: with the usual litter of helmets and weapons, stacks of ammunition, papers fluttering in the snow, pocketbooks from dead Germans and any number of smashed corpses lying where they fell or stacked up in great frozen heaps for later burial.[10]

Whatever the outcome, the cleanup had to begin. The city's sewerage system in some districts had been severely compromised, with pipes cracked or broken and tunnels collapsed as a result of the fighting. Sewage that had flowed through cellars, stairwells, rooms of buildings, and out into the streets but then frozen during the bitter winter fighting was now a real danger with the springtime thaw on the horizon. The environmental cleanup could not begin until each area of risk was assessed by specialist demolition teams for German booby traps as well as the unexploded ordinance that littered the city.[11] From February 15 to April 4, the battlefield was semi-sealed off from outsiders as a program of mass removal of enemy corpses was implemented by the Stalingrad Defense Committee, with special detachments removing and transporting them outside the city for burial or in some cases to be burned in communal pyres due to concerns of infectious disease. The bodies of officers and men of the Red Army that were also in situ across the dozens of battlefield sites of the city were collected and buried in communal graves, normally with a ceremony attended by local officials and army commanders. Groups of German prisoners were retained in Stalingrad first to support this clearing-up program, before then turning toward rebuilding the city. One such prisoner, a member of Major General Roske's 71st Division, recalled the everyday horror of the cleanup that eventually became a normal day's work:

> Into one ravine alone we threw approximately thirty-thousand corpses—Russian and German—and chucked earth over them. I had kept a register of all the many thousands of German men killed in action, in order to be able to inform their relatives back home later. But this register was taken from me by the Russians.[12]

It was a common site to have what few civilians there were still in the city in attendance, too, or to maintain these mass graves as time went on. The Russian ones, that is.

Despite the levels of death and destruction, and the depopulation of the city itself, over the days and weeks, once the northern pocket had finally been cleared of those German troops still fighting NKVD units,[13] by April 1943 a semblance of new life seeped back into the place on a surge of euphoria that the Red Army had finally beaten the Germans. As Paul Winterton's report captured:

> There's a real holiday atmosphere among these people today. They're the proudest men and women I've ever seen. They know they've done a terrific job and have done it well. Their city's been destroyed but they smashed the invader by sheer stubbornness and unconquerable courage. These men and women fought and worked for months with their backs to the river, that they'd sworn never to retreat across. Facing an enemy who held the only dominating height in Stalingrad and could pound them with shells and mortars unceasingly by day and night. They clung to their narrow foothold and their feet never slipped.[14]

The process of shipping out the German and Axis prisoners of war had begun almost immediately for fear of infections and disease spreading to the Russian population. They were to be transported across the Volga and into the Soviet hinterland, though a portion of the ninety-one thousand Axis prisoners remained in the city to work on its reconstruction. Having survived the inferno of defending the city and the horrors he had witnessed, Guards Lieutenant Antatoliy Merezhko now looked on his tormentors with pity:

> Before, I had thought I could rip their throats open with my bare teeth, but when I saw them convoyed across the Volga, in those tattered pathetic overcoats, knowing that the nearest habitable place where they could rest was 10–15 kilometers away. . . . And so, this column marches . . . into this endless Kazakh steppe. . . . And you think to yourself: "You'll never make it, fellas. . . ." And at the same time, you experience the triumphant feeling of victory. . . . As I was standing there on a Volga scarp, I decided that I would stay alive to the end of the war! I ordered myself: "Stay alive to the end of the war!"[15]

*   *   *

Reconstruction took place slowly. In January 1947, some 330,000 people were living in Stalingrad, in very cramped conditions, and tens of thousands were still living in the basements and stairwells of ruined buildings or in makeshift dormitories.[16] Yet, from the massive rebuilding program that would be needed in the city would arise a community-based spirit to not only rebuild Stalingrad to the glory it had previously been, but to commemorate and celebrate the victory, too. What would evolve would be a local campaign to rebuild one iconic house in the center of the city that had epitomized the desperate struggle to defeat the fascist invaders. This campaign would be galvanized by the stories of the house's defense that had by now been reported all across Russia, with its defenders lionized to instill hope and fervor. As with the rest of the city, the house was a ruin.

From its ashes would arise a new patriotic campaign to not only rebuild Pavlov's House but to then reconstruct Stalingrad and every town and city in western Russia that had suffered at the hands of the Germans. It would be ordinary Russian citizens who would spark this monumental effort, and the Russian state that would support and nurture the campaign in order to not only rebuild the country but also shape the postwar narrative that enhanced the reputation of Stalin, his leadership, and the mighty role the Communist Party had played in the country's victory over Nazi Germany. Pavlov's House would become an emblem of this strategy.

The Legend of the "Lighthouse"

No one is forgotten, and nothing is forgotten.[1]
—Panorama Museum, Volgograd

During the length of the Great Patriotic War, the Russian government was possibly better placed to undertake the propaganda war as it was to hold off the German onslaught across its western borders. Since the Bolshevik revolution of 1917 the Party had developed and weaponized its mass media to control and direct its population. From Stalin's accession to the leadership, to his Five-Year Plans that drove the country into the twentieth century and his subsequent brutal purges killing millions, the use of print and radio had promoted his message and thus maintained his control. Now that the country was at war with Nazi Germany, the government apparatus simply supercharged its message and the noble, even holy cause every single Russian citizen was now invested in.

Stalin's government would not only rally its men and women to the Motherland in order to rebuild the horrific losses the Red Army would suffer in the first two years of the war, but also work toward controlling and manipulating what the country would be told of its performance. Millions of ordinary people, much like the citizens of the other great power in World War II, the United States, would enlist to create an enormous "citizen's army." This newly raised people's militia would evolve through many catastrophic mistakes, bloody losses, and costly victories to defeat a most professional and lethal army at the gates of

Stalingrad in February 1942.[2] The demographic and ethnic diversity of this new Red Army mirrored the vastness of the country itself: a population of 170 million, comprised of at least ten main ethnic groups (Russian being the dominant grouping) and speaking more than fifty languages. The government and the armed forces needed to establish an "unbreakable bond" with their people, across all boundaries and borders. This would be achieved by the media—whether by persuasion or coercion—through its political organs.

During the course of the war, more than thirteen hundred newspapers and journals were produced by the Red Army, reaching a readership of at least 4.3 million people. There would be a wide array of national and regional weekly editions, as well as standard daily newspapers covering the main stories of the war, in every theater Soviet forces were engaged in, all heavily censored but truthful enough to maintain the country's mindset since Stalin's call to arms in July 1941 that the Motherland was in danger. Added to this, to tie troops to their units and areas of service, the army would provide dedicated and distinctive editions for all units. Normally printed as a two-, four- or six-page edition, these published relevant stories promoting units' (company, battalion, regiment, division, etc.) feats of bravery against the fascist invader, and where relevant, individuals were praised and celebrated, while the publications would promote the Party line and if necessary promulgate whatever storyline was needed to shore up morale, both in the civilian and military spheres. The disasters of the first eighteen months of the war—Barbarossa, Moscow almost captured, Leningrad under siege, the failed spring offensives of 1942, and of course the retreat to Stalingrad—all fostered a sense of the country under siege and how the government (Stalin) and the Red Army would stem the tide.

To service the thirst for news a crusade across Russia was launched for stories of heroism, sacrifice, patriotism, and of course the glorification the Red Army, the Party, and Stalin himself. This improved, well-oiled media machine needed content. The Red Army would employ more than five thousand reporters, writers, poets, playwrights, and radio scriptwriters to go out into the country, into the various theaters of conflict, to the actual front line itself to find the people and the stories. More than a million serving Russian personnel were encouraged to keep diaries and write stories and letters for public consumption. As Brandon M. Schecter summarized in *The Stuff of Soldiers*:

> The new Soviet world was built as much on paper as it was in the physical world; fighting through writing was every bit as soldierly as wielding a rifle, driving a tank, or manning a cannon. . . . The military alone was publishing 465 frontline papers, and thousands of local papers continued their work even under the harshest of conditions and even in besieged Stalingrad. Of the 943 professional writers inducted into the Soviet Armed Forces 255 would be killed in combat.[3]

These "soldier writers" were put to work by all the big media organs: the Defense Ministry's newspaper, *Krasnaya Zvezda*; the government's daily mouthpiece, *Izvestiya*; and the Communist Party's own conduit for all news, *Pravda*. Under fire and covering the major events on the front line, from the Baltic to the Caspian Seas, men such as Konstanin Simonov, Boris Polevoy, David Ortenberg, Ilya Ehrenburg, and of course, Vasily Grossman would establish their reputations on the back of their acclaimed reports covering the war, especially at Stalingrad. Some would later fall foul of the censors and the Party—Ortenberg and Grossman in particular would come in for rough treatment—but at this time, their stories in the daily newspapers were read by millions—whether working in factories in the Urals or fighting in the trenches outside Leningrad or Kharkov. Those who could not afford to purchase the cheaply produced editions would regularly visit public notice boards to read pinned-up versions. Much as Nazi doctrine would degrade the Russian as backward and illiterate, a quarter of the population could read and write, approximately 1 million people had a higher education, and 13 million had received a full secondary education.[4]

Upon the commencement of the German offensive in the summer of 1942, and Army Group B's advance toward the Volga, the five-month fight for Stalingrad would take on almost a religious fervor as these writers, and many minor ones besides, were drawn to the battlefield to capture what really was a life-and-death struggle for the city and river that encapsulated modern Russia. The city itself would become the embodiment of the country's struggle, which soldier writers such as Vasily Grossman recognized quickly, his arrival in August as the Luftwaffe laid waste to Stalingrad inspiring him to coin the phrase "the dead city." It would be his articles that brought into the homes of millions of Russians the vicious struggle—such as the fight for the Grain Elevator in the southern district, or the Tractor Factory in the north—lionizing each unit entering the fight and tying its fate into the themes of sacrifice and commitment to the country.

Chuikov's change of tactics to develop storm groups for his waging of an "active defense" against the Sixth Army soon took hold of writers' and reporters' imaginations, as the fighting for every house, floor, and room grabbed the attention of the country. As Professor Ian R. Garner describes:

> The development of the house defence story provided the reader with a new means to project their own experience onto Stalingrad (and vice versa). The battle for single houses became synonymous with the militarisation and defence of both the nation and the individual's own home. . . . "Every house at Stalingrad is a fortress!" declared masthead slogans alongside photographs of destroyed homes, kicking off a period of focus on the house as central to Stalingrad.[5]

The fighting for the iconic buildings in and around Stalingrad served as a perfect backdrop to lionize the ability of the Russian soldier while also tying in the theme of belonging to a great cause and drilling down to a personal angle that every citizen could relate to. Defending one's own town, city, and—more important—home. Before the Red Army had even launched its dramatic counterattack in mid-November to encircle the Sixth Army, the operations undertaken by Chuikov's storm groups from late September onward, to reclaim whatever pieces of the west bank they could hold on to, had grabbed the attention of war reporters on the Stalingrad Front.

What became known as the "house-defense narrative" would not only play a vital part in maintaining the morale of the country but also boost the confidence of the Red Army itself, still reeling from its losses in Southern Russia all summer long. With Paulus cementing German occupation of the vast bulk of the city, his final phase to then capture the northern industrial sectors looked to be succeeding. The Luftwaffe still dominated the skies, Soviet reinforcements were being decimated with days of landing on the western bank, and despite a spirited Russian defense, Army Group A's progress in the Caucasus remained unchecked. A critical question was being asked not just in Russia but in Britain and America, too: Could the Russians hold out?

We still do not know whether there was a political decision made to instruct Red Army correspondents to begin a series of witness testimonies that would celebrate the fighting spirits and successes of the Stalingrad defenders, but amid these terrible months of savage fighting, with the city on the precipice, Soviet reporters began to find stories of heroic deeds performed by Chuikov's defenders, holding out against overwhelming odds and protecting the "home" against the fascist invaders. Ilya Grigoryevich Ehrenburg's polemic "Kill the German," published on July 24, 1942, had provided a call to arms for the country not to give up the fight as Army Groups A and B plowed through Southern Russia. Then, as winter approached, Russians needed some shred of news that promised success, to galvanize the defense of the Volga and the Eastern Front as a whole. The 13th Guards, holding their tiny strip of land in the center of the city, would be one of several units of Chuikov's army whose fighting performance would thus be lionized in the Soviet press. Their sacrifice, and more important their successes, in holding the city, protecting the "home," and taking the fight to the enemy would become the focus—celebrating deeds and individuals. The house-to-house fighting in Stalingrad would serve as a perfect metaphor for the country's fight for survival, as Professor Ian Gardener concluded:

> By documenting the house as a home, introducing memories or remnants of its inhabitants or pre-war life, the defence of Stalingrad and

therefore the entire nation is transposed onto a single familiar site. To the reader whose home was under threat from invasion, loss, bombing or evacuation, any house could stand in for the entire war. . . . When victory at Stalingrad looked a certainty, the heady cocktail of individual sacrifice, epic battle, and doughty Russian military bravery—the "Stalingrad spirit" as it would become known—could in turn be projected onto action across the Eastern Front.[6]

Alongside other feats of bravery such as the bitter fighting north of the city in the Kotluban Operations, which had cost more than two hundred thousand Red Army casualties, or the defense of the Grain Elevator in the south, where a small Russian garrison of the 10th Rifle Brigade had mauled a whole division, so the defense of Pavlov's House overlooking 9th January Square would be brought to the public's attention. On October 18, as the fight for the northern districts was going badly for Chuikov, three weeks into the "siege," *Izvestia* reported on the house for the first time, but did not mention Junior Sergeant Pavlov himself or anyone else for that matter. The combat log of the 13th Guards does not record the house, and neither do the diary entries of the 71st or 295th Infantry Divisions of LI Corps. The personal papers of Major General Roske, whose I.R. 194 had positions near to the square, do not comment on it.

There are no reports of it being discussed at LI Corps or indeed Sixth Army headquarters. Nevertheless, as described in this book, the battle for the house was indeed happening amid the daily ebb and flow of the fighting for the city's central buildings, where the 13th Guards still held on to their positions in the NKVD complex, the Brewery, and Gerhardt's Mill. More than a month after Elin's 7th Company 42nd Guards Rifle Regiment had taken ownership of the building, the stakes were raised, to a degree, by a soldier writer from the 62nd Army's own newspaper, *Stalinskoe Znamya (Stalin's Banner)*.

On October 31, 1942, under the headline "Pavlov's House," the paper published "This Is Heroic Stalingrad," by Juliy Chepurin, Stalingrad.

For more than thirty days, a group of guardsmen from the unit of Hero of the Soviet Union Rodimtsev, under the command of the guard Sergeant Pavlov, have been defending one of the houses that are important in the defense of Stalingrad. In the part, this house is called "Pavlov's House." It is not an accidental episode in the struggle of the guardsmen. On the contrary, there is nothing of chance here. Here the commander's plan is combined with his exemplary execution. "Pavlov's House" is a symbol of the heroic struggle of all defenders of Stalingrad. It will go down in the history of the defense of the glorious city as a monument to the military skill and valor of the guards.

This dilapidated house stands almost in the very center of the city. For more than thirty days without sleep, without rest, the Russian people Pavlov, Aleksandrov, Afanasiev, the Ukrainians of Sabgaid, Glushchenko, the Georgians Mosiyashvili, Stepanoshvili, the Uzbek Turgunov, the Kazakh Murzaev, the Abkhazian Sukba, the Tajik Turdyev, the Tatar of their fighting friends and their friends have been defending Stalingrad.

This is Pavlov's House.[7]

Juliy Petrovich Chepurin was a twenty-eight-year-old special correspondent for the 62nd Army's newspaper, hailing from Saratov, 380 kilometers (approximately 240 miles) north of the fighting. In 1939 he was called up for active military service as a private, and by the time of the battle in 1942 had been accepted by the Communist Party and risen to an officer's rank. Along with many other journalists in mid-October, he had been drawn to the central district occupied by the 13th Guards as it was now the quietest sector in Chuikov's area of operations. The fighting in the north had intensified, with enemy aerial activity concentrated there. One can assume Major General Rodimtsev's division, now facing two exhausted German units (71st and 295th) and themselves heavily depleted, was a safe bet for writers to find time to talk to the troops and hear their stories. Studying the combat logs, the Germans now seem entrenched in their lines and were content to offer stout resistance if attacked but resorted more to lobbing over mortar rounds and sporadic artillery barrages. Rodimtsev wanted to stabilize his line to offer a coordinated defense, hence the need to capture the house in the first place, as it offered an excellent spotter's position. One can imagine the fighting for a four-storey building on Penzenskaya Street, still 90 percent intact, overlooking the city's main square might tick all the boxes for readers. All around it was the debris of war, but the house was standing, having been brilliantly captured with its defenders occupying every floor, not hiding in the cellars, or creeping through the sewers to fight the Germans.

Chepurin's piece on Pavlov's House took up two pages and praised the capture of the house, its fortifications, and the small garrison protecting it. At this point in the story the house was titled after Junior Sergeant Pavlov, who was name-checked as the garrison commander, when in reality it would have been Lieutenant Afanasiev, Senior Lieutenant Naumov of the 7th Company, and ultimately battalion commander Senior Lieutenant Zhukov, whom both officers reported to, based a few hundred yards away at Gerhardt's Mill. The story for the first time also tied in the nation's contribution, as Chepurin celebrated the loyal effort of Pavlov's fellow guardsmen's ethnic origins: Chechens, Georgians, Tartars, Tajiks, Uzbeks, and Ukrainians. The 13th Guards had suffered appalling casualties since they had come ashore on September 14–15, and many replacements were from these territories, so Chepurin's story was perhaps sailing close to the wind in terms of accuracy, but it was also giving his 62nd Army audience what they wanted to read. They were all in it together.

Within days of the piece being published, the government's and the Red Army's need for better news meant that Chepurin's story gained a bigger audience. The feats of Rodimtsev's division were now recognized on a national level due to their survival and success in holding the city. Word spread to Moscow-based writers also looking for positive news from the front line, *Pravda* tracking down Colonel Elin's own political instructor, Leonid Koren of the 42nd Guards Rifle Regiment, who published a series of vignettes titled "Stalingrad Days." Perhaps picking up on the earlier piece, Chepurin covered the story of the capture and defense of the Party's own building on Penzenskaya Street. Soviet audiences were now brought the incredible deeds of the 13th Guards and in

particular one sergeant who was leading a heroic defense of a key fortification within the city, now named after him: Pavlov's House. While
General Zhukov's counteroffensive was underway and the Sixth Army
melted back into their doomed pocket, this one story was picked up by
Soviet national radio, and a piece of Koren's was read to a captivated
nation by the country's premier broadcaster, Yuri Levitan.

The story might have ended there, as Pavlov was wounded after fifty-
eight days serving on the front line in the city, and shipped back to the
rear, with the defense of the house and the fight for the city continuing
for more than two more months. The war progressed, and Pavlov would
not rejoin the 13th Guards on returning to duty in 1943, but would serve
with the artillery as the Red Army pushed toward Berlin in 1945. He
survived the war, as did many of his comrades who had fought with
him in Stalingrad and in the house overlooking the Volga. But, as the
war began to move westward toward Germany, Stalingrad was emerg-
ing from the rubble, its people returning to bring the city and Pavlov's
place in it back to life.

On a normal day in the offices of *Stalingradskaia pravda* there landed
on the desk of the editor a handwritten letter titled "Our Contribution,"
which would have historical significance for the city and for Russia. It
read:

> Yesterday, one of the kindergarten workers, the chairman of the
> neighborhood committee, Alexandra Maksimovna Cherkasova,
> who was awarded the medal "For the Defense of Stalingrad," sub-
> mitted a wonderful idea, which we happily supported. Comrade
> Cherkasova decided to organize a volunteer work brigade that
> would meet during our free hours and days off.
>
> We call for the socialist competition of a brigade of builders who
> are working to restore the legendary "House of Pavlov," and we call
> all the working people of the city, all the people of Stalingrad, to
> follow our example.
>
> Heroic defenders of Stalingrad, defending our city, went ahead,

to the west, and proposed to fight with the enemy, not knowing rest,
day or night, not sparing their strength or their life.

So, we will prove ourselves worthy, we heroic Stalingradtsy
[Stalingraders], we will work toward the restoration of our native
city as selflessly as our husbands, fathers and brothers fight against
the enemy!

It was signed by nineteen women and by Cherkasova herself. The following day, Tuesday, June 15, 1943, the letter was reproduced on the newspaper's front page. Within days the group's petition had been acted upon by the local authorities, with a brigade formed that comprised nineteen veterans, teachers, and technical workers of children's institutions, and ordinary young Stalingrad mothers. The newly set-up group immediately got to work and began to restore the building on Penzenskaya Street. It would be the first house or building to be rebuilt from the destruction wrought by the German invaders. It would not be the last but the beginning of a movement that would sweep western Russia.

Stalingradskia pravda's next issue focused heavily on this new phenomenon of the birth of the "Cherkasova Brigade," devoting 90 percent of its front page to stories, letters, and photographs of it. The local Party authorities quickly got on board, Stalingrad's Restoration Bureau of the City Committee issuing a statement praising the group's "patriotic initiative" and pushing the locals to get behind the project, which more or less guaranteed it would get all the support it required to get up and running, Cherkasova herself becoming an overnight sensation, with *Stalingradskaia pravda* likening her contribution to the city to the same level as the military that had secured its victory months before. Within a week of publishing her first letter, the city held the first "mass Sunday" event for ordinary workers and housewives to join construction workers and the thousands of Axis prisoners of war already being put to work. More than eight thousand took part.

In the month after Cherkasova's letter was published, hundreds of her fellow citizens, titled the *Stalingradtsy*, followed what her new group was doing. Hundreds soon became thousands, all volunteering their spare time to join projects to clear and rebuild the city to what it once had been, very much in the same vein as German women (*Trümmerfrau*)[8] would do after the end of the war. Banners strung across rubble-strewn streets and graffiti scrawled across the ruins of buildings now sprang up across the city, their message vowing the same thing: "We will revive you, our beloved Stalingrad!"

The "Cherkasova Movement," as it came to be known, was the vanguard for the city's and eventually the country's desire to rebuild and repay those who had sacrificed their lives in the fighting. The movement quickly expanded out of the city and into Southern Russia and the Ukraine, as more brigades were set up, the war pushed farther west, and the people moved back to their destroyed homes. Though the Party did attempt to guide and control this much welcomed human resource, it had to tread carefully in not being seen to too overtly micromanage what projects each brigade decided to take on—the celebratory mood of victory needed to be maintained. Still, newspapers, reminiscent of the Five-Year Plans of the thirties, praised the exploits of exceptionally productive brigades and individuals, stoking up competition between working parties to see who could mobilize more laborers and how many tasks could be completed. A "Cherkasova ledger" was soon put in place that almost acted like time-keeping workbooks, thus giving the Party and administrative planners data with which to give the movement some sense of focus.[9]

In the post-Communist age, as witnessed in some of the memoirs of the men who fought for the city with the 13th Guards, the reality of life in a "Cherkasova brigade," when measured against political and media manipulation, can diverge. Civilians who enthusiastically volunteered contrasted with those who felt press-ganged to contribute. Many celebrated their achievements and the new skills they developed, but others felt that working on such projects simply guaranteed a smoother path in education and their chosen careers.

Nevertheless, the movement spread throughout the country, and by the time the Red Army had reached Berlin, the Cherkasova brigades had become a staple of Russian life, in the news and on the street, as renovation and new construction projects took shape in Leningrad,

Kiev, Smolensk, and Sevastopol. Cherkosova's role in this regeneration from the ashes of the great sacrifice would be firmly cemented once she officially met with (now Junior Lieutenant) Yakov Pavlov in Stalingrad in the summer of 1945, when he officially accepted from Cherkosova the completed building he had defended with such tenacity, an event the local and national press covered—one legend joined by another.

By the decree of the Presidium of the Supreme Soviet of the USSR of June 17, 1945, Junior Lieutenant Yakov Fedotovich Pavlov was awarded the prestigious title of "Hero of the Soviet Union" as well as the Gold Star for his actions at Stalingrad in 1942. He had already been awarded for his later service as an artillery officer two Orders of the Red Star, and an Order of Lenin for further wounds received in the fighting with the 3rd Ukrainian and 2nd Belorussian Fronts from 1943 to 1945. The move to grant him one of the country's highest awards had come from Marshal Chuikov himself who had met and talked with him in Poland as his 8th Guards Army rolled westward. The move seemed to have been questioned to a degree, as Pavlov's old 42nd Regiment commander from the time, Colonel Elin, had told reporters (and his veterans at subsequent reunions) he knew nothing of the recommendation for such a high honor. Pavlov was demobilized from the Red Army in August 1946, having turned down an offer to remain with his unit based in Stettin. In reality he was worn out from the eight years of service, mainly on the front line, that he had given his country, and he was still recuperating from the last of three serious wounds he had suffered in the war. He had by now joined the Communist Party and, like the majority of his comrades, wanted to embark on a new life as a civilian, but his life seems to have been mapped out for him due to his postwar popularity.

In 1947 he married, and the following year published with a Stalingrad publishing house a short memoir of his wartime service. The couple moved for nine years to Moscow, where Pavlov studied at the Party's prestigious Higher Party School and his wife taught Russian to foreign students from Vietnam and North Korea. It was here their son Yuri was born. He traveled frequently on behalf of the Party, both around

Russia and through the Eastern Bloc and into Western Europe, and even to Cuba, where he befriended Fidel Castro. Yuri Pavlov, now a retired engineer still living in his father's hometown of Novgorod, provided a picture of his father as an ordinary man who lived an extraordinary life:

> He never boasted of the Golden Star in front of people, but at the same time he highly appreciated it. He lived modestly. He worked a lot, was engaged in social activities, took an active part in instilling a sense of patriotism and love for the Motherland among young people. He often told me: "We, the soldiers of the Soviet Army, did not think that this was a feat, but simply performed our military duty." He never said: "I defended the house." Rather: "We defended." My father became friends with the legendary sniper Vasily Zaitsev, with whom he usually attended various events in Volgograd.[10]

On May 7, 1980, Pavlov was awarded the title of "Honorary Citizen of the Hero City of Volgograd," for the "special services shown in the defense of the city and the defeat of the Nazi troops in the Battle of Stalingrad." These are the accepted facts if one visits the city and tours the battle sites around 9th January Square and the central district.

However, when I was researching the testimonies of those who served with the 13th Guards Rifle Division in Stalingrad during the battle, one anecdote sprung out at me. It was from a letter written in 1957 to the director of the newly established Panorama Museum in the city, by Captain Alexei Efimovich Zhukov, commander of the 3rd Rifle Battalion of the 42nd Guards Rifle Regiment, who had operational responsibility in the area of 9th January Square. Senior Lieutenant Zhukov, like a great many other veterans of the battle, was being requested by the museum to supply answers to a series of questions that would enable their archive to establish a bank of memories of the battle. One of the questions regarded the heroic fight for Pavlov's House, about which even 62nd Army's commander Chuikov himself had stated the often-quoted line that more German soldiers had died attempting to take the position than had been killed capturing Paris in 1940.[11]

In his reply to the then director of the museum (between 1956 and

1958), Nadezhda Mikhailovna Shevtsova, Senior Lieutenant Zhukov stated:

> You wanted to know all the participants in the defense of Pavlov's House. Comrade Shevtsova, believe me, this is simply not possible. After all, the people there were not the same, they dropped out every day and the house was replenished with new ones, how can you remember all of them? I can remember about ten people, those you already know about: Pavlov, Romodonov, Sabgayda, Glushchenko, Voronov, Kalinin, medical instructor Ivaschenko, Formusatov, machine gun platoon commander Afanasiev, political instructor Avagimov, company commander Naumov, fighter Voedinov, who later was a liaison with Senior Lieutenant Dorokhov.
>
> At the time when the medical orderly Kalinin reported to regiment commander, Guards Colonel Elin, that the building at 61 Penzenskaya Street had been seized by Sergeant Pavlov and three other soldiers who had taken up defence there, a correspondent was present, and the next day a front-line newspaper carried an article entitled "Sergeant Pavlov's House." Neither we nor the command thought at the time that the house would go down in history under this name.[12]

Though timelines were confused on occasion, Senior Lieutenant Zhukov and other contributors to the archives and in subsequent interviews praised all the combatants of the siege, and Pavlov's heroism, but what they did question was the now established storyline portrayed: How long did the siege last? Who was the commander? And how many men fought there? Basically, what was the truth behind these accepted tropes that had been constructed and first published in *Stalin's Banner*, *Red Star*, and *Pravda* in November 1942 and then repeated through time?

Another key eyewitness who had already survived the fighting in mid-September when the 13th Guards landed on the west embankment was Lieutenant A. K. Dragan of the 1st Company, 1st Battalion of

Colonel Elin's 42nd Regiment. His testimony highlights the obvious discrepancy in the siege of the house being fifty-eight days in length. Perhaps with Pavlov there it was, but the fighting for the building and the area itself would carry on for many more days and weeks into 1943. Once the building's original commander, Senior Lieutenant Naumov, had been killed assaulting the Milk House (where Pavlov himself had been seriously wounded and evacuated from the city), Dragan had been transferred by Elin to the 7th Company to take over the defense of the house:

> In the second half of December . . . Elin gave me the order to defend "Pavlov's House" and make it a stronghold of our defense. . . . From that moment on, the defense of Pavlov's House began, but Pavlov himself was no longer in this house from that time. . . . I personally with my 7th Company defended it until the end of the Battle of Stalingrad.[13]

Dragan followed this statement with a further assessment of the collective performance of his unit, which fought in the house:

> For more than four months, the guardsmen of the 7th Company and the 3rd Machine-gun Company defended a four-storey building, called "Pavlov's House," on the square of 9th January of Heroic Stalingrad.[14]

The testimony of Georgi Potanski in Michael K. Jones's excellent oral history of Red Army veterans who fought at Stalingrad confirms that the size of the garrison was also airbrushed from official history:

> I was in the Mill when we heard "Pavlov's House" had been taken. We got another seven men in within a few hours, and the next day sent another thirty. A further force of fifty, and then another seventy, followed shortly. Our field engineering unit had constructed a 100-metre trench from the cellar of the Mill to "Pavlov's House," and we moved in reinforcements: machine gunners, anti-tank gunners, infantrymen and artillery spotters. . . . The twenty-four names were

deliberately selected from the garrison to emphasise the point of the Soviet Union republics.[15]

The question of who commanded the garrison is answered by the man on the ground who actually gave the order, the commander of the 42nd Guards Rifle Regiment, Colonel Elin. In his own testimony to the museum's director in the 1950s he stated it was he alone who instructed Senior Lieutenant Zhukov to commence the operation to stabilize his defensive line and to have a senior officer running the newly acquired position now protruding into no-man's-land:

> After its capture, the house entered the system of the defensive area of the 3rd Rifle Battalion. Responsibility for the defense was assigned to the battalion commander Zhukov, and they assigned it to the commander of the 7th Rifle Company, Naumov.[16]

Finally, Potanski confirms the main question of who actually commanded the house. Potanski was a reconnaissance and artillery spotter within the 42nd Guards Rifle Regiment who entered the house in the early days of the operation. He confirms to Jones the character and bravery of Pavlov: "He was my fighting buddy—brave, straightforward and honest."[17] But he then admits a truism that has quite possibly been bubbling to the service over decades among the veterans, since the end of the war, about who gets to record history and tell "their" story: "There were many others like him in our garrison who haven't entered the history books: it was the spirit of comradeship which made our forces so strong."[18]

This narrative was never meant to besmirch one man's reputation or poke holes in a country's pride in its recent military history—though its current leader seeks to use such history as a pretext to invade a sovereign nation at the time of this book's completion. The Battle of Stalingrad in my opinion is quite simply the most staggering feat of human endurance, sacrifice, and arms in the history of warfare. On both sides of the conflict, men, women, and children displayed a unique level of courage and devotion to their comrades, unit, city, and country. The losses and suffering are unimaginable for today's history students to contemplate, though the devastation inflicted upon the Ukrainian cities of Kharkiv and Mariupol in 2022 gives one an idea. But it is fundamental to ensure with research of existing material and new testimonies being discovered that we get to the truth of all aspects of the battle. For me, Pavlov's House represents a moment where the imagined storyline was deemed more important than the actual truth, in order to shore up a nation and a battered army's morale at a critical time in the Second World War on the Eastern Front. It served a purpose, but then in the Communist era became a story too big to fail. One cannot simply construct a legend to then tear it down. All the men who fought there and those who served with the 42nd Regiment, 13th Guards, who populate this story, are heroes, Junior Sergeant Pavlov included. But he is not the only hero. There is now even a campaign underway to have the building renamed to "Afanasiev's House." Though in the current climate one could argue it will never happen while President Putin remains in power.

The final page of Afanasiev's memoir sums up the price each man of the Red Army paid to defend the city and how, despite the destruction, new life emerged and the city was reborn:

In 1946, when returning from holiday, I had to transit through the city on the Volga. As soon as the train stopped at the railway station, I was immediately drawn to 9th January Square. My wife and I walked slowly through the city. There were ruined buildings everywhere, but our attention was attracted by numerous construction sites. Here and there the foundations of new houses were laid, new streets were built, the old ones were restored.

We got very emotional as we approached the memorable building. The house was already restored, but the bullet and shrapnel marks on the walls reminded of everything we had gone through. The names of my close comrades-in-arms, the brave defenders of the legendary bastion were written by a careful hand on the end wall facing the

Volga. Next to them, there was a more recent inscription: "We will revive you, dear Stalingrad!"

After going out of the house we went around it and stood in the square for a while. Convoys of lorries loaded with construction materials moved along the cleared streets; people with hand barrows and shovels bustled about in the rubble. The residents were restoring their city.[19]

Acknowledgments

I must thank Nikolai Chuikov, for taking the time to answer my questions as to his grandfather's performance and legacy from the fighting at Stalingrad. It was a thrill to have him involved in the project. I would also wish to express thanks to Yuri Pavlov, for being willing to answer my questions about his father, during and after the battle. A key contributor to my research who has offered a quite unique and revealing voice from the battle from the German perspective is Doctor Uwe Roske. His father, Major General Friedrich Roske, was captured and imprisoned for twelve years, returning to West Germany in 1955. He left behind a quite remarkable collection of diaries, drawings, letters home, and an unpublished memoir before committing suicide in 1956. The bulk of this collection has never been published before and I thank the Roske family for allowing me to now bring his story to the general public. The personal papers of Unteroffizier Albert Wittenberg were invaluable in allowing me to appreciate the ordinary German soldier's experience during that summer offensive as they rumbled toward Stalingrad and the disaster that awaited them. Much thanks to his son Frank, for supplying the material.

The research for this book has led me down many pathways, made slightly difficult by the restrictions of movement that lockdown imposed upon any historian trying to visit archives, in Britain and elsewhere. Despite this, I was very fortunate to travel to the archives of the Panorama Museum in Volgograd in the winter of 2020. My grateful thanks to all the staff who aided my weeklong stay in their offices and who then subsequently supported me with my many follow-up queries on material. I wish to thank Mikhail Shuvarikov and his battlefield tour company, Volgograd Sputnik Travel, for all their assistance and care before, during, and after my visit to the city of Volgograd. The amount of first-person testimonies I researched from the archives was incredible as well as daunting to translate, and I must thank Andrey Efimenko for his work. Lawrence G. Kelley was also an ever-present expert who took the time to explain in detail the material I was reading so I could fully understand its meaning and incorporate it into my narrative accurately. From a German perspective I wish to thank both Bernd Kostka and Uda Delbanko, for their exemplary work in providing expert translation of the many letters, memoirs, and diaries I received from various families whose relatives fought with the Sixth Army in 1942–43.

Doctor Ian Garner from the University of Toronto, who is an expert on Soviet and Russian literature and culture connected to the Great Patriotic War, was incredibly supportive in answering all my questions as well as sharing his latest work on research into Soviet press coverage of the Battle of Stalingrad. Many thanks to director Christoph Meissner at the German-Russian Museum in Karlshorst, who offered contacts and ideas for more research in Russia. Doctor Matthew D. Cotton from the University of Washington was incredibly helpful in sharing his research on the rebuilding program for Stalingrad after the battle. Aleksey Shirokormadov was very helpful in pinpointing and supplying various Soviet testimonies and newspaper articles from the battle. Special thanks go to Jason Mark for his expert analysis of the battle narrative.

I would like to thank several colleagues who are also historians and authors in their own right and have supported this project: James Barr, Jonathan Dimbleby, Karen Farrington, Robert Forczyk, James Holland, Michael K. Jones, Giles Milton, Al Murray, Laurence Rees, and William Taubman. Many thanks to Marcus Cowper, publisher of Osprey Military, for being quick to support my research with various titles from his excellent range. I am also grateful for the assistance given from Tony Pastor at Goalhanger Films who has been a big supporter of this project and also Robert Attar at *BBC History Magazine*.

My hat is tipped to Craig Fraser for such a beautiful jacket cover and to Martin Lubikowski at ML Design for the excellent and informative maps.

Finally, I am indebted to the belief and support received from my literary agent, Mark Lucas at the Soho Agency, who has been a font of wisdom throughout this process, and to George Lucas at Inkwell Management in New York. I am equally grateful for the support I have received from Andreas Campomar at Constable, his editor Holly Blood, and my publicist Henry Lord. At Scribner in New York, I will always be thankful for having such a brilliant editor as Colin Harrison, ably supported by Emily Polson and Jason Chappell.

I dedicated this book to my children, both budding historians, but will end this long list by thanking the one person who was always on hand to listen to my woes during lockdown as well as to encourage my trip to Russia: my wife, Jo. I wouldn't have been able to write this book without her. I am a lucky man.

Iain MacGregor
London, March 2022

Notes

1 *Stalin's Banner*, October 31, 1942, MZSB KP 213/58.

Prologue: We Bury Our Own

1 Interview with Nikolai Chuikov, July 2021.
2 The eighth of twelve children, Chuikov was born February 12, 1900, in the village of Serebryanye Prudy in the Tula region south of Moscow.
3 The 62nd Army was redesignated the Soviet 8th Guards Army, part of the 1st Belorussian Front. Chuikov received the German unconditional surrender on May 2, 1945.
4 Between 1949 and 1953 Chuikov served as commander in chief of the Group of Soviet Forces in Germany.
5 The Chuikov family had petitioned Brezhnev for his body to be buried on the Mamayev Kurgan.
6 An ancient burial mound allegedly named for the Tartar commander defeated at the Battle of Kulikovo in 1380.
7 He would move his command post four times during the fighting due to enemy action.
8 "CP 62" refers to the command post of General Chuikov's 62nd Army on the Mamayev Kurgan.
9 (1908–1974). Among his other works was the Soviet War Memorial in Treptower Park, Berlin, built between 1946 and 1949, which won him international fame and recognition from the Communist hierarchy.
10 A prime example of socialist realism, the eight-thousand-ton statue is the tallest in Europe at 85 meters (279 feet), higher than New York's Statue of Liberty and Rio de Janeiro's Christ the Redeemer.
11 Colonel General Mikhail Shumilov, who commanded Stalingrad's 64th Army, was part of the official planning committee for the Mamayev Complex's construction and would ultimately not sign off the budget in protest at Chuikov's dominance of its design.
12 In his memoir *The Battle for Stalingrad* Chuikov painted a vivid image

of the victory ceremony and the emotion he felt: "Seeing the formed-up columns of soldiers, with whom I had survived 185 fiery days and nights, I broke into a sweat. I began my speech with the following words. 'We vowed to stand to the death, to not surrender Stalingrad to the enemy. We have stood. We have kept our word to the Motherland.'"

13 Interview with Nikolai Chuikov, July 2021.

14 Scott W. Palmer, "How Memory Was Made: The Construction of the Memorial to the Heroes of the Battle of Stalingrad," *Russian Review* 68 (July 2009): 373–407.

15 Between November 10 and December 17, 1942, it is estimated Zaitsev killed 225 enemy soldiers.

16 Stalingrad veterans recognized the symbolic relationship of the statue, standing more than 16.5 meters (more than 50 feet) in height, to their old commander and annually gathered there up until the mid-aughts.

Introduction

1 John Erickson, *The Road to Stalingrad* (Cassell Military Classics, 2003), p. 41.

2 Casualties at Stalingrad for the Red Army accounted for 2.5 million.

3 Professor Richard Vinen, *A History in Fragments: Europe in the Twentieth Century* (Little, Brown, 2010).

4 As part of the de-Stalinization after the dictator's death, Stalingrad was renamed Volgograd in 1961.

5 Stalin was acclaimed "Man of the Year 1942" by a grateful *Time* magazine. Hitler had enjoyed the same honor in 1938.

6 Interfax news agency, as reported in Damien Sharkov, "What Happened at Stalingrad?," *Newsweek*, February 2018.

7 Thirteen-day siege of a religious outpost near San Antonio by Mexican troops during the Texas Revolution in 1836.

8 February 21–December 18, 1916, the longest battle of the Great War on the Western Front in France.

9 Brandon M. Schecter, *The Stuff of Soldiers: A History of the Red Army in WWII Through Objects* (Cornell University Press, 2019), p. 21.

10 More than fifty divisions were destroyed, approximately 147,000 killed, and 91,000 captured. Richard Overy, *Russia's War 1941–45* (Penguin, 1997), p. 186.

11 John Erickson, *The Road to Stalingrad* (Cassell Military, 2003), p. 43.

12 Russian Ставка, derived from Russia's imperial past, the Stavka was the high command of the Soviet Armed Forces during the Second World War, responsible for strategy, supplies, and the direct supervision of the main military commands led by Joseph Stalin (*Stavka Verkhovnogo Glavnoko-mandovaniya*).

13 GlavPU RKKA, the Main Political Directorate of the Red Army.

14 Russian фронтовик (*Frontoviki*) was not the same generic name as the American "G.I. Joe," the British "Tommy," and the German "Landser." This was a specific term given to those Red Army soldiers in combat on the front line.

15 The life span of a front-line Red Army soldier in Stalingrad was measured in hours.

16 "Stalingrad Days" was a series of essays for *Pravda* written by Moscow-based journalist VN Kuprin.

17 *Daily Mail*, front page headline, February 1, 1943.

18 *New York Times*, February 3, 1943.

19 A double-edged, two-handed broadsword, approximately four feet long, with a solid silver cross guard. On display today at the Panorama Museum in Volgograd.

20 Stalin's favorite broadcaster, who had announced the German invasion on June 22, 1941, and would read every major government proclamation during the war.

21 The British film critic Richard Taylor described the film as "a personality cult film." *Film Propaganda* (London), p. 48.

22 *Krasnaya Zvezda*, first published on January 1, 1924, is still the central news organ for the Ministry of Defense.

23 *Life and Fate* was first published in Russian, in Switzerland after being smuggled out of the country under the noses of the KGB in 1980. An English-language edition was published in 1985. Critics liken Grossman's work to the writing of Leo Tolstoy.

24 Lancaster spent three weeks on location, filming in eight Soviet cities. See episode 5: "The Defense of Stalingrad."

25 In 2021, the critic and editor Robert Gottlieb, writing in the *New York Times*, referred to *Life and Fate* as "the most impressive novel written since World War II."

26 The Cherkasova Movement will be discussed in the Epilogue.

27 Visit to the interactive museum, "Russia Is My History," February 2, 2018.

28 He was elected three times as deputy to the Supreme Soviet of the Russian Soviet Federative Socialist Republic.

29 The city reverts to calling itself 'The Hero City Stalingrad' six days of the calendar year—all relevant to The Great Patriotic War and the battle for the city itself: February 2 for victory at Stalingrad; May 9 for Victory in Europe; June 22 for Germany's initial invasion; July 17 marks the beginning of the Battle of Stalingrad; August 23 the air raids on the city; and November 19 the beginning of Operation Uranus.

30 *Tsentral'nyy Arkhiv Ministerstva Oborony Rossiyskoy Federatsii* (The Central Archives of the Russian Ministry of Defense).

31 Russian *агитпроп*—the promulgation in the media of government ideas that favor Communism.
32 Soviet political officers.

PART I: BLACK SUMMER FOR THE RED ARMY

1 Quote from interview by Jochen Hellbeck taken from website Facing Stalingrad.com.

Chapter One: Rolling the Dice—The Battle of Moscow 1941

1 "Molotov Addresses the Soviet People," June 22, 1941, RG-60.0880, US Holocaust Memorial Museum.
2 In the first three days of Barbarossa the Luftwaffe reportedly destroyed 3,100 aircraft. Christer Bergström, *Barbarossa—The Air Battle: July–December 1941* (Classic Publications, 2007).
3 Hitler had dismissed the term several times. Blitzkrieg had been in use by the German Army since the Great War, but to refer to an infantry attack–based offensive against strategic weak points which would be developed for larger encirclement.
4 Named after Emperor Barbarossa, the twelfth-century medieval leader of the Holy Roman Empire's Third Crusade.
5 David M. Glantz and Jonathan M. House, *Stalingrad* (University Press of Kansas, 2017), pp. 5–6.
6 The cull had included three of five marshals of the Soviet Union, all eleven deputy ministers of Defense, seventy-five of the eighty members of the Military Soviet, all the commanders of the military districts, thirteen of the fifteen army commanders, half the corps commanders, and 30 percent of officers below brigade level.
7 At least 28 percent of German armor (1,023 tanks) consisted of the inferior Panzer Mks. I and II.
8 Ben H. Shepherd, *Hitler's Soldiers: The German Army in the Third Reich* (Yale University Press, 2016) p. 115.
9 Catherine Merridale, *Ivan's War—The Red Army 1939–45* (Faber & Faber, Ltd., 2005), pp. 59–60.
10 Albert Axell, *Russia's Heroes 1941–45* (Constable & Robinson, 2001), p. 33.
11 Charles Messenger, *The Last Prussian: A Biography of Gerd von Rundstedt* (Pen & Sword Military, 2018), p. 209.
12 Initially Army Group North would capture Leningrad and the areas around it and link up with the Finns, thus eliminating the Russian fleet in the Baltic and increasing German influence in Scandinavia. The Central and Southern Army Groups would advance only to a line running from south to north: Odesa on the Black Sea, Kiev, Orsha, Lake Ilmen,

and Leningrad. Then if time allowed, Army Group North could advance southeast from Leningrad toward Moscow while Army Group Center moved eastward on the capital. All further operations would be postponed until the following year when headquarters would draft new plans based on the situation map.

13 Nigel Askey, *Operation Barbarossa: The Complete Organisational and Statistical Analysis, and Military Simulation*, II B (Lulu Publishing, 2014).

14 Joel S. A. Hayward, *Stopped at Stalingrad: The Luftwaffe and Hitler's Defeat in the East 1942–43* (University of Kansas Press, 1998), p. 2.

15 The *Guidelines for the Behaviour of the Fighting Forces* stated that Bolshevism was, "the mortal enemy of the National Socialist German people," and that the German soldier must show "ruthless and energetic action against Bolshevik agitators, guerrillas, saboteurs, Jews and the complete liquidation of any active or passive resistance." As for Russian POWs, "Extreme reserve and most alert vigilance are called for towards all members of the Red Army—even prisoners."

16 Geoffrey Roberts, *Victory at Stalingrad*, 1st edition (Routledge, 2002), pp. 29–30.

17 Germany and Japan, alongside Mussolini's Italy, had signed the Tripartite Pact on September 27, 1940. It was one of a number of agreements among the three powers to counter the economic threat of the United States.

18 Stalin's belief that the Battle of Britain was a prelude to a seaborne invasion strengthened his confidence that the Red Army's own blitzkrieg could work if Hitler's focus was facing west. His chief of the general staff Zhukov and defense commissar Semyon Timoshenko, with Stalin's hand guiding them, had ordered the military to draw up plans for a preemptive strike that would defeat German forces in occupied western Poland and East Prussia in less than forty days.

19 The original recipe of the Molotov cocktail was a mixture of ethanol, tar, and gasoline in a 750-milliliter (25-ounce) bottle. More than 450,000 were made during the Winter War.

20 An ex-Tsarist cavalry officer who fought for the Bolsheviks in the Russian Civil War, Budyonny was a survivor and confidant of Joseph Stalin. After being told of the importance of the tank in the coming war in 1939, he remarked, "You won't convince me. As soon as war is declared, everyone will shout, 'Send for the Cavalry!'" Events of the winter counteroffensive proved him correct to a degree.

21 B. Bonwetsch, "The Purge of the Military and the Red Army's Operational Capability During the 'Great Patriotic War,'" in B. Wegner, ed., *From Peace to War: Germany, Soviet Russia and the World, 1939–1941* (Oxford, 1997), pp. 396–98.

22 Future first secretary of the Soviet Union Nikita Khrushchev would be one

such appointment on the Stalingrad Front, working alongside Marshal Andrey I. Yeremenko.

23 The Russian commander of the Western Front, General Dimtry Pavlov, together with his deputies, was recalled to Moscow, tried, and executed by the NKVD (the forerunner of the KGB) for apparent complacency. A raft of other Soviet Western Front commanders would share a similar fate that summer.

24 Doc. No. N-16845-F, "The War Journal of Generaloberst Franz Halder, Chief of the General Staff of Supreme Command of the German Army (OKH), Vol VI" (Archives Section Library Services, Fort Leavenworth, Kansas).

25 Ibid.

26 Interview with Nikolai Vasilievich Orlov taken from the iRemember website.

27 By September 30, Army Group South had lost 35,000 men and 250 tanks and artillery pieces.

28 Literally meaning "traffic stoppages," *Rasputitsa* was a Russian term for conditions in the spring and autumn when heavy rain and melting snow made unpaved roads impassable.

29 Doc. No. N-16845-G, "The War Journal of Generaloberst Franz Halder, Chief of the General Staff of Supreme Command of the German Army (OKH), Vol VII" (Archives Section Library Services, Fort Leavenworth, Kansas).

30 Hitler had planned the fate of Leningrad on September 22, issuing a directive for the city to be erased by artillery and airstrikes and its population liquidated.

31 Walter Kerr, *The Secret of Stalingrad* (Doubleday & Company, Inc., 1978), p. 5.

32 Including twenty-four thousand killed and five thousand MIAs.

33 Georgy Zhukov, *The Battle for Stalingrad* (Holt, Reinhart & Winston Inc., 1963).

34 The pocket containing more than one hundred thousand men of the 16th Army was surrounded between February 8 and April 21, 1942. They were supplied by an air bridge at the cost of 106 transport aircraft and 387 airmen, but the Germans' success at resupplying a trapped army would have fatal repercussions by the end of the year at Stalingrad.

35 This one operation, involving hundreds of thousands of workers loading and transporting hundreds of factories, oil refineries, and steel plants on trains and vehicles, had achieved the impossible in the harshest winter conditions. It had come at great human cost, but it guaranteed the country still had the capacity to wage war.

36 The fight to retake this valuable ground dominating arterial supply routes would last fifteen months and cost more than 1.5 million casualties. It was grimly nicknamed by its combatants the "Rzhev Meat Grinder."

37 More than forty generals, including Field Marshals von Bock and von Rundstedt, and the supreme commander of the German Army Walther von Brauchitsch, were dismissed or "retired" from service.

38 Although prevailing conditions were in no way comparable to those of the winter of 1941–42 at Stalingrad.

Chapter Two: History Repeating Itself—March 15–May 28, 1942

1 Adolf Hitler, *Reden und Proclamationen, 1932–45*, II, pp. 1,871–74 (Domarus, ed.), taken from Earl F. Ziemke, *Stalingrad to Berlin: The German Defeat in the East* (Center of Military History, United States Army, 2002).

2 "Speech for the Heroes' Memorial Day," Berlin, March 15, 1942.

3 Richard Overy, *Russia's War 1941–45* (Penguin, 2010), p. 154.

4 von Brauchitsch had suffered a heart attack on November 19 and was retired to the Führereserve (officers reserve) on Hitler's order in December following the failure of Operation Typhoon.

5 By November 1941 as few as thirty-three thousand trained replacements were available from the Zone of Interior.

6 The man hours for building a U-boat equaled the time for constructing two Panzers (depending on type).

7 David M. Glantz and Jonathan M. House, *Stalingrad* (University Press of Kansas, 2017), pp. 8–9.

8 Between December 1941 and June 1942 more than five hundred thousand German men were removed from the armaments industry and agriculture to fill the vacancies in the armed forces.

9 There was even an argument put forward by Field Marshal von Rundstedt that the German Army should retire to their original Polish front line to reduce their lines of defense and supply.

10 Field Marshal Reichenau, Sixth Army, commenting to his staff officer Captain Jordan, in Guido Knopp, *Hitler's Warriors: Paulus the Defector* (Sutton Publishing, 2005).

11 Paramilitary death squads used throughout German-occupied Europe, specifically in the east, under the leadership of Reichsfuhrer-SS Heinrich Himmler.

12 Reichenau officially complained about the shortages of ammunition for the Sixth Army due to SS units shooting Jews.

13 Wilhelm Adam and Otto Ruhl, *With Paulus at Stalingrad* (Pen & Sword Ltd., 2015).

14 As far back as the initial planning phase for Barbarossa in July 1940, Hitler had outlined the need to seize the oil fields in the Caucasus. His *Fuhrer Directive 32* had stated how this would be achieved and then for Army Group South to push on to neighboring Iran and into the Middle East

to threaten the assets of British-run Palestine. While his armies fought outside the gates of Moscow in November 1941, his military planners in Berlin issued further reports on what specialized units would be needed within Army Group South to seize, repair, and then run the Baku and Maikop oil fields. Such optimism had been dissipated with the subsequent Soviet counterattack that winter, but now, faced with a "winner takes all" gambit in the spring of 1942, Hitler convinced himself it could still be achieved.

15 The FHO prepared situation maps of the Soviet Union, Poland, Scandinavia, and the Balkans and assembled information on potential adversaries.

16 Operation Kremlin, involving increased Luftwaffe reconnaissance flights, and the movement of two German Panzer divisions.

17 *Stalin's Correspondence with Churchill, Attlee, Roosevelt and Truman, 1941–45* (Lawrence & Wishart, 1958), doc. 36, p. 41.

18 A. Beevor, *Stalingrad* (Penguin Books, 1998), p. 63.

Chapter Three: The Move South

1 Order of the Day, No. 55, February 23, 1942.

2 Interview of Lieutenant Yampolsky taken from the iRemember website.

3 Holding facilities for personnel arriving from enemy encirclement or captivity, until their "trustworthiness" had been verified.

4 Interview of Lieutenant Yampolsky taken from the iRemember website.

5 *Diary of Unteroffizier Albert Wittenberg* (Copyright Frank Wittenberg, Germany, 2021).

6 The German 11th Army suffered seventy-five thousand casualties of which twenty-five thousand were killed.

7 *Diary of Unteroffizier Albert Wittenberg* (Copyright Frank Wittenberg, Germany, 2021).

8 Ibid.

9 William Craig, *Enemy at the Gates: The Battle for Stalingrad* (Hodder & Stoughton, 1973), p. 13.

10 This did not prevent more than fifty thousand people gaining permission to leave throughout August—mainly senior Party and administrative officials and their extended families.

11 Hugh Trevor-Roper, *Hitler's War Directives, 1939–45* (Sedgewick & Jackson, 1964), pp. 129–30.

12 Ibid.

Chapter Four: "Not One Step Back!"

1 Situation room briefing, Sixth Army HQ, August 19, in Wilhelm Adam and Otto Ruhl, *With Paulus at Stalingrad* (Pen & Sword Ltd., 2015), p. 48.

2 Interview with Lieutenant Ivan Vladimirovich Maslov taken from the iRemember website.

3 Pogoniï, *Stalingradskaia epopeia*, in John Hannstad, *The Power of Persuasion: Remembering the Battle of Stalingrad During the Thaw, 1958–1966* (University of North Carolina, 2014), p. 443.

4 Vasily Grossman, "On the Volga," *Krasnaya Zvezda*, August 21, 1942.

5 Yeremenko still limped from the wounds he had received fighting outside Moscow the previous winter.

6 Interview with Lieutenant Ivan Vladimirovich Maslov taken from the iRemember website.

7 BfZ, Sterz Collection. Sold. Christian B., 198. Inf. Div., 23.8.42.

PART II: ALL ROADS LEAD TO THE VOLGA

1 Excerpt from report "Remembering the Horrors of Stalingrad" by Daniel Sandford, BBC News, Volgograd, January 31, 2013.

Chapter Five: A City of Revolution—The Birth of Stalingrad

1 Nikolai Alekseevich Nekrasov (1821–1878) was one of nineteenth-century Russia's finest poets. "On the Volga" was written in 1860. His family's countryside estate was on the river, and he played along its banks as a child.

2 Janet M. Hartley, *The Volga* (Yale Press, 2021), p. 2.

3 Russian: Ива́н Васи́льевич (August 25, 1530–March 28, 1584). The first Tsar of Russia 1547–75.

4 Tsaritsyn was nicknamed the "Chicago of the Volga" for good reason.

5 The White forces were a Russian "Volunteer Army" planning to march on Moscow—their leaders objecting to socialism, internationalism, and instead demanding the restoration of the monarchy.

6 Jonathan Bastable, *Voices from Stalingrad* (Greenhill Books, 2019).

7 Robert Service, *Stalin: A Biography* (Pan MacMillan, 2004), p. 169.

8 W. Craig, *Enemy at the Gates: The Battle for Stalingrad* (Hodder & Stoughton, 1973), pp. 35–36.

9 Martin Sixsmith, *Russia: A 1,000-Year Chronicle of the Wild East* (The Overlook Press, 2014).

10 "Collectivization," the term given to forcing millions of Russia's peasants onto state-run farms, resulted in widespread famine and more than eleven million deaths by 1934. Eric Hobsbawn, *Age of Extremes* (Allen Lane, 1994).

11 "Stalingrad," in Leon E. Seltzer, ed., *Columbia Lippincott Gazetteer of the World* (Columbia University Press, 1952), p. 1818.

12 Волгоградский тракторный завод (историческая справка) [Volgograd

Tractor Plant (history reference)]. Real Economy Information Portal, 2007, archived from the original on June 5, 2008.

13 A. S. Chuyanov, *Two Hundred Days of Fire: Accounts by Participants and Witnesses of the Battle of Stalingrad* (Moscow, 1970), p. 225.

14 Sited in front of the station was the soon to become iconic Barmaley Fountain sculpture showing a circle of young children dancing around a snapping crocodile.

15 The 24th and 64th armies would come under the command of General Yeremenko of the Southeastern Front. R. Forczyk, *Campaign 368: Stalingrad*, Volume 2 (Osprey Publishing, 2021), p. 23.

16 He served as the first secretary of the Stalingrad Regional Committee of the Communist Party from 1938 to 1946.

17 Commanded by Major Vasily Ivanovich Zaitsev, the division had performed well in the fighting that summer on the retreat to Stalingrad.

18 Just prior to the first attack on Stalingrad, more than 2,700 arrests of those without valid papers were made in and around the city.

19 Quote from Samsonov, *Stalingradskaia bitva*, p. 153.

Chapter Six: Rain of Fire

1 John Erikson, *The Road to Stalingrad* (Cassell, 1975), p. 347.

2 Joel S. A. Hayward, *Stopped at Stalingrad: The Luftwaffe and Hitler's Defeat in the East 1942–43* (University Press of Kansas, 1998), p. 183.

3 *Fliegerkorps* VIII suffered two planes shot down. A good return compared to the Soviet 8th Air Army losses of ninety plus planes and killed pilots in the one-sided opener.

4 USAFHRA K113.309-3 vol. 5: *Hauptmann Herbert Pabst, Staffelkapitan u.Gruppenkommandeur in einer Sturzkampfstaffel: Berichte aus Russland, 1942, 23 August 1942*; Joel S. A. Hayward, *Stopped at Stalingrad: The Luftwaffe and Hitler's Defeat in the East 1942–43* (University Press of Kansas, 1998), p. 188.

5 Vasily Grossman, *A Writer at War: A Soviet Journalist with the Red Army, 1941–1945*. Antony Beevor and Luna Vinogradova, editors and translators, (New York, 2005) ("Grossman"), pp. 130-131

6 Dr. Wigand Wuster, *An Artilleryman in Stalingrad* (Leaping Horseman Books, 2007), p. 82.

7 Walter Kerr, *The Secret of Stalingrad* (Doubleday & Co. Ltd., 1978), p. 125.

8 Antony Beevor, *Stalingrad* (Viking, 1998), p. 109.

9 Robert Forczyk, *Campaign Series: Stalingrad*, Volume 1 (Osprey Publishing, 2021), p. 79.

10 H. Pabst Hauptmann, quoted in Joel S. A. Hayward, *Stopped at Stalingrad: The Luftwaffe and Hitler's Defeat in the East 1942–43* (University of Kansas Press, 1998), p. 188.

11 *Fliegerkorps* VIII bombed the besieged Soviet forces of Sevastopol with impunity, flying 23,751 sorties and dropping 20,528 tons of bombs in June alone.

12 William Craig, *Enemy at the Gates: The Battle for Stalingrad* (Hodder & Stoughton, 1973), p. 57.

13 Laurence Rees, *War of the Century—When Hitler Fought Stalin* (BBC Books), p. 143.

14 Burkov and Miakushkov, *Letopistsy pobedy*. 52, from I. R. Garner, *Stalingrad Lives* (Yale University Press, 2021), p. 46.

15 The dropping of the world's first atomic bomb, christened "Little Boy," by the USAAF's *Enola Gay* directly killed seventy thousand plus people. The Atomic Bombing of Hiroshima Archive, March 3, 2016, U.S. Department of Energy, Office of History and Heritage Resources.

16 Casualties for all six of the city districts from August 24 to 26 were as follows. Tractor District: 68 killed, 247 wounded. Barricades District: 200 killed, 120 wounded. Red October District: 62 killed, 126 wounded. Dzerzhinsky District: 70 killed, 68 wounded. Yermansky District: 302 killed, 257 wounded. Voroshilov District: 315 killed, 463 wounded. Making a total of 1,017 killed and 1,281 wounded. Walter Kerr, *The Secret of Stalingrad* (Doubleday & Co. Ltd., 1978), p. 135.

17 During the Battle of Stalingrad Lieutenant Merezhko served in the 62nd Army's headquarters. Promoted to captain, he would take part in the Battle of Berlin in 1945.

18 Excerpt from interview by Jochen Hellbeck taken from the website FacingStalingrad.com.

19 Party officials had tried to cover up the fact that by mid-August almost eight thousand families from the city's Party and business elite had been permitted to evacuate the city.

20 *Rechnoi transport SSSR 1917–1957: sbornik staei o razvitii rechnogo transporta SSSR za 40 let* (Moscow, 1957), p. 33.

21 МЗСБ НВФ 17123: "Memoirs of Vladimir Konstantinovich Shustov—a former Red Army soldier of the 34th rifle regiment of the 13th Guards Rifle Division" (Panorama Museum Archives, Volgograd).

22 Russian Всесоюзный ленинский коммунистический союз молодёжи, these were cells of the Leninist Young Communist League. The final age group of the three youth organizations was as follows: Little Octoberists (9 years of age), Youth Pioneers (9–14), and then Komsomol (14–28). Then they would become fully fledged members of the Communist Party.

23 Excerpt from report "Remembering the Horrors of Stalingrad" by Daniel Sandford, BBC News, Volgograd, January 31, 2013.

24 Situation room briefing, Sixth Army HQ, August 19, in Wilhelm Adam and Otto Ruhl, *With Paulus at Stalingrad* (Pen & Sword Ltd., 2015), pp. 60–61.

25 Catherine Merridale, *Ivan's War: The Red Army 1939–45* (Faber & Faber, 2005), p. 150.
26 Ian R. Garner, *Stalingrad Lives* (Yale Press, 2021), p. 48.

PART III: "LIVING CONCRETE"—THE SEPTEMBER BATTLES

1 Ilya Ehrenburg, "The Russian Anthaeus," *Krasnaya Zvezda,* September 20, 1942.

Chapter Seven: The King of Stalingrad!

1 Laurence Rees, *War of the Century—When Hitler Fought Stalin* (BBC Books, 1997).
2 *Hauptfeldwebel* Friederich Hundertmark, letter supplied courtesy of Frank Wittenberg.
3 General Rolf Wuthmann, 295th Infantry Division, in Ben H. Shepherd, *Hitler's Soldiers: The German Army in the Third Reich* (Yale University Press, 2017).
4 Vasily Ivanovich Chuikov, *The Battle for Stalingrad* (Ballantine, 1968).
5 Anatoliy Grigoryevich Merezhko, excerpt from interview cited in Jochen Hellbeck, "Facing Stalingrad: One Battle Births Two Contrasting Cultures of Memory," *Berlin Journal* 21 (Fall 2011).
6 *Hauptfeldwebel* Friederich Hundertmark, letter supplied by Frank Wittenberg.
7 XXXXVIII Panzer Corps and IV Army Corps (comprising 4th Pnz. Div., 14th Pnz. Div., 29th Motorized Inf. Div., 94th Inf. Div., and the Romanian 20th Inf. Div., a total of eighty thousand soldiers). Robert Forcyzk, *Campaign 368: Stalingrad,* Volume 2 (Osprey Publishing, 2021).
8 Dr. Wigand Wuster and Jason Mark, *An Artilleryman in Stalingrad* (Leaping Horseman Books, 2007), p. 94.
9 Unpublished memoir of Major General Friedrich Roske (by permission of Dr. Uwe Roske, 2021).
10 Recollections of Ernest-August Deppe, Ronald MacArthur Hirst papers, Box 12, Folder "Hartmann, Alexander von," Hoover Institution Library & Archives, USA.
11 Ibid.
12 *The 71st Infantry Division 1939–1945; Combat and Experience Reports from the Battles of the "Lucky Division" from Verdun to Stalingrad, from Monte Cassino to Lake Balaton* (in German) (Dörfler, 2006), pp. 462–63.
13 Dr. Wigand Wuster and Jason Mark, *An Artilleryman in Stalingrad* (Leaping Horseman Books, 2007), p. 93.
14 The Sturmgeschütz III was turretless, providing a low profile for protec-

tion and concealment. Carrying a powerful 75mm gun, it proved highly effective in the initial stages of the battle. It was Germany's most-produced, fully tracked armored vehicle of the Second World War.

15 Unpublished memoir of Major General Friedrich Roske (Courtesy of Dr. Uwe Roske, Germany, 2021).

16 Captain Gerhard Münch, excerpt from interview cited in Jochen Hellbeck, "Facing Stalingrad: One Battle Births Two Contrasting Cultures of Memory," *Berlin Journal* 21 (Fall 2011).

17 Unpublished memoir of Major General Friedrich Roske (Courtesy of Dr. Uwe Roske, Germany, 2021).

18 Little was he to know, but four months later, Roske would be situated a few hundred meters from this position, surrounded by Russian tanks and making ready to surrender with the few men that remained of his division.

19 Unpublished memoir of Major General Friedrich Roske (Courtesy of Dr. Uwe Roske, Germany, 2021).

20 Ibid.

21 Dr. Wigand Wuster and Jason Mark, *An Artilleryman in Stalingrad* (Leaping Horseman Books, 2007) p. 101.

22 General Hans Doerr, chief of the German liaison staff to the Romanian 4th Army, in Geoffrey Roberts, *Victory at Stalingrad*, 1st edition (Routledge, 2002).

23 Unpublished memoir of Major General Friedrich Roske (Courtesy of Dr. Uwe Roske, Germany, 2021).

24 Ibid.

Chapter Eight: Send for the Guards

1 МЗСБ НВФ 990, "Memories of Colonel Ivan Pavlovich Elin, commander of the 42nd Guards Rifle Regiment of the 13th Guards Rifle Division," April 7, 1961 (Panorama Museum Archives, Volgograd).

2 Marshal Vasily Ivanovich Chuikov, *The Battle for Stalingrad* (Ballantine Books, 1968), p. 145.

3 Ibid., p. 146.

4 Escaping the Kharkov debacle had cost the division more than 70 percent casualties fending off German counterattacks. See МЗСБ НВФ 990, "Memories of Ivan Pavlovich Yelin, commander of the 42nd Guards Rifle Regiment of the 13th Guards Rifle Division," April 7, 1961 (Panorama Museum Archives, Volgograd).

5 Serving under the cover name "Pablito," he had been a key Soviet military adviser at the Battle of Guadalajara in 1937, when the Spanish Republicans defeated Mussolini's expeditionary corps.

6 The 5th Parachute Brigade (numbering approximately seventeen hundred men) of the 3rd Airborne Corps.

7 МЗСБ НВФ 12219/2, "Memoirs of Senior Lieutenant Alexei Efimovich Zhukov, commander of the 3rd Rifle Battalion of the 42nd Guards Rifle Regiment of the 13th Guards Rifle Division" (Panorama Museum Archives, Volgograd).

8 In the 1st Company, 1st Battalion, of the 42nd Guards Regiment, for example, from a total of 85, all ranks, ethnic groups consisted of: 40 Russians, 15 Ukrainians, 5 Belarusians, 1 Tajiks, 1 Jew, 4 Uzbeks, 5 Tatars, 3 Georgians, 2 Kazakhs, 2 Bashkirs, 2 Chuvashes.

9 Brandon. M. Schechter, *The Stuff of Soldiers: A History of the Red Army in WWII Through Objects* (Cornell University Press, 2019), p. 42.

10 Boris Sokolov, *Myths and Legends of the Eastern Front: Reassessing the Great Patriotic War 1941–45*, translated by Richard Harrison (Pen & Sword Ltd., 2020).

11 By the time of D-Day, 1944, the United States had sent to the Soviets under the Lend-Lease program more than three hundred thousand trucks and other military vehicles—the majority of which were the 2.5-ton 6x6 Studebaker. American Historical Association.

12 "Alexander Rodimtsev," in I. Afanasiev, *House of Military Glory*, 3rd edition (DOSAAF Publishing House, 1970).

13 The legend of two guardsmen sharing one rifle going into battle, as depicted in the film *Enemy at the Gates*, is patently ludicrous. The division would have been fully armed.

14 At the time of the battle Krasnaya Sloboda was still a small town situated on the eastern bank of the Volga, opposite the Central Ferry Crossing into the city. Surrounded by forests, it was an ideal way station for Red Army units to remain hidden before transit into Stalingrad.

15 МЗСБ НВФ 12219/2, "Memoirs of Senior Lieutenant Alexei Efimovich Zhukov—commander of the 3rd Rifle Battalion of the 42nd Guards Rifle Regiment of the 13th Guards Rifle Division" (Panorama Museum Archives, Volgograd).

16 The Russian самовар, meaning "self-brewer," is an elaborate metal container whose invention in Russia spread throughout the peoples of the Soviet Union. This author has enjoyed many cups of dark tea from one of them!

17 *Two Hundred Days of Fire: Accounts by Participants and Witnesses of the Battle of Stalingrad* (Moscow, 1970), p. 168.

18 "Alexander Rodimtsev," in I. Afanasiev, *House of Military Glory*, 3rd edition (DOSAAF Publishing House, 1970).

19 Marshal of the Soviet Union Vasiliy Ivanovich Chuikov, *The Battle for Stalingrad* (Holt, Rinehart and Winston, 1964).

20 "Alexander Rodimtsev," in I. Afanasiev, *House of Military Glory*, 3rd edition (DOSAAF Publishing House, 1970).

21 Obviously Rodimtsev was in no position to realize how stubbornly the defense of the Factory District to the north was going. For him, the col-

lapse in the center of the city would spell disaster for the whole of the 62nd Army's position. That is what Chuikov himself had outlined to him.

22 МЗСБ НВФ 12219/2, "Memoirs of Senior Lieutenant Alexei Efimovich Zhukov, commander of the 3rd Rifle Battalion of the 42nd Guards Rifle Regiment of the 13th Guards Rifle Division" (Panorama Museum Archives, Volgograd).

23 More than 470,000 of the Degtyaryov Single Shot Anti-Tank Weapon System model of 1941 would be in service with the Red Army by 1945.

24 МЗСБ НВФ 990, "Memories of Colonel Ivan Pavlovich Elin, commander of the 42nd Guards Rifle Regiment of the 13th Guards Rifle Division," April 7, 1961 (Panorama Museum Archives, Volgograd).

25 Ibid.

26 Chervyakov was a regular soldier, having enlisted in 1933 and graduating from the Kharkov Infantry School. In his memoirs, Rodimtsev described him as "a rare combination . . . full of youth and daring, with the restraint and discipline of a warrior."

27 Alexander Rodimtsev, in I. Afanasiev, *House of Military Glory*, third revised edition (DOSAAF Publishing House, 1970).

28 A brick warehouse where nails and wiring were stored.

29 МЗСБ НВФ 990, "Memories of Colonel Ivan Pavlovich Elin, commander of the 42nd Guards Rifle Regiment of the 13th Guards Rifle Division," April 7, 1961 (Panorama Museum Archives, Volgograd).

30 Alexander Rodimtsev, *In with the Guards!* (Moscow Publishing House, 1967).

31 And which in some cases have persisted to this day.

32 Boris Sokolov, *Myths and Legends of the Eastern Front: Reassessing the Great Patriotic War*, translated by Richard Harrison (Pen & Sword Ltd., 2019), p. 131.

33 МЗСБ НВФ 535/1, "Memoirs of Lieutenant Anton Kuzmich Dragan, commander of the 1st Company of the 1st Battalion of the 42nd Rifle Regiment, 13th Guards Rifle Division" (Panorama Museum Archives, Volgograd).

34 Alexander Rodimtsev, *In with the Guards!* (Moscow Publishing House, 1967).

35 The siege of the Grain Elevator is too epic a tale to do justice to in one or two paragraphs. David M. Glantz and Jonathan House's *Stalingrad* trilogy (University of Kansas Press, 2017) is required reading to understand its significance.

36 Alexander Rodimtsev, *In with the Guards!* (Moscow Publishing House, 1967).

37 МЗСБ НВФ 535/1, "Memoirs of Lieutenant Anton Kuzmich Dragan, commander of the 1st Company of the 1st Battalion of the 42nd Rifle Regiment, 13th Guards Rifle Division" (Panorama Museum Archives, Volgograd).

38 Ibid.

39 Lieutenant Anton Kuzmich Dragan, in Michael K. Jones, *Stalingrad: How the Red Army Triumphed* (Pen & Sword Ltd., 2007), p. 121.

40 Officially titled "Children's Khorovod" ("Children's Round Dance"), the fountain was installed in 1939. Based on a Russian folktale, the fountain depicts six laughing children linking arms as they dance around a snapping African crocodile.

41 МЗСБ НВФ 683, "Memories of Ilya Vasilievich Voronov, machine gunner of the 1st Rifle Company, then squad commander of the 42nd Guards Regiment of the 13th Guards Rifle Division" (Panorama Museum Archives, Volgograd).

42 МЗСБ НВФ 763, "Memoirs of Lieutenant General Alexander Ilyich Rodimtsev. Commander of 13th Guards Rifle Division" (Panorama Museum Archives, Volgograd).

43 Alexander Rodimtsev, *The Guards Fought to the Death!* (Moscow Publishing House, 1969).

44 Antony Beevor, *Stalingrad* (Viking, 1998), p. 137.

45 The Barmaley Fountain, the statue consisting of a circle of six children dancing the khorovod around a crocodile.

46 J. Bastable, *Voices from Stalingrad: First-hand Accounts from World War II's Cruelest Battle* (David & Charles, 2007).

47 W. Craig, *Enemy at the Gates: The Battle for Stalingrad* (Hodder & Stoughton, 1973).

48 Dr. Wigand Wuster and Jason Mark, *An Artilleryman in Stalingrad* (Leaping Horseman Books, 2007), p. 109.

49 Boris Sokolov, *Myths and Legends of the Eastern Front: Reassessing the Great Patriotic War*, translated by Richard Harrison (Pen & Sword Ltd., 2019).

50 The remnants of: 10th NKVD Division; 91st Railroad Security Regiment; 178th, 249th Convoy Regiment; 112th Rifle Division; 244th Rifle Division; 133rd and 137th Tank Brigade; 42nd Rifle Brigade; 92nd and 95th Rifle Division; 6th Guards Tank Brigade; and the People's Militia—collectively the strength of three full divisions (thirty thousand men).

51 Marshal of the Soviet Union Vasiliy Ivanovich Chuikov, *The Battle for Stalingrad* (Holt, Rinehart and Winston, 1964).

52 The Sixth Army suffered almost two thousand casualties from snipers in Stalingrad.

53 *The 71st Infantry Division 1939–1945: Combat and Experience Reports from the Battles of the "Lucky Division" from Verdun to Stalingrad, from Monte Cassino to Lake Balaton* (in German) (Döfler, 2006), p. 478.

54 Ilya Ehrenburg, "Stalingrad (I)," *Krasnaya Zvezda*, September 6, 1942.

Chapter Nine: Success Measured in Meters and Bodies

1 Rodimtsev, *Two Hundred Days and Nights* (Moscow, 1970), p. 174.

2   Lidin, "They Know at Home How You Are Fighting," *Pravda* (September 1942): quoted in Alexander Werth, *The Year of Stalingrad: A Historical Record and a Study of Russian Mentality, Methods, and Policies* (Alfred A. Knopf, 1947), p. 225.

3   Rodimtsev believed that Fedoseyev and all his men died in the battle. Fedoseyev actually was captured alive and survived the war.

4   МЗСБ НВФ 535/1, "Memoirs of Lieutenant Anton Kuzmich Dragan, Commander of the 1st Company of the 1st Battalion of the 42nd Rifle Regiment, 13th Guards Rifle Division" (Panorama Museum Archives, Volgograd).

5   Ibid.

6   Ibid.

7   Michael K. Jones, *Stalingrad: How the Red Army Triumphed* (Pen & Sword Ltd., 2007), p. 142.

Chapter Ten: Change at the Top

1   Combat diary of the 71st Infantry Division, 1942.

2   The Upper Command of the Armed Forces was mockingly titled by the staff of Halder's headquarters "the military bureau of Corporal Hitler." B. H. Liddell Hart, *The German Generals Talk* (William Morrow, 1975).

3   Heinz Schroter, *Stalingrad: The Epic Story of Germany's Greatest Military Disaster* (Ballantine, 1958) p. 42.

4   Ibid., p. 49.

5   Ibid.

6   Walter Goerlitz, *Paulus and Stalingrad* (Methuen, 1960), p. 65.

7   Zeitzler acted as chief of staff to General Paul Ludwig von Kleist's 1st Panzer Army, which had spearheaded the innovative German thrust into France from the Ardennes in 1940.

8   Albert Speer, the Reich's minister for armaments and war production, cynically quoted the Fuhrer's thoughts, in Albert Speer, *Inside the Third Reich* (Weidenfeld & Nicolson, 1995), p. 333.

9   Heinz Schroter, *Stalingrad: The Epic Story of Germany's Greatest Military Disaster* (Ballantine, 1958), p. 49.

10 Combat log, 71st Infantry Division, 1942.

11 Ibid.

Chapter Eleven: The Storm Group and the Art of Active Defense

1   General Vasily Chuikov, interview January 5, 1943, in Jochen Hellbeck, *Stalingrad: The City That Defeated the Third Reich* (PublicAffairs, 2015).

2   For a full understanding of this issue, see David R. Stone, "Stalingrad and the Evolution of Soviet Urban Warfare," *Journal of Slavic Military Studies* 22, no. 2 (2009): 195–207, DOI: 10.1080/13518040902918089.

3 On the lack of a clear Soviet doctrine for fighting in cities, see G. Efimov, "Nekotorye Voprosy Taktiki Oborony Gorodov v Pervom Periode Voiny," Voenno-Istoricheskii Zhurnal (hereafter VIZh)2 (1977): 21–29.

4 Transcript of interview with Comrade Lieutenant General Vasily Ivanovich Chuikov, in Jochen Hellbeck, Stalingrad: The City That Defeated the Third Reich (PublicAffairs, 2015), p. 285.

5 Marshal of the Soviet Union Vasiliy Ivanovich Chuikov, The Battle for Stalingrad (Holt, Rinehart and Winston, 1964), p. 146.

6 "Order 166 of 62nd Army," September 26, 1942, part. 7, in ibid., p. 150.

7 Between 1941 and 1945 the Soviet Union produced more than twelve million rifles and carbines.

8 The PPSh-41 and later PPS-43 models were a radical design. Using lighter stamped rather than heavier machined parts, they could be produced in massive numbers—over six million were made between 1941 and 1945. They were easy to maintain and clean, with innovative chromed barrels.

9 A thin sheet of metal 20cm (approx. 8 inches) long and 15cm (approx. 6 inches) wide, drawn over a 30cm (approx. 12 inches) handle, the spade could have a square or a sharp head.

10 Brandon M. Schecter, The Stuff of Soldiers: A History of the Red Army in WWII Through Objects (Cornell University Press, 2019), p. 130.

11 Konstantin Simonov, "Days and Nights," Krasnaya Zvezda, September 24, 1942.

12 Po-platunski (an extremely low belly-crawl).

13 "Transcript of interview with Comrade Lieutenant General Vasily Ivanovich Chuikov, Stalingrad, January 5, 1943," in Joachim Hellbeck, Stalingrad: The City That Defeated the Third Reich (PublicAffairs, 2015), p. 277.

14 "Stavka directive 170635 to Stalingrad Front, October 5, 1942," Velikaia Otechestvennaia 5, no. 2: doc. 589, p. 411.

15 VPnaV, p. 472.

16 "Defense of a Large Populated Area," pp. 136, 139; see also "Instructions from the Headquarters of the Supreme High Command on the Defense of Large Populated Areas," Soviet Documents, pp. 240–41.

PART IV: KEEP YOUR ENEMY CLOSE

1 Marshal of the Soviet Union Vasiliy Ivanovich Chuikov, The Battle for Stalingrad (Holt, Rinehart and Winston, 1964).

Chapter Twelve: The Legend Begins: The Capture of the "Lighthouse"

1 This motto taken from the eighteenth-century Russian military commander General Aleksandr Suvorov was adopted by Red Star for the front

of their October 3, 1942, edition detailing the Red Army's performance at Stalingrad.

2 *Cheval de fries* (plural: *chevaux de fries*) was a makeshift defensive obstacle to plug gaps in barbed wire fortifications—sometimes made of wood, or wire, and even broken glass, studding the top of a wall. Highly effective to hold up infantry attacks in the open and then bring down artillery and machine gun fire.

3 I. Afanasiev, *House of Military Glory*, third revised edition (DOSAAF Publishing House, 1970).

4 *Combat Log for the 13th Guards Division, Stalingrad*, September 1–December 31, 1942.

5 МЗСБ НВФ 990, "Memories of Colonel Ivan Pavlovich Elin, commander of the 42nd Guards Rifle Regiment of the 13th Guards Rifle Division" (Panorama Museum Archives, Volgograd).

6 МЗСБ НВФ 12219/2, "Memoirs of Senior Lieutenant Alexei Efimovich Zhukov, commander of the 3rd Rifle Battalion of the 42nd Guards Rifle Regiment of the 13th Guards Rifle Division" (Panorama Museum Archives, Volgograd).

7 Ibid.

8 МЗСБ НВФ 1062, "Memoirs of Terenty Illarionovich Gridin, rifleman of the 7th Company of the 42nd Guards Rifle Regiment of the 13th Guards Rifle Division" (Panorama Museum Archives, Volgograd).

9 МЗСБ НВФ 12219/2, "Memoirs of Senior Lieutenant Alexei Efimovich Zhukov, commander of the 3rd Rifle Battalion of the 42nd Guards Rifle Regiment of the 13th Guards Rifle Division" (Panorama Museum Archives, Volgograd).

Chapter Thirteen: Trouble in the North

1 Quoted from Ilya Ehrenburg, "*Ubei!*" ("Kill!"], *Krasnaia Zvezda*, July 24, 1942.

2 Diary of *Unteroffizier* Albert Wittenberg (Copyright Frank Wittenberg, Germany, 2021).

3 Johan Heesters, "*Man müsste Klavier spielen können.*"

4 Diary of *Unteroffizier* Albert Wittenberg (Copyright Frank Wittenberg, Germany, 2021).

5 Ibid.

6 Ibid.

7 Ibid.

8 Ibid.

9 Ibid.

10 Ibid.

11 Ibid.

12 On October 19, 1942, Wittenberg was taken on a hospital train to Oderberg in Upper Silesia (now in the Czech Republic), where he arrived six days later. In 1943 he was moved again, near Kandrzin-Cosel (now in Poland), and he remained there until toward the end of the war. In April 1945, Polish militias took over the hospital and handed it to the Red Army, after which Wittenberg opted to flee to the West and the advancing American forces.

13 Vasily Ivanovich Chuikov, *The Battle for Stalingrad* (Ballantine, 1968), p. 156.

Chapter Fourteen: The Last Assault of the Sixth Army: Operation Hubertus

1 The official newspaper of the SS, cited in Jochen Hellbeck, "Facing Stalingrad: One Battle Births Two Contrasting Cultures of Memory," *Berlin Journal* 21 (Fall 2011).

2 Adolf Hitler, November 8, 1942, speech, on the occasion of the ninth anniversary of the Beer Hall Putsch.

3 Brandon M. Schechter, *The Stuff of Soldiers: A History of the Red Army in WWII Through Objects* (Cornell University Press, 2019), p. 179.

4 Vasily Ivanovich Chuikov, *The Battle for Stalingrad* (Holt, Rinehart and Winston, 1964).

5 Created in the summer of 1942 on the back of Stalin's Order No. 227 and primarily consisting of commissioned officers who had fallen afoul of the regime. Service was for one to three months on the front line, and in many cases the battalions were highly valued by Red Army commanders due to the combat experience of the men serving in them. Casualties were high in the fighting for Stalingrad.

6 Excerpt from report "Remembering the Horrors of Stalingrad," by Daniel Sandford, BBC News, Volgograd, January 31, 2013.

7 For Red Army losses see David M. Glantz and Jonathan M. House, *Stalingrad* (University of Kansas Press, 2017), p. 284.

PART V: THE GREATEST VICTORY

Chapter Fifteen: "Twentieth Century Cannae": Operation Uranus

1 Geoffrey Roberts, *Victory at Stalingrad*, 1st edition (Routledge, 2002), p. 118.

2 Jochen Hellbeck, *Stalingrad: The City That Defeated the Third Reich* (PublicAffairs, 2015), pp. 279–80.

3 David M. Glantz and J. M. House, *When Titans Clashed: How the Red Army Stopped Hitler* (Kansas University Press, 1995), p. 134.

4 Excerpt from interview by Jochen Hellbeck taken from website Facing Stalingrad.com.

5 Heinz Schroter, *Stalingrad: The Epic Story of Germany's Greatest Military Disaster* (Ballantine, 1958), pp. 74–75.

6 William Craig, *Enemy at the Gates: The Battle for Stalingrad* (Hodder & Stoughton, 1973), pp. 204–5.

7 Göring's decision to announce that the Luftwaffe could achieve this task countered the arguments from his own staff. The Sixth Army required 750 tons per day; Göring agreed 500 tons was possible; his staff analyzed the tools they had to do the job, factored in all elements, and settled at 350 tons maximum.

8 Horst Boog et al., *Germany and the Second World War*, Vol. 5 (Clarendon Press, 2001), p. 1148

9 V. E. Tarrant, *Stalingrad: Anatomy of an Agony* (Pen & Sword Ltd., 1992), pp. 142–43.

10 Personal papers of Colonel Friedrich Roske, I.R. 194, 71st Division (Courtesy of Dr. Uwe Roske, Germany, 2021).

11 William Craig, *Enemy at the Gates: The Battle for Stalingrad* (Hodder & Stoughton, 1973), p. 211.

12 Colonel Friedrich Roske, in ibid.

Chapter Sixteen: The Relentless Fight

1 "*Kazhdyi dom Stalingrada—Krepost!,*" *Izvestia*, September 1942.

2 МЗСБ НВФ 990, "Memories of Ivan Pavlovich Elin, commander of the 42nd Guards Rifle Regiment of the 13th Guards Rifle Division" (Panorama Museum, Volgograd).

3 A quotation from Ulrich von Hutten, a German knight from the fifteenth century, who was a scholar, poet, and satirist, and later became a follower of Martin Luther and a fierce Protestant reformer.

4 The PAK 38 (55mm artillery piece) was the standard antitank gun used by the Wehrmacht during the fighting.

5 МЗСБ НВФ 990, "Memories of Ivan Pavlovich Elin, commander of the 42nd Guards Rifle Regiment of the 13th Guards Rifle Division" (Panorama Museum, Volgograd).

Chapter Seventeen: Hope Extinguished: Christmas in the *Kessel*

1 Geoffrey Roberts, *Victory at Stalingrad*, 1st edition (Routledge, 2002), p. 125.

2 Unpublished memoir of Major General Friedrich Roske (Courtesy of Dr. Uwe Roske, Germany, 2021).

3 The *Winterhilfswerk des Deutschen Volkes*, commonly known by its abbre-

viated form *Winterhilfswerk*, was an annual donation drive by the National Socialist People's Welfare to help finance charitable work.

4 Philip Westrich, bicycle battalion of the 100th Jaeger Division.

5 Willi Jettkowski, IR 191, *KLEEBLATT* Nr 75/1971, taken from the book ... *Ich Kam Durch!* (Erich Pabel 1970).

6 Captain Hindenlang began the battle as a first lieutenant and was subsequently promoted to the rank of captain by the beginning of January 1943.

7 Unpublished memoir of Major General Friedrich Roske (Courtesy of Dr. Uwe Roske, Germany, 2021).

8 Laurence Rees, *War of the Century—When Hitler Fought Stalin* (BBC Books, 1997), p. 182.

9 Unpublished memoir of Major General Friedrich Roske (Courtesy of Dr. Uwe Roske, Germany, 2021).

10 Ibid.

11 Vasily Grossman, *Red Star*, January 1, 1943.

12 Wilhelm Adam and Otto Ruhle, *With Paulus at Stalingrad*, translated by Tony Le Tissier (Pen & Sword Ltd., 2015), p. 168.

13 Ibid.

14 The Don Front now enjoyed a superiority of 8 to 1 in manpower, 5 to 1 in armor, and 20 to 1 in artillery. David M. Glantz and Jonathan M. House, *Stalingrad* (University Press of Kansas, 2017), pp. 455–57.

15 Pitomnik had actually been "captured" by a single T-34 tank two days previously, when German personnel defending the airfield fled in terror. A coordinated counterattack soon drove it off and the airfield was made operational again for two more vital days.

16 David M. Glantz and Jonathan M. House, *Stalingrad* (University Press of Kansas, 2017), 469–70.

17 Paulus's army HQ consisted of approximately 120 staff, together with his chief of staff Lieutenant General Arthur Schmidt and his senior ADC Colonel Wilhelm Adam. Both men would be captured alongside Paulus.

18 Wilhelm Adam and Otto Ruhle, *With Paulus at Stalingrad*, translated by Tony Le Tissier (Pen & Sword Ltd., 2015), p. 181.

19 William Craig, *Enemy at the Gates: The Battle for Stalingrad* (Hodder & Stoughton, 1973), p. 364.

20 As a colonel and commander of a news department, he was flown into the Stalingrad pocket on December 28 as the newly appointed news chief of the Sixth Army.

21 Unpublished memoir of Major General Friedrich Roske (Courtesy of Dr. Uwe Roske, Germany, 2021).

22 Ibid.

23 Ibid.

24 Ibid.

25 Ibid.

26 Wilhelm Adam and Otto Ruhle, *With Paulus at Stalingrad* (Pen & Sword Ltd., 2015), translated by Tony Le Tissier, pp. 2–3.

27 Ibid.

28 Heinz Schroter, *Stalingrad: The Epic Story of Germany's Greatest Military Disaster* (Ballantine, 1958).

Chapter Eighteen: The Last Commander of the "Lucky Division"

1 Heinz Schroter, *Stalingrad: The Epic Story of Germany's Greatest Military Disaster* (Ballantine, New York, 1958).

2 Dr. Wigand Wuster and Jason Mark, *An Artilleryman in Stalingrad* (Leaping Horseman Books, 2007), p. 162.

3 Letters, diaries, and testimonies from the Ronald MacArthur Hirst papers, Box 12, Folder "Hartmann, Alexander von"; Hoover Institution Library & Archives, USA.

4 Heinz Schroter, *Stalingrad: The Epic Story of Germany's Greatest Military Disaster* (Ballantine, 1958), pp. 221–22.

5 Letters, diaries and testimonies from the Ronald MacArthur Hirst papers, Box 12, Folder "Hartmann, Alexander von"; Hoover Institution Library & Archives, USA.

6 Ibid.

7 HELANO, 71. ID in *KLEEBLATT* Nr. 45/1965 (part 7).

8 Major General Roske's private papers (Courtesy of Dr. Uwe Roske, Germany, 2021).

9 Ibid.

10 Ibid.

11 Ibid.

12 Ibid.

13 According to his memoir, Roske had actually taken an armed group and approached a nearby T-34 under a flag of truce and spoken with a commander on the ground—Senior Lieutenant Fyodor Ielchenko of the 29th Rifle Division—in order to get a message out he now wished to parlay.

14 Captain Lukyan Petrovich Morozov of the 38th, Senior Lieutenant Fyodor Ielchenko of the 29th, and Captain Rybak of the 38th.

15 Lieutenant Colonel Leonid Abovich Vinokur, deputy political officer for the 38th Motor Rifle Brigade.

16 Testimony from Lieutenant Colonel Leonid Abovich Vinokur, in Jochen Helllbeck, *Stalingrad: The City That Defeated the Third Reich* (Public-Affairs, 2015), pp. 244–45.

17 Field Marshal August von Mackensen was a Prussian and one of Imperial Germany's most prominent generals in World War I. He was interned by

the Allies after his defeat at the Battle of Mărășești in Romania in September 1917.

18 F. Gilbert, ed., *Hitler Directs His War: The Secret Records of His Daily Military Conferences* (Oxford University Press, 1950), pp. 18–19.

19 Major Unruh.

20 Various junior Red Army officers who had already arrived at the department store prior to Laskin have since stated they had met with Paulus beforehand. There is a great deal of competition between these memoirs as to whose claim is the truth. What we do know is Laskin had not yet met with Paulus while the surrender was taking place. He had abdicated responsibility to Schmidt and Roske, and Schmidt had subsequently stepped aside for Roske to act as the main Sixth Army intermediary.

21 Excerpt from report "Remembering the Horrors of Stalingrad" by Daniel Sandford, BBC News, Volgograd, January 31, 2013.

22 Brandon M. Schechter, *The Stuff of Soldiers: A History of the Red Army in WWII Through Objects* (Cornell University Press, 2019), p. 222.

23 Roske would sadly never see them again. Upon Roske's death by suicide in 1956 in West Germany, Captain Hindenlang would carry his commander's medals behind his coffin.

24 *KLEEBLATT* Nr 147/1988.

25 After his initial imprisonment in Beketovka, between January 1943 and October 1955, Roske would be moved around the prison system in Russia as a POW: Iwanowo (northeast of Moscow) in March 1946–47; Stalingrad, September 1948 (where he was sentenced to twenty-five years imprisonment); March 1949 to a brick factory camp at Workuta, north of the Arctic Circle; 1951, a camp in Asbest in the Urals; 1954, a camp in Sochi on the Black Sea, until October 1955 (Courtesy of Dr. Uwe Roske, Germany, 2021).

26 Major General Roske's private papers (Courtesy of Dr. Uwe Roske, Germany, 2021).

Chapter Nineteen: The End

1 Foreman of Workshop No. 7 at the Red October Steel Plant, in Jochen Hellbeck and Christopher Tauchen, *Stalingrad: The City That Defeated the Third Reich* (PublicAffairs, 2014).

2 Dr. Wigand Wuster and Jason Mark, *An Artilleryman in Stalingrad* (Leaping Horseman Books, 2007).

3 Interview with Joseph Mironovich Yampolsky taken from the iRemember website.

4 F. Gilbert, ed., *Hitler Directs His War: The Secret Records of His Daily Military Conferences* (Oxford University Press, 1950), pp. 18–19.

5 William Taubman, *Khrushchev: The Man and His Era* (The Free Press, Simon & Schuster, 2003).

6 Brandon. M. Schechter, *The Stuff of Soldiers: A History of the Red Army in WWII Through Objects* (Cornell University Press, 2019).

7 "*Dokladnaia zapiska zaveduiushchego originstruktorskim otdelom Stalingradskogo obkoma* TsK VKP (B) Tingaeva v TsK VKP (B) *Shambergu o rabote po vosstanovleniiu goroda*," July 1943, F.17, Op.88, D.226, RGASPL.

8 Samsonov, *Stalingradskaia bitva* (Moscow, 1971), p. 316.

9 A later NKVD report cited that German troops continued to resist in mopping-up operations that lasted well into March 1943—with NKVD security troops killing more than two thousand and capturing a further eight thousand.

10 "The Battle for Stalingrad," by Paul Winterton, BBC report from Stalingrad, broadcast on February 9, 1943. Excerpt from *Witness History*, BBC Worldwide, February 2, 2013.

11 Even today. In November 2020 this author discovered the tailfin of a German heavy mortar when walking along the western slopes of the Mamayev Kurgan.

12 Medical Staff Sergeant Meyer, from the I.R. 194, from the unpublished memoir of Major General Friedrich Roske (Courtesy of Dr. Uwe Roske, Germany, 2021).

13 NKVD reports by March 1943 state that more than 11,000 German troops held out after the official surrender—holed up in cellars, sewers, and ruins. The Soviets killed 2,418 and captured a further 8,646. *Stalingrad*, Episode 3: "*Der Untergang*," German television documentary, directed by Sebastian Dehnhardt and Manfred Oldenburg.

14 "The Battle for Stalingrad," by Paul Winterton, BBC report from Stalingrad, broadcast on February 9, 1943. Excerpt from *Witness History*, BBC Worldwide, February 2, 2013.

15 Exceprt from interview by Jochen Hellbeck taken from the website Facing Stalingrad.com.

16 Robert Dale, *Divided We Stand: Cities, Social Unity and Post-War Reconstruction in Soviet Russia, 1945–1953* (Cambridge University Press, 2015), p. 506.

Epilogue: The Legend of the "Lighthouse"

1 Russian: "Никто не забыт и ничто не забыто," the well-known saying at the Panorama Museum archives.

2 By the time of the victory at Stalingrad, the Red Army had suffered 5,639,782 killed, missing, captured, or invalided out of service.

3 Brandon M. Schechter, *The Stuff of Soldiers: A History of the Red Army in WWII Through Objects* (Cornell University Press, 2019), p. 189.

4 Ibid., p. 22.

5 Ian R. Garner, *Stalingrad Lives* (Yale University Press, 2021), p. 35.

6 Ibid., pp. 36–7.

7 "This is Pavlov's House," *Stalin's Banner*, October 31, 1942, MZSB KP 213/58, USSR, RSFSR.

8 "Rubble women." Even this legend has come into question from German historians whose research has uncovered data showing only a small percentage of women actually worked to rebuild the country's destroyed infrastructure.

9 According to estimates compiled by the city's executive committee in 1951, by the end of 1943, nearly 15,000 registered volunteers worked in 821 officially recognized labor brigades within Stalingrad, providing 480,000 man-hours to the restoration of the city. By 1944, the number of brigades had risen to more than 20,000. Collectively, they would add more than a million man-hours to the city's labor pool.

10 Interview with Yuri Pavlov, September 2020.

11 Which he subsequently repeated in his military memoirs, *The Battle for Stalingrad*, in the early 1960s.

12 Memoirs of Senior Lieutenant Alexei Efimovich Zhukov, commander of the 3rd Rifle Battalion of the 42nd Guards Rifle Regiment of the 13th Guards Rifle Division (Panorama Museum Archives, Volgograd).

13 ЗСБ НВФ 535/1, "Memoirs of Lieutenant Anton Kuzmich Dragan, commander of the 1st Company of the 1st Battalion of the 42nd Rifle Regiment, 13th Guards Rifle Division" (Panorama Museum Archives, Volgograd).

14 МЗСБ НВФ 9146, "Memoirs of Lieutenant Anton Kuzmich Dragan, commander of the 1st Company of the 1st Battalion of the 42nd Rifle Regiment, 13th Guards Rifle Division" (Panorama Museum Archives, Volgograd).

15 Georgi Potanski, in Michael K. Jones, *Stalingrad: How the Red Army Triumphed* (Pen & Sword Ltd., 2007), p. 255.

16 МЗСБ НВФ 990, "Memories of Colonel Ivan Pavlovich Elin, the 42nd Guards Rifle Regiment of the 13th Guards Rifle Division" (Panorama Museum Archives, Volgograd).

17 Georgi Potanski, in Michael K. Jones, *Stalingrad: How the Red Army Triumphed* (Pen & Sword Ltd., 2007), p. 255.

18 Ibid.

19 Excerpt from I. Afanasiev, *House of Military Glory*, 3rd edition (DOSAAF Publishing House, 1970).

Bibliography

Aboulin, Mansur. *Red Road from Stalingrad—Recollections of a Soviet Infantryman*. Pen & Sword Ltd., 2004.

Afanasiev, I. *House of Military Glory*, 3rd edition. DOSAAF Publishing House, 1970.

Antill, Peter. *Campaign Series 184: Stalingrad 1942*. Osprey Publishing Ltd., 2007.

Bastable, Jonathan. *Voices of Stalingrad: First-hand Accounts from World War II's Cruellest Battle*. Pen & Sword Ltd., 2019.

Beevor, Antony. *Stalingrad*. Viking, 1998.

Beevor, Antony & Vinogradova, Luba. *A Writer at War: Vasily Grossman with the Red Army 1941-45*. Harvill Press, 2005.

Bergstrom, Christer. *Black Cross Red Star Air War Over the Eastern Front: Volume 4, Stalingrad to Kuban 1942–1943*. Vaktel forlag; Illustrated edition, 2019.

Boog, Horst, et al. *Germany and the Second World War*, Vol. 6. Clarendon Press, Oxford, 2001.

Busch, Reinhold. *Survivors of Stalingrad: Eyewitness Accounts from the Sixth Army, 1942–43*. Frontline Books, 2012.

Chuikov, Vasily. *The Battle for Stalingrad*. Holt, Rinehart and Winston, 1964.

Craig, William. *Enemy at the Gates: The Battle for Stalingrad*. Hodder & Stoughton, 1973.

Dimbleby, Jonathan. *Barbarossa: How Hitler Lost the War*. Viking, 2021.

Erikson, John. *The Road to Stalingrad: Stalin's War with Germany*, Vol. 1. Orion, 1975.

Erikson, John. *The Road to Berlin: Stalin's War with Germany*, Vol. 2. Orion, 1983.

Forczyk, Robert. *Campaign Series 254: Kharkov 1942*. Osprey Publishing Ltd., 2014.

Forczyk, Robert. *Campaign Series 359: Stalingrad 1942–43*, Vol. 1. Osprey Publishing Ltd., 2021.

Forczyk, Robert. *Campaign Series 368: Stalingrad 1942–43*, Vol. 2. Osprey Publishing Ltd., 2021.

Garner, Professor Ian. *Stalingrad Lives*. McGill-Queen's University Press, 2022.

Gerlach, Heinrich. *Breakout at Stalingrad*. Apollo, 2018.

Glantz, David M., and Jonathan M. House. *Stalingrad Trilogy*. University Press of Kansas, 2017.

Goerlitz, Walter. *Paulus and Stalingrad*. Methuen & Co. Limited, 1963.

Grossman, Vasilly. *Life and Fate*. Vintage, 2006.

Grossman, Vasilly. *Stalingrad*. Harvill Secker, 2019.

Hartley, Janet M. *The Volga*. Yale University Press, 2021.

Hayward, Joel S. A. *Stopped at Stalingrad: The Luftwaffe and Hitler's Defeat in the East*. University Press of Kansas, 1998.

Hellbeck, Jochen. *Stalingrad: The City That Defeated the Third Reich*. Public-Affairs, 2015.

Hill, Alexander. *The Red Army and the Second World War (Armies of the Second World War)*. Cambridge University Press, 2019.

Holmes, Richard. *The World at War*. Ebury Press, 2007.

Joly, Anton. *Stalingrad Battle Atlas*, Volume 1. STALDATA.COM, 2013.

Jones, Michael. K. *Stalingrad—How the Red Army Triumphed*. Pen & Sword Ltd., 2007.

Kerr, Walter. *The Secrets of Stalingrad*. MacDonald & Jane's Publishers Limited, 1978.

Kershaw, Ian. *To Hell and Back: Europe 1914–1949*. Allen Lane, 2015.

Khrushchev Nikita. *Khrushchev Remembers*. Little, Brown, 1970.

Kirchbuel, Robert. *Atlas of the Eastern Front 1941–45*. Osprey Publishing Ltd., 2015.

Liddell Hart, B. H. *The German Generals Talk*. Morrow, 1975.

Makarov, Ivan Philippovich. *Born Under a Lucky Star: A Red Army Soldier's Recollections of the Eastern Front of World War II*. Anastastia Walker, 2020.

Mark, Jason D. *Death of the Leaping Horseman—The 24th Panzer Division in Stalingrad*. Stackpole Books, 2014.

Merridale, Catherine. *Ivan's War—The Red Army 1941–45*. Faber & Faber Ltd., 2005.

Muller, Rold-Dieter. *Hitler's War in the East, 1941–1945: A Critical Assessment*, 3rd Edition. Berghahn Books, 2009.

Overy, Richard. *Russia's War 1941–45*. Penguin, 1997.

Popov, P. P., A. V. Kozlov, and B. G. Usik. *Turning Point: Recollections of Russian Participants and Witnesses of the Stalingrad Battle*. Leaping Horseman Books, 2008.

Rees, Laurence. *War of the Century: When Hitler Fought Stalin*. BBC Worldwide Ltd., 1999.

The Road to Stalingrad. Time Life Books (illustrated series).

Roberts, Geoffrey. *Victory at Stalingrad*. Routledge, 2002.

Roberts, Geoffrey. *Stalin's Wars*. Yale University Press, 2006.

Rodimtsev, Alexander. *In With the Guards!* Moscow Publishing House, 1967.

Rottman, Gordon L. *Warrior Series 123: Soviet Rifleman 1941–45.* Osprey Publishing Ltd., 2007.

Ruhl, Otto, and Adam Wilhelm. *With Paulus at Stalingrad.* Methuen & Co. Ltd., 1963.

Schechter, Brandon M. *The Stuff of Soldiers: A History of the Red Army in World War II Through Objects.* Cornell University Press, 2019.

Schroter, Heinz. *Stalingrad—The Epic Story of Germany's Greatest Military Disaster.* Ballantine, 1958.

Seebag Montifiore, Simon. *Stalin—The Court of the Red Tzar.* Weidenfeld & Nicolson, 2003.

Service, Robert. *Stalin: A Biography.* Macmillan, 2004.

Sevruk, Vladimir. *Moscow to Stalingrad 1941–1942—Recollections, Stories, Reports.* 1970.

Shepherd, Ben H. *Hitler's Soldiers: The German Army in the Third Reich.* Yale University Press, 2016.

Sokolov, Boris. *Myths and Legends of the Eastern Front.* Pen & Sword Ltd., 2019.

Speer, Albert. *Inside the Third Reich.* Weidenfeld & Nicolson, 1995.

Stargardt, Nicholas. *The German War—A Nation Under Arms 1939–45.* Vintage, 2015.

Taubman, William. *Khrushchev—The Man and His Era.* Simon & Schuster, 2003.

Trevor-Roper, Hugh. *Hitler's War Directives, 1939–45.* Sedgewick & Jackson, 1964.

Turner, Jason. *Stalingrad: Day by Day.* Chartwell Books, 2012.

Two Hundred Days of Fire: Accounts by Participants and Witnesses of the Battle of Stalingrad. Progress Publishers, Moscow, 1970.

Vinen, Professor Richard. *A History in Fragments: Europe in the Twentieth Century.* Little, Brown, 2010.

Walsh, Stephen. *Stalingrad 1942–43.* St. Martin's Press, 2001.

Werth, Alexander. *The Year of Stalingrad: On the Ground Reporting in 1942–43.* Hamish Hamilton, 1946.

Werth, Alexander. *Russia at War 1941–45.* Skyhorse Publishing, 2017.

Wuster, Wigand. *An Artilleryman in Stalingrad.* Leaping Horseman Books, 2007.

Zaitsev, Vasili. *Notes of a Russian Sniper.* Pen & Sword Ltd., 2009.

Zemke, Earl F. *Stalingrad to Berlin: The German Defeat in the East.* Center of Military History, United States Army, 2002.

Zhukov, Georgy. *The Battle for Stalingrad.* Holt, Reinhart & Winston Inc., 1963.

Interviews

Nikolai Chuikov, Moscow, September 3, 2021
Yury Pavlov, Novgorod, September 29, 2021
Juliy Chepurin, Moscow, October 13, 2021
Dr. Uwe Roske, December 1–9, 2021

Other Sources

Combat Log of the 13th Guards Division, Stalingrad. September 1–December 31, 1942.

"The Battle of Stalingrad," by Paul Winterton. *Witness History.* BBC Worldwide, February 2, 2013.

Hellbeck, Jochen. "Facing Stalingrad: One Battle Births Two Contrasting Cultures of Memory." *Berlin Journal* 21 (2011).

Kahl, Hans, Lieutenant-Colonel. *Stalin, the Soldier.* The Russia Today Society, London, 1945.

Roske, Friedrich, Colonel of I.R. 194 and later Major General of the 71st Infantry Division, unpublished memoir and personal papers. Permission kindly given by Dr. Uwe Roske.

Stone, David R. "Stalingrad and the Evolution of Soviet Urban Warfare." *Journal of Slavic Military Studies* 22, no. 2 (2009): 195, 207. DOI: 10.1080/13518040902918089.

Wittenberg, Albert, *Unteroffizier,* 50th Infantry Division. Unpublished papers. Permission kindly given by family.

Yampolsky, Joseph Mironovich, Lieutenant, 23rd Tank Corps. Interview taken from iRemember website.

Letters, diaries, and testimonies from the Ronald MacArthur Hirst papers, Box 12, Folder "Hartmann, Alexander von." Hoover Institution Library & Archives, USA.

Letters, diaries, and testimonies from the Ronald MacArthur Hirst papers, Box 19, Folder "Roske, Friedrich." Hoover Institution Library & Archives, USA.

Letters, diaries, and testimonies from the archives of the State Historical and Memorial Museum-Reserve of the Battle of Stalingrad.

Ref.	Title
КП-1094	Scheme - the defense area 'Pavlov's House' in Stalingrad.
КП-19024	BOOK. Saveliev L.I. *Pavlov's House*, M., Sov. Russia, 1970.
НВФ-11961	Poem *Pavlov's House.* Author - Zemlyakov B. A.
НВФ-2800 /1	Memories of V.K. Kotsarenko about the battles in the city center, for the 'L' -Shaped House, 1965. Typescript.
КП-21954	Book *House of Soldiers' Glory,* author - Ivan Filippovich Afanasiev, with a dedicatory inscription. 1960.
НВФ-3276	Memoirs of Yakov Pavlov.
НВФ-654	Memoirs of Ivan Filippovich Afanasiev - Guard Lieutenant, commander of a machine-gun platoon of the 3rd Rifle Battalion of the 42nd Guards Rifle Regiment.
НВФ-1045	Memoirs of A. V. Boldyrev.
НВФ-683	Memories of Ilya Vasilyevich Voronov - machine gunner of

the 1st Rifle Company, then squad leader of the 42nd Guards Rifle Regiment.

НВФ-1062   Memories of T. I. Gridin - Guards of the Red Army, rifleman of the 7th Company of the 42nd Guards Rifle Regiment.

НВФ-17798   Memoirs of Aleksey Alekseevich Dorokhov - Guard Senior Lieutenant of the 42nd Guards Rifle Regiment of the 13th Guards Rifle Division.

КП-6403/4   Memories of Fayzerakhman Zulabakharovich Ramazanov - Guard Corporal, assistant commander of the anti-tank rifle regiment of the 42nd Guards Rifle Regiment.

НВФ-1319   Memories of Alexei Ivanovich Ivaschenko - Guard Sergeant, gunner of the heavy machine gun of the 3rd Machine Gun Company of the 3rd Rifle Battalion of the 42nd Guards Rifle Regiment of the 13th Guards Rifle Division.

НВФ-1015   Memoirs of Alexei Efimovich Zhukov - Commander of the 3rd Infantry Battalion of the 42nd Guards Rifle Regiment.

НВФ-1210   Scheme of underground mine work in the area of oil tanks in the defense zone of the 13th Guards Rifle Division.

КП-1374   The scheme of blocking the enemy strong point in the building of the State Bank. September 18, 1942.

КП-5182   Lists of participants in the Battle of Stalingrad, 42nd Guards Rifle Regiment, 13th Guards Rifle Division.

КП-427   Materials about the combat exploits of sappers of the 8th Guards Sapper Battalion of the 13th Guards Rifle Division.

НВФ-1218   The scheme of strengthening and location of the defense of the 'L'-Shaped House.

НВФ-12022/2   Memoirs of I. G. Glazkov about the storming of the 'L'-Shaped House.

НВФ-7639   Scheme of the defense of the 3rd Rifle Battalion of the 42nd Guards Rifle Regiment in the area of 9th January Square.

МЗСБ НВФ 763   Memoirs of Major General Alexander Ilyich Rodimtsev. During the Battle of Stalingrad, 13th Guards Rifle Division.

МЗСБ НВФ 1051   Memoirs of Zimnyur Yunusovich Tyapaev - gunner of 82mm mortar of the Mortar Company of the 13th Guards Rifle Division.

МЗСБ НВФ 1025   Reminiscence of A. P. Seredintsev - a soldier of the 13th Guards Rifle Division.

МЗСБ НВФ 1789/1   Memoirs of Mikhail Alekseevich Andreyev, a former machine gunner of the 20th Machine-gun Company of a separate machine-gun battalion of the 13th Guards Rifle Division.

МЗСБ НВФ 1951   Memoirs of Grigory Arsentievich Gulko, a former soldier of the 8th Guards Separate Sapper Battalion of the 13th Guards Rifle Division.

МЗСБ НВФ 11146   Memories of Ivan Terentyevich Artyomenko, Senior Lieu-tenant, political instructor of the 39th Guards Rifle Regiment of the 13th Guards Rifle Division.

МЗСБ НВФ 3219   Memoirs of Pyotr Ivanovich Kuznetsov - Guards Lieutenant, commander of a Machine-gun Company of the 13th Guards Rifle Division.

МЗСБ НВФ 3220   Memories of Matvey Alekseevich Rusakov - Guards Captain of the Mortar Company of the 13th Guards Rifle Division.

МЗСБ НВФ 4045   Memoirs of Ivan Nesterovich Kopeikin - Commander of the Divisional School for junior command personnel of the 13th Guards Rifle Division.

МЗСБ НВФ 12022/2   Memoirs of Ivan Grigorievich Glazkov, a former intelligence officer of the 34th Rifle Regiment of the 13th Guards Rifle Division.

МЗСБ НВФ 4316   A letter to the 'Komsomol and Youth of Moscow' from the Komsomol members of the Guards Unit of the 13th Guards Rifle Division.

МЗСБ КП 4574   Order of the headquarters of the 13th Guards Rifle Division from December 22, 1942. on submission to the commander of the 3rd Battalion of the 42nd Rifle Regiment of a heavy machine gun with a machine-gun crew, who was at the firing position in the 'Pavlov House.'

МЗСБ КП 28356   Combat characteristics on combat performance on Dronov Viktor Ivanovich - the commander of the Rifle Battalion of the 42nd Rifle Regiment, 13th Guards Rifle Division.

МЗСБ КП 11401/2   A letter from the front from Nikitin Vladimir Kuzmich, a soldier of the 13th Guards Rifle Division.

МЗСБ НВФ 16611   Memoirs of Tikhon Stepanovich Goloborodko - Jr. sergeant of the 7th Machine Gun Company, the 3rd Rifle Battalion of the 42nd Rifle Regiment, the 13th Guards Rifle Division.

МЗСБ НВФ 1310   Memoirs of Yusup Shaikhovich Bakeev - gunner of the 9th Battery of the 3rd Division of the 32nd Artillery Regiment of the 13th Guards Rifle Division.

МЗСБ НВФ 17123   Memories of Vladimir Konstantinovich Shustov - a former Red Army soldier of the 34th Rifle Regiment of the 13th Guards Rifle Division.

к МЗСБ НВФ 12604   Memoirs of Sergei Nikitovich Ashikhmanov - an operative of the KGB of Stalingrad for the 13th Guards Rifle Division.

МЗСБ НВФ 535/1   Memoirs of Anton Kuzmich Dragan, commander of the 1st Company of the 1st Battalion of the 42nd Rifle Regiment, 13th Guards Rifle Division.

МЗСБ НВФ 17798   Memoirs of Aleksey Alekseevich Dorokhov - guard senior lieutenant, commander of the 3rd Machine Gun Company of the 42nd Rifle Regiment, 13th Guards Rifle Division.

МЗСБ НВФ 12219/1 A copy of the front letter of Alexei Efimovich Zhukov - the commander of the 3rd Rifle Battalion of the 42nd Guards Rifle Regiment of the 13th Guards Rifle Division dated September 17, 1942.

МЗСБ НВФ 12219/2 Memoirs of Alexei Efimovich Zhukov - commander of the 3rd Rifle Battalion of the 42nd Guards Rifle Regiment of the 13th Guards Rifle Division.

МЗСБ НВФ 683 Memories of Ilya Vasilievich Voronov, machine gunner of the 1st Rifle Company, then squad commander of the 42nd Guards Regiment of the 13th Guards Rifle Division

Reference titles from State Historical and Memorial Museum-Reserve of the Battle of Stalingrad

Library *Code of historical and architectural heritage of Tsaritsyn - Stalingrad - Volgograd* (1589–2004) - Volgograd: Publishing house "Panorama," 2004. 240 p.

Library Oleinikov P. P. *The architectural heritage of Stalingrad* [Text]: monograph / P. P. Oleinikov. - Volgograd: Publisher, 2012. 557, [1] page. : illustration, portrait, table, fax., color. illustration.

Library *"Hero City on the Volga": A guide to history. places of Volgograd.* - Moscow: Military Publishing, 1962. 144 p.

Library "Volgograd is a hero city": *A Guide to History and Places of the City* / T. N. Naumenko, I. M. Loginov, L. N. Merinova.—M.: Soviet Russia, 1973. 287 p., 1 section.

Library Pavlov J. F. In Stalingrad: (Front notes) / Ya. F. Pavlov, Hero of the Soviet. Union. - Stalingrad: Regional publishing house. 32 p. : illustration (picture).

Library Panchenko Yu. N. *163 days on the streets of Stalingrad* / Yuri Panchenko. - Volgograd: PrinTerra, 2006 (Volgograd: Typ. Of the PrinTerra publishing house). 321, [1] p., [8] l. Portrait illustration

Photography Credits

Index

Page numbers in *italics* refer to maps. Page numbers beginning with 305 refer to notes.

341

About the Author

IAIN MacGREGOR has been an editor and publisher of nonfiction for over twenty-five years. He is the author *Checkpoint Charlie*, the acclaimed oral history of Cold War Berlin. As a history student he visited the Baltic and the Soviet Union in the early 1980s and has been captivated by Soviet history ever since. He has published books on every aspect of the Second World War on the Eastern Front 1941–45 and has visited archives in St. Petersburg, Moscow, and Volgograd. He is a Fellow of the Royal Historical Society, and his writing has appeared in *The Guardian*, *The Spectator*, and *BBC History Magazine*. He lives with his wife and two children in London.